I0061518

"Under the deft guidance of one of America's great psychologists, this book explores a question that, at one time or another, enters the minds of most human beings: What's it all about? The answer is Significance. And in making the case, Kruglanski and Raviv cover – in a delightfully accessible way – material from modern psychological research to the ancient philosophies of Rome and Asia. Stunning insights never stop coming. You can't read this book without understanding your life and society more deeply... and without experiencing an inspiring sense of both challenge and reassurance."

Claude Steele, Lucie Stern Professor Emeritus in Psychology, Stanford University, California.

"What matters most to all of us? Simply, and profoundly: for our lives to matter and that we be treated with respect. This fundamental insight in Arie Kruglanski and Dan Raviv's landmark new book, *The Quest for Significance*, is the foundation for a penetrating rethinking of where human choices come from, from choosing friends and lovers to choosing to become a terrorist. This scholarly, beautifully written, and fascinating book tells us what it means to be human. It is a need to know."

E. Tory Higgins, author of *Shared Reality: What Makes Us Strong and Tears Us Apart*.

"By weaving together engaging accounts from history, politics, and psychology, Kruglanski and Raviv offer compelling evidence for a remarkably encompassing assertion: that almost all of human expression, practice, and goal formation can be traced to the need for personal and social Significance. It's a *tour de force*."

Robert Cialdini, author of *Influence* and *Pre-Suasion*.

"In this groundbreaking exploration of human motivation, Arie Kruglanski and Dan Raviv reveal how our universal need to feel significant shapes everything from our most intimate relationships to world-changing historical events. By illuminating this fundamental drive, the authors provide a master key that unlocks deeper insights into relationships, parenting, careers, leadership, mental health, social movements, and even the roots of extremism – empowering us to navigate life's complexities with greater wisdom, empathy, and effectiveness. This book will change the way you view yourself and others, offering a powerful lens through which to understand human behavior in a rapidly changing world."

Michele J. Gelfand, author of *Rule Makers, Rule Breakers*....

THE QUEST FOR SIGNIFICANCE

The Quest for Significance: Harnessing the Need that Makes the World Go Round is a fascinating exploration of why we all seek Significance – a fundamental human motivation – and how we can understand it to help us lead better lives. Renowned psychologist Arie Kruglanski and journalist Dan Raviv show how the Quest for Significance propels our actions, governs our feelings, and dominates our thoughts: pervasively affecting our happiness, pursuits, and relationships.

Drawing on both academic research and the personal experiences of the authors, including Kruglanski's childhood in Poland during the Holocaust, the authors help readers to understand themselves and people around them – to promote happiness, gain friendship, and find love.

This one-of-a-kind book is fascinating reading for students, professionals, and anyone interested in how they can better appreciate themselves and those close to them, and live a fulfilling life.

Arie W. Kruglanski is a globally esteemed authority on human motivation, goal systems, cognitive closure, and terrorism. A Distinguished University Professor at the University of Maryland, his many awards include the American Psychological Society honoring "his lifetime of significant intellectual contributions to the basic science of psychology."

Dan Raviv is a bestselling author and covered war, espionage, diplomacy, and politics for CBS News for 40 years.

THE QUEST FOR SIGNIFICANCE

Harnessing the Need that Makes the World Go Round

Arie W. Kruglanski and Dan Raviv

Routledge
Taylor & Francis Group

NEW YORK AND LONDON

Designed cover image: Getty Images © xxmmxx

First published 2025
by Routledge
605 Third Avenue, New York, NY 10158

and by Routledge
4 Park Square, Milton Park, Abingdon, Oxon, OX14 4RN

Routledge is an imprint of the Taylor & Francis Group, an informa business

© 2025 Arie W. Kruglanski and Dan Raviv

The right of Arie W. Kruglanski and Dan Raviv to be identified as authors of this work has been asserted in accordance with sections 77 and 78 of the Copyright, Designs and Patents Act 1988.

All rights reserved. No part of this book may be reprinted or reproduced or utilised in any form or by any electronic, mechanical, or other means, now known or hereafter invented, including photocopying and recording, or in any information storage or retrieval system, without permission in writing from the publishers.

Trademark notice: Product or corporate names may be trademarks or registered trademarks, and are used only for identification and explanation without intent to infringe.

ISBN: 9781032531694 (hbk)
ISBN: 9781032508788 (pbk)
ISBN: 9781003410706 (ebk)

DOI: 10.4324/9781003410706

Typeset in Joanna
by Deanta Global Publishing Services, Chennai, India

We dedicate this book to Hannah and Dori, our wives and most significant others.

This book was completed while Arie W. Kruglanski was a residential fellow at the Rockefeller Foundation Center at Bellagio, Italy.

CONTENTS

PREFACE

This book has had a long past and a short history. The past goes back to World War II and Arie Kruglanski's childhood. As a Jewish boy growing up in the 1940s in the ill-fated Lodz Ghetto in Poland at the time of the Holocaust, fear and anxiety suffused the very air he breathed. The likelihood of annihilation weighed heavy on everyone's minds; and the angst of being reduced to nothingness, of utter *insignificance*, was omnipresent.

Yet strangely, in those dark years of violence and dread, young Arie was made to feel significant and worthy. As his parents' only child, at a time when having children was outrageously unwise, he was surrounded by love, warmth, and admiration, and treated as someone very special. The jarring dissonance between his sense of worth at home – and his worthlessness outside of it – posed for him a puzzle that for long decades remained unsolved.

Fast forward to the early 2000s, with the world still recovering from the trauma of Al Qaeda's attack on the United States on 9/11. To understand how this unimaginable tragedy could have happened, scientists of various ilks dropped what they were doing to refocus their attention on terrorism, its causes, and its consequences. By now a seasoned professor of psychology, Arie was among those who did so – in his case to turn to terrorism's psychological underpinnings, and more specifically to terrorists' motivations. Early terrorism scholars explained this form of mass murder by compiling lists of specific motives including vengeance, religion, adoration of the leader, and expected perks of paradise, among others. But Arie's epiphany was when he hit upon what appeared to be the common denominator of those reasons: the terrorists' Quest for Significance (QFS) and mattering that they believed would be enhanced by acts of martyrdom and perverted heroism.

That discovery marks the start of this book's short history. Whereas initially the Quest for Significance was invoked in relation to violent extremism, it became clear that violence and aggression pave merely one path to Significance, and there are many others laid out by cultural values and narratives.

What followed was a full-fledged theory of QFS, the "mother" of all social motivations. Truly, Significance deserves a capital "S," as its pursuit affects individuals, communities, and nations – its impacts charting the course of history. At long last, the puzzle of Significance that troubled Arie as a child has been resolved.

After discussing this with a friend, Dan Raviv, a distinguished foreign correspondent who has witnessed many historical figures and events up close, we decided to recount the Significance story in the book you are holding, the fruit of a long journey into the mysteries of the human psyche. In it, we aim to convey to you, dear reader, what the Quest for Significance means to you, how it affects your life's experiences, and how it impacts your relations with friends, lovers, adversaries, and the world at large.

1

WINNING FRIENDS AND INFLUENCING PEOPLE

Dale Carnegie's 1936 self-help volume, *How to Win Friends and Influence People*, is one of the best-selling books of all time – bought by 30 million readers in over a dozen languages. Seventy-five years after the appearance of its first edition, it was number 19 on TIME magazine's list of the 100 most influential books. What made this work so incredibly successful? Part of the answer is that it is very easy to read, very direct and practical, a "self-help" book in the truest meaning of the term. Each chapter ends with a principle that is simple, understandable, and seemingly easy to implement: "Don't criticize, condemn, or complain," "Give honest and sincere appreciation," "Arouse in the other person an eager want," "Become genuinely interested in other people," and "Smile."

However useful, these are mere techniques: means to a specific end, "winning friends and influencing people." So, the real question is why millions of readers all over the world seek this particular end to begin with? You may think of that as a trick question – that everyone would agree that

DOI: 10.4324/9781003410706-1

it is nice to have friends and the power to influence, whereas being friend-less, loveless, and without influence would feel terrible.

Whereas this may be true, there is a better reply to the question, one that took this entire book to write. In brief, having friends who appreciate you, and having people accept your opinion and be influenced by it, is proof that you *matter*. You are *somebody*. You have *Significance*.

That is a better answer, because it gets to the crux of the issue. All of us – whether our achievements so far seem high, middle, or low – are on a Quest for Significance (QFS). We believe our book can help by identify-ing and highlighting the techniques people use in that lifelong QFS. We explain why and how they work, and also under what circumstances they might not.

In addition, we illuminate the importance of seeing how other people react to your behavior, and how you react to theirs. In effect, we connect and amplify Carnegie's techniques – which he refined into bite-sized advice – and tie them to the encounters, dilemmas, predicaments, and experi-ences at the core of being human.

Our natural actions and reactions include love and hate, kindness and aggression, pride and jealousy, elation and exploitation, selflessness and nihilistic martyrdom. The choices we make in our QFS lead to our joys and disappointments, and on a broader canvas, they relate to political activism, the striving for social justice, wars, and revolutions.

This goes well beyond Dale Carnegie's counsel to be nice and consider-ate to people. Indeed, the simple techniques he proposed are but the tip of an iceberg, concealing a mammoth amount of underlying psychology that governs our thoughts, feelings, and actions. The purpose of this book is to uncover this psychology, spell out how it may increase your understanding of yourself and other people, and ultimately suggest how that can make you a more effective parent, spouse, colleague, and citizen.

The Quest for Significance

The desire for our lives to matter – the uniquely human Quest for Significance – is the pursuit of dignity, respect, and appreciation from people who mat-ter to us. Experts on behavior call it our craving for social worth. The 18th-century philosopher Jean-Jacques Rousseau made the quest sound egotistical, dubbing it "self-love" (*amour propre*).[1] Many centuries of history and culture show that QFS is one of the most fundamental human motivations, truly making the world go round, both for good and for ill, in every stage of every person's life. Questing for Significance not only underlies romantic love, friendship, and devotion, but it also promotes hate and violence. It propels the generous dedication of artists and humanitarians, yet it also feeds tyrants' and dictators' insatiable appetite for power.

As we show throughout this volume and illustrate via copious examples, the desire to believe that you are significant is really why "winning friends and influencing people" is so universally appealing. Showing people respect and appreciation is giving them what they most desire, thus turning them into your friends who respect you in return and value your opinion.

There is a negative mirror image: Denying people respect – humiliating or insulting them – is extremely hurtful and often the cause of great emotional suffering that can erupt in aggression against themselves or others. This dynamic has been an inseparable part of human nature for millennia, as the following story illustrates.

The Oldest Complaint in History

An archaeological fragment dating back to roughly 1750 BCE was found in the ancient city of Ur, located in what is now Iraq. The small clay tablet (4.6 by 2 inches) is part of the permanent collection of the British Museum. The language on the tablet is Akkadian, the earliest known Semitic language (a Middle Eastern group that includes Hebrew, Arabic, and Aramaic). It is written in cuneiform script and has been deciphered by scholars to reveal a litany of complaints from a man named Nanni about a merchant known as Ea-nasir. Ea-nasir, the tablet alleges, delivered to Nanni the wrong grade of copper and was also responsible for delays in a later delivery. And worst of all, he was rude to the servant whom Nanni sent to collect the product. This insult in particular occasioned Nanni's sense that he had lost Significance and motivated his angry complaint.

"What do you take me for, that you treat somebody like me with such contempt?" said Nanni.[2] "I have sent as messengers gentlemen like ourselves to collect the bag with my money, but you have treated me with contempt by sending them back to me empty-handed several times, and that through enemy territory. Is there anyone among the merchants who trade with Telmun who has treated me in this way? You alone treat my messenger with contempt!

How have you treated me for that copper? You have withheld my money bag from me in enemy territory. It is now up to you to restore [my money] to me in full. ...I will not accept here any copper from you that is not of fine quality. I shall [from now on] select and take the ingots individually in my own yard, and I shall exercise against you my right of rejection because you have treated me with contempt."

There is little doubt that Nanni feels slighted and treated as unworthy by Ea-nasir, that he detests that feeling, and therefore he vows to restore his self-pride in future transactions. However, his plans to do so appear gentle and civilized.

Human reactions look very different when the insulted individual is a powerful despot, the leader of a well-armed nation with a nuclear arsenal at his disposal. A recent case in point is that of Vladimir Putin, who, upon feeling slighted by the West and in order to restore his and fellow Russians' feelings of Significance, initiated a major war that killed and wounded around 500,000 people in its first 18 months.[3]

Putin's War

In February 2022, Putin ordered the invasion of Ukraine and blamed the brutal war that ensued on a Ukrainian fantasy of being part of the West, which he called a clear threat to Russia's security. Yet, there are strong, Significance-based reasons to believe that the cause of the war was something completely different: Putin's outsized dream of glory, seeking a place in history as one of his country's most heroic leaders.

Putin apparently nourished for decades his vision for restoring the greatness of a collapsed empire. When the Soviet Union was disbanded in 1991, most officials in St Petersburg's city hall were quick to replace the portraits of Vladimir Lenin and other Communist heroes with an official photograph of Boris Yeltsin, the new Russian president. However, there was one exception. The mayor's personal assistant, young Vladimir Putin, chose for his wall a portrait of Peter the Great: one of Russia's most important czars who created a powerful European empire.[4] This incident now seems like a portent, highlighting a streak of Putin's personality that 30 years later would make him the alarming center of global attention: his unquenchable thirst for Significance.

The human desire for dignity and worth is universal. No one wants to be humiliated, ignored, or patronized. But only a tiny minority are willing to risk everything for the sake of glory. Putin is one of those select few. When appointed prime minister in 1999, he described his new job as a "historical mission" to save Russia from "bandits" – the Chechen Islamists who had attacked the Russian Republic of Dagestan. "I realized I could do this only at the cost of my political career," Putin told an interviewer. "It was a minimal cost to pay."[5] He ordered the destruction of an entire city, Grozny, to defeat the rebels. An estimated 8,000 residents were killed.[6] It was clear, from the start, that this newly minted leader was willing to take risky steps that could bring him glory.

Putin has often portrayed himself as the savior of the Russian homeland from a scheming West bent on destroying Russia's "traditional values." In a speech on the day that the 2022 invasion began, he claimed he had no choice, as "a matter of life and death, a matter of our historical future as a nation."[7]

In most cultures, Russia and the United States included, one of the most sacred values is patriotism. Serving one's country with devotion and self-denial bolsters a person's social worth – in their own eyes and in the eyes of others – claiming a place in history and the aura of a hero. Patriotism is particularly put to the test when your country is in dire straits and threatened by enemies, or when your leader declares that the straits are dire.

For those who crave Significance, the perception of national humiliation offers a golden opportunity for greatness. The whole nation seeks a turnaround story, a comeback offering leaders a chance to achieve glory.

Vladimir Vladimirovich Putin soared through the ranks of Russian politics at just such a propitious moment. The obvious loser of the Cold War, Russia quickly saw its vast empire in Eastern Europe come unglued. The country was left with fewer than 150 million citizens, half the population of the old Soviet Union, and for many of them, the breakup was a shattering cultural trauma that would last for decades. The loss of empire and global status offered an opportunity for Putin to lead an effort aimed at reversing that catastrophe, and thus to attain greatness and recover all or some of the nation's lost Significance.

In such circumstances, a person on his Quest for Significance often casts blame on foes and rivals, and Putin increasingly flared with resentment directed at the United States – because even if the United States did not cause Russia's precipitous fall, the Americans were rubbing it in. Just after Putin first sought to regain power and pride by seizing parts of eastern Ukraine in 2014, President Barack Obama delivered a calculated insult by declaring: "Russia is a regional power that is threatening some of its immediate neighbors, not out of strength but out of weakness."[8] Not a world power? Only regional?

These perceived slights poured oil on the flames of Putin's discontent and reinforced his resolve to make Russia great again, which for Putin meant a show of force. The rest is history, of course, and a tragic one at that.

Aggressing for Significance

It is no coincidence that Putin used aggression as a way of seeking Significance. Violence and aggression are the primordial ways of gaining dominance and Significance among humans and animals alike.[9] China's Chairman Mao Zedong famously proclaimed in 1927 that "political power grows out of the barrel of a gun."[10] In his preface to Franz Fanon's anti-colonialist classic, *The Wretched of the Earth*,[11] the existentialist philosopher Jean-Paul Sartre supported the book's call for the oppressed to "become men" by exercising "mad fury." The writer Isaac Asimov dubbed aggression as "the last refuge of the incompetent,"[12] and the renowned psychologist William James quipped that "war is the romance of history" because its horrors are endlessly fascinating.[13]

Throughout history, leaders have fanned the flames of humiliation-driven anger to whip their followers into clamoring for aggression. For example, Adolf Hitler cultivated the legend of the stab-in-the-back (*Dolchstoßlegende*) of the German Army by the Jews to explain the capitulation of Germany in World War I and thus to encourage oppression and mass murder of these alleged culprits. Hitler used the humiliation of Germany in the Versailles Treaty of 1919 as justification for his invasions that triggered World War II. Japan, which had fought alongside the Allies in World War I, launched expansionist policies in the Pacific and joined the German–Italian Axis in World War II – partly because of the feeling among Japan's leaders that their nation, too, was humiliated by its former allies when they refused to reject racism in the Versailles Treaty.[14]

Everyday aggression is also fueled typically by the perpetrator's prior humiliation or Significance loss. This is particularly true among men. When mass shooters have been captured or killed, their neighbors often say that the fellow was reacting to a lifetime of being bullied. Within married couples, murder is more likely to be the result of a wife's infidelity or suspected infidelity – immortalized in Shakespeare's renowned play, "Othello" – rather than infidelity by the husband.

Evidence also suggests that young men who come from disadvantaged family backgrounds have lower IQs, are of lower socioeconomic status, and therefore have less opportunity to succeed in society on a traditional career path. They are thus more likely to be involved in gang activity and violent crime. A key part of their goal is to enhance their Significance in the eyes of females and other gang members.[15]

Margo Wilson and Martin Daly, a wife-and-husband team of behavioral scientists, examined all the homicides committed in the city of Detroit in one year, 1972. Their analysis revealed that the majority of these violent crimes were committed in the course of "social conflict" where status (that is, Significance) was at stake. Actors in these murderous dramas – both perpetrators and victims – were predominantly young males, unemployed and single, likely to feel insignificant and low in social worth.

Even though the link between aggression and dominance (and hence Significance) may be primordial and universal, especially for men, the specific culture in which people find themselves matters a lot. Militaristic cultures such as Germany of the 1930s or Russia have held the value of aggressiveness in high esteem and honor the lives and memory of courageous soldiers and victorious generals. A study of violence in America's Southern states coined the term "culture of honor" to describe the regional norms' belief in fighting to cancel humiliations and insults.[16]

Sex and Significance

Desire for sexual pleasure is, of course, one of the most dominant forces affecting human life. Hundreds of billions of dollars a year are spent on sex globally, including money spent on pornography, human trafficking, prostitution, and sex toys. In all known societies, sex is the subject of laws, norms, and taboos that impact the lives of billions of people around the planet.

Whereas sex is often considered a physical and biological need, it has a substantial psychological underlay related to the Quest for Significance, particularly for men. Sex may confer Significance directly, through evidence of their own attractiveness and charm that are admired and envied, or indirectly, through the demonstration of their power and dominance in the case of rape, or through the propagation of multiple children who symbolically and biologically extend their existence and world impact.

Seduction

In Mozart's illustrious opera *Don Giovanni*, Leporello, Giovanni's faithful servant, sings the seducer's praise by cataloging the women his master slept with, as follows: "In Italy, six hundred and forty / In Germany, two hundred and thirty-one; a hundred in France; in Turkey, ninety-one / But in Spain already one thousand and three."

Don Giovanni's sexual exploits are obviously a source of his pride and claims to Significance. However, the use of sex as a path to Significance goes well beyond the world of opera. Researchers Pamela Regan and Carla Dreyer asked college students (men and women) how and why they chose romantic and sexual partners. They found that young men in particular admitted they were mostly following the behavior of their peers, so that they could enhance their prestige.[17]

In a study conducted in 2007, Cindy Meston and David Buss asked approximately 1,500 people why they had sex. Major gender differences emerged: Men more than women reported that sexual liaisons were a way to improve their social status. The males agreed more with statements such as, "I wanted to enhance my reputation," "I wanted to brag to my friends about my conquests," and "I needed another notch on my belt."[18]

Again and again, men who are sexually active are found to regard that as a way of proving and enhancing their sense of masculinity and vitality.[19] Indeed, the common phrase "sexual conquests" strongly suggests that sexual success is seen as a triumphant source of Significance and social worth. The seducer is viewed as a "conqueror" to whom glory is due.

Rape

One of the most prevalent yet underreported crimes, rape, is not primarily a sexually motivated act – many scholars say – but an act of aggression intended to degrade, humiliate, and subjugate the victim, to exercise dominance and, in this way, to assert one's own supposed superiority. Analyses of gang rapes suggest that participants in this odious crime are trying to prove their masculinity to the other rapists. Gang rapes often follow a ritualized pattern in which the sequence of carrying out the offense is determined by each man's status in the group.[20]

Consistent with the notion that rape is a way that a criminal – often a man who is pathetic and powerless in most of his life's domains – tries to build up his own Significance, social psychologists have distinguished between rape-free and rape-prone societies. Rape-free societies are ones where women are respected and enjoy a recognized and positive status in their culture. Rape-prone societies are ones where women are held in low esteem and are subordinate in almost every way; where male power has been toppled from its former overlord status; and/or where societies have rigid conceptions of "masculinity" versus "femininity."

Researchers conclude that most Western societies are among the rape-prone, in part because of strong women's movements pointing out gender-based discrimination, plus a sense among some men that they have lost their former power. And so, rape is among the most frequent crimes of violence in the United States.[21]

Rape committed as part of war has a second-level intention. War criminals are not only besmirching the humanity of female victims. The attackers are also attempting to humiliate the male-led armies and governments of their enemy – as if to trumpet the insulting notion that the enemies are incapable of "protecting their women." Thus, the goal is to diminish the Significance of both the women and the men of their adversary.

The fact that rape during wartime is so common attests to the enduring power of this appalling phenomenon. Historical accounts report that over two million women were raped by Soviet troops when the Red Army liberated Berlin in 1945. Between 250,000 and 500,000 women and girls were raped in the 1994 genocide in Rwanda, more than 60,000 in a civil war in Sierra Leone, between 20,000 and 50,000 in the war in Bosnia and Herzegovina, and at least 200,000 in the Democratic Republic of the Congo since 1996.[22] More recently, a United Nations commission issued a report attesting to the massive occurrence of rape of Ukrainian women and children by Russian soldiers.[23]

Significance by Impregnation

Another UN report declared that a massive number of rapes and the forced impregnation of women during war amounted to "ethnic cleansing" and genocide. Armed groups and forces strategically use the forced impregnation of women to destabilize communities, in that children born as a result of war-related rape are often treated as the next generation of the rapists' side in conflict. When the kids grow up, they are recruited as soldiers for the aggressors.[24] That is yet another ugly way in which sexual violence is used to elevate the Significance of a violent invasion.

A very different case of Significance by impregnation is related to a movement calling itself "longtermism," based on the ethical view that positively influencing the long-term future is a key moral priority of our time. Elon Musk is a devoted "longtermist" who believes that smart people like himself should have more children. "If each successive generation of smart people has fewer kids, that's probably bad," he was quoted as saying.[25] At the time of publication, Musk was the multi-billionaire father of 11 children with three different mothers via multiple different means (including IVF and surrogacy).

Another prominent advocate for longtermism was Nick Bostrom, an Oxford University philosopher and head of the Musk-funded Future of Humanity Institute. In 2017, Bostrom commented on how too many lower-IQ people were having children in "modern societies," and earlier in his career, Bostrom warned about less "intellectually talented individuals" having a greater number of children than more "intellectually talented" people.[26] While ostensibly worried about the future of humanity, the longtermist argument appears to be little more than an attempt by people who view themselves as superior to propagate further their "brand," and hence Significance, through spawning a maximal number of progeny.

Physical Frailty

The Quest for Significance appears in many guises and generally needs to be awakened or activated by various circumstances. QFS can also result in a range of behaviors that are aimed at attaining Significance in given situa-tions. Having the power to aggress, for instance, with no one to stop you, may encourage you to do so as a way of feeling dominant and superior. The perception of being slighted by others may incite you to vengeful actions against those culprits or alternatively seek their approval by demonstrating your virtues and capabilities.

A feeling of Significance loss may also be aroused by failing at an impor-tant task or not measuring up to a cherished value (for instance, courage or honesty). Keep in mind also that through no fault of their own, a person may never possess a culturally valued attribute (such as being a man, being white, or being Christian).

Also, a person could lose his or her socially valued attributes – such as obvious brainpower or physical strength – and hence feel less significant and diminished for reasons of health or age. It is common for a person's loss of Significance to trigger a stronger QFS, and the quest could help shore up strength or mental sharpness.

A fascinating observation is that when people feel that their abilities are slipping, they feel a greater need for connections with other people to whom they might matter. Researchers Laura Carstensen and Barbara Fredricksen published evidence in 1998 that physical weakness stemming from declining health (either because of being elderly or having tested positive for HIV) is associated with giving greater importance to the per-son's relations with close others.[27] The authors suggested that it was not exactly the person's age. It was their perception of proximity to the end of life – feeling vulnerable and frail, especially – that gave them a feeling of impending insignificance. That is what drove them to seek affirmation of their Significance from trusted people.

Sometimes, that kind of positive turn toward others can take subtle forms. For instance, some participants in a research study were shown evi-dence that there was a chance they would be injured in a war. That group became more willing to volunteer to help victims of the conflict. The researchers found a positive correlation between participants' perceived likelihood of getting hurt or sick and their willingness to donate to a local charity. Moreover, when participants' sense of physical vulnerability was experimentally enhanced by asking them to imagine themselves in the shoes of someone who had a high risk of developing skin cancer, those people showed a higher willingness to donate to a health organization.[28]

Apparently, people can become nicer to others when their sense of Significance is threatened. It seems that we need others' appreciation when we sense that our powers are waning. Indeed, research findings show[29] that older people are seen as low on competence but warm. That suggests, as social psychologists would explain, that older folks often suffer losses in the competence domain, but they seek to compensate for their Significance loss by exhibiting warmth – another Significance-conferring attribute.

Even in Asia, where the influence of Confucian values leads to treating elderly people with respect and obeying them, studies indicate that senior citizens are perceived as more warm than competent.[30]

In the 2017 film, "Phantom Thread," the protagonist is a London couturier named Reynolds Woodcock. He is an egomaniacal and tyrannical artist who is highly dismissive of his wife, Alma, and is about to leave her. However, this dynamic quickly changes when she comes up with a winning, albeit wacky, idea: to weaken his invincible sense of agency by poisoning him (non-fatally) and rendering him temporarily helpless. The ruse works wonders. Woodcock's flagging love for his spouse is quickly reignited, and he regains full appreciation for her indispensability.[31] This entertaining premise is not as outlandish as it might appear. In fact, it is grounded in acute psychological insight, as the documented relationship between fragility and neediness demonstrates.

Money Talks: On Wealth and Significance

Across cultures and historical periods, people have been gaining their sense of Significance from wealth, whereas poverty has been generally seen as a Significance-reducing stigma.[32] Money allows a person to obtain all kinds of goods and physical comforts. But it also fuels the attainment of cherished values, such as security and independence.

Being wealthy almost always attracts the attention of other people interested in benefiting from the rich person's affluence and influence. So, people with a lot of money can feel confident that they gain Significance through being admired by anyone they help; and they may well feel positive reactions from the wider society. In short, money reduces a person's dependence on other people; it gives them freedom and the power to do what they want. They are assured of having the admiration of others, and they do not need to make great efforts to attain it. Hence, they do not generally strive to win the friendship and goodwill of others.

Echoing this state of mind that affluence can engender, portrayals of the rich in the world's literature have been typically negative. Wealthy people are often caricatured, if not overtly demonized.[33] Authors such as Balzac, Dickens, and Dostoyevsky have characterized their affluent characters as cunning and morally lax. Anthony Chuzzlewit and his son Jonas, in Dickens's Martin Chuzzlewit, are described as greedy and miserly, for example. Authors such as F. Scott Fitzgerald and John O'Hara, who were fascinated by the rich, usually depicted them as cynical or jaded – as hedonists such as Tom and Daisy Buchanan in The Great Gatsby, or as ill-bred strivers of the nouveau riche variety, such as Julian English in Appointment in Samarra. These authors were not wrong. Research shows that wealthy and powerful people are indeed less empathetic[34] and (sorry, rich folks) less altruistic.[35]

Intriguing psychological findings suggest that just thinking of money has far-reaching effects. Essentially, people who do that feel empowered. Experiments in which participants were made to think about money reported that they felt stronger,[36] more self-confident, self-efficacious,[37] and self-sufficient; in sum, more significant.[38]

It is less pleasing to read other experimental results: having money on their mind makes people feel less of a need for social contact. They even deprecate other people. Simply mentioning cash or financial topics, and then questioning participants on various issues, exposed a lower need to belong with other people,[39] and the test subjects with money on their mind chose more individually oriented leisure activities and took a seat farther from other participants.[40] In yet other studies, "money-priming" remarks were found to reduce people's intentions to socialize, to engage in intimate relations,[41] to show concern for others,[42] and to feel compassion and empathy.[43]

Having an "Attitude"

In short, mere thoughts about money affect not only our self-perceptions but also our attitudes toward other people. The concept of money is associated in people's minds with wealth, wealth is linked to Significance, and that, in turn, is associated with a sense of independence and a lower neediness for support from other people. The research shows that merely contemplating a subject – certainly if it is money or another universal marker of success – can affect how we see ourselves and feel toward others.

These effects do not only concern money, whether real or contemplated. People's attitudes toward themselves and toward others are also affected by having high status (versus low status) in their group or society, or a higher degree of competence (versus people who seem less able).

In all those cases, people with a high presumed sense of Significance – high status, any measure of social power, or feeling competent and successful – display less care about others. Ample research[44] reveals that individuals who score high on these dimensions pay less attention to other people and are less responsive to their needs.

These research findings mean that whereas "winning friends and influencing people" is generally desirable, it is desired less by some people compared with others. "People who need people," sang Barbra Streisand in a hit from the 1970s, "are the luckiest people in the world." Yet, research suggests otherwise. The "lucky" ones – the rich, the famous, the powerful – seem to need people less than the fragile, the weak, and the downtrodden. The former already feel significant and respected; they do not require repeated affirmation of this fact from new friends and acquaintances. They are not as concerned about "winning friends and influencing people" as are people low on Significance, simply because the rich and famous already feel admired and influential.

Everyday Significance

Our Quest for Significance enters into the deepest and most intimate nooks and crannies of our experience. Our mood fluctuates on an almost minute-by-minute basis, reflecting the smiles and the snubs we receive from people around us. An unanswered e-mail may make us feel "ghosted" or willfully ignored. A kind gesture from a stranger may make us feel worthy and appreciated. A rejection letter can toss us into a black hole of despair. And an invitation to some project or event, being included and recognized, may make us elated and optimistic.

The seemingly trivial bits of "good" or "bad" news in our day-to-day lives determine our momentary mood and sense of well-being, all because of their implications for our Significance. Behind the superficial cravings for wealth, happiness, power, or beauty, people have a deeper innate need to achieve social worth, dignity, and the sense that they matter.

In short, the sense of *mattering* constitutes a center of gravity for people's existence. It is a framework that organizes life's options and desires, affecting the choices we make and the sacrifices and trade-offs that those involve.

That is why we need to decode how we – and the people around us – define Significance in our own individual ways. Only then can we truly understand ourselves and others. And only after that can we take better control of how we react to others and how they to us, day to day and year to year.

Dale Carnegie's highly influential self-help book intuited the tremendous importance of the Quest for Significance, without using that term, and he delivered techniques for satisfying that need – through direct contact with and potential impact on people we meet. Yet, however insightful and useful that book has been, it was based on the psychology of the 1930s. The science of psychology has advanced appreciably over the last century.

In the book you are now holding, we are taking advantage of the great progress in the science of human motivation that occurred over the last century and applying it toward understanding the Quest for Significance, this "mother" of all social motivations. In examining the deep basis of Significance strivings, we go beyond mere techniques for "winning friends and influencing people." We address their limits and the circumstances in which they may work just fine.

Moreover, whereas Carnegie's work focused on *what you can do to others*, our analysis affords insights also into *what they can do for you*; in this way deepening your self-knowledge, as Socrates recommended, while also teaching you to adjust your reactions, fulfill your Significance goals, and add to your sense of well-being.

Summary

The Quest for Significance is a fundamental social motivation that all humans possess, though not everyone possesses it to the same degree. It is a motivation that affects much of our lives, in matters small and large. It has a major effect on people's everyday sense of feeling happy and proud, whereas feeling insignificant and humiliated makes them upset and dejected.

QFS also energizes major social movements, wars, and revolutions. Big things happen when one group of people – members of a particular nation, race, ethnicity, religion, or gender – feel that they are woefully deprived of Significance by others, or that other groups or identities do not give them the Significance that they deserve.

What makes people feel significant depends largely on the values that a culture or subculture uses to measure a person's worth. Some of those values are moral, like honesty, generosity, or kindness. Others are material, like money or net worth. Yet others are aesthetic, such as beauty, or political, like the right to wield power.

Understanding how the Quest for Significance works – and how deep is its influence on people's lives – is helpful in navigating everybody's relations with everybody else. That applies at home with the family, at work, or at leisure, in fact, in all social circumstances, whatever the relationships and venue might be.

Notes

1 Rousseau discussed *amour propre* in his 1750 essay, *Discourse on the Sciences and Arts*, where he suggested that excessive self-regard fuels selfishness, which is anything but virtuous.

2 Oppenheim, A. Leo, *Letters from Mesopotamia* (Chicago: University of Chicago Press, 1967). Oppenheim, a distinguished Assyriologist, translated the cuneiform on the fragment from Ur.

3 Cooper, Helene; Gibbons-Neff, Thomas; Schmitt, Eric; Barnes, Julian E., "Troop Deaths and Injuries in Ukraine War Near 500,000, U.S. Officials Say," *New York Times* (August 18, 2023); found at www.nytimes.com/2023/08/18/us/politics/ukraine-russia-war-casualties.html.

4 Cohen, Richard, "Vladimir Putin's Rewriting of History Draws on a Long Tradition of Soviet Myth-Making," *Smithsonian Magazine* (March 18, 2022).

5 Putin, Vladimir; Gevorkyan, Natalia; Timakova, Natalya; Kolesnikov, Andrei, *First Person: An Astonishingly Frank Self-Portrait by Russia's President Vladimir Putin* (New York: PublicAffairs, 2000).

6 Zürcher, Christoph, *The Post-Soviet Wars: Rebellion, Ethnic Conflict, and Nationhood in the Caucasus* (New York: NYU Press, 2007).

7 Galeotti, Mark, "Putin Is on a Quest for Historical Significance by Invading Ukraine and Gambling on His Own and Russia's Glory," *The Conversation* (March 1, 2022). Galeotti is a British historian specializing in Russian politics.

8 A news report from The Hague on March 25, 2014, found at www.reuters.com/article/idUSBREA2O19J.

9 Kruglanski, Arie W.; Ellenberg, Jordan; Szumowska, Ewa; Molinario, Ettore; Speckhard, Anne; Leander, N. Pontus; Pierro, Antonio; Di Cicco, Giorgio; Bushman, Brad J., "Frustration-Aggression Hypothesis Reconsidered: The Role of Significance Quest," *Aggressive Behavior*, Vol. 49, No. 5 (2023), pp. 445–468.

10 Zedong, Mao, "Problems of War and Strategy," in *Selected Works, Volume 2* (Beijing: Foreign Languages Press, 1965), p. 224.

11 Fanon, Frantz, *The Wretched of the Earth* (New York: Grove Press, 1961).

12 Asimov, Isaac, *Foundation* (New York: Gnome Press, 1951).

13 William James (1842–1910), in his essay "The Moral Equivalent of War," first published in 1910, and available as a thin book from several publishers.

14 Many historians have established that Japan proposed a statement in the Versailles Treaty ending World War I that would have condemned racism. However, the controlling powers were so racist against Japan that they rejected the proposal. We are indebted to John Levine, a professor emeritus at the University of Pittsburgh, for these suggestions.

15 Daly, Martin; Wilson, Margo, "Crime and Conflict: Homicide in Evolutionary Psychological Perspective," *Crime and Justice*, Vol. 22 (1997), pp. 51–100. Also: Macfarlane, Angus, "Gangs and Adolescent Mental Health: A Narrative Review," *Journal of Child & Adolescent Trauma*, Vol. 12, No. 3 (2018), pp. 411–420.

16 Nisbett, Richard; Cohen, Dov, *Culture of Honor: The Psychology of Violence in the South* (New York: Routledge, 1996).

17 Studies include several by Pamela Regan, a professor at California State University, including Regan, P.; Dreyer, C.S., "Lust? Love? Status?: Young Adults' Motives for Engaging in Casual Sex," *Journal of Psychology and Human Sexuality*, Vol. 11, No. 1 (1999), pp. 1–24.

18 Meston, Cindy M.; Buss, David M., "Why Humans Have Sex," *Archives of Sexual Behavior*, Vol. 36 (2007), pp. 477–507.

19 Jonason, Peter K., "A Mediation Hypothesis to Account for the Sex Differences in Reported Number of Sexual Partners: An Intrasexual Competition Approach," *International Journal of Sexual Health*, Vol. 19, No. 4 (2008), pp. 41–49.

20 Seifert, Ruth, *War and Rape: Analytical Approaches* (Geneva: Women's International League for Peace and Freedom, 1993).

21 Porter, Roy. "Rape—Does It Have a Historical Meaning?" In Tomaselli, Sylvana; Porter, Roy (eds.), *Rape* (Oxford: Basil Blackwell, 1986), pp. 216–236.

22 United Nations Development Fund for Women, "Rape as a Tactic of War," *Conflict and Post Conflict* (undated); found at www.unwomen.org/sites/default/files/Headquarters/Media/Publications/UNIFEM/EVAWkit_06_Factsheet_ConflictAndPostConflict_en.pdf.

23 United Nations High Commissioner for Human Rights, "Report on Human Rights Violations and War Crimes in Ukraine," October 2022.

24 United Nations Security Council, "Women and Girls Who Become Pregnant as a Result of Sexual Violence in Conflict and Children Born of Sexual Violence in Conflict," Report of the Secretary-General on Conflict-Related Sexual Violence

(April 2020); found at www.un.org/sexualviolenceinconflict/wp-content/uploads/2022/02/report/auto-draft/N2223437.pdf.

25 Many websites include this quotation from Vance, Ashlee, *Elon Musk: Tesla, SpaceX, and the Quest for a Fantastic Future* (New York: HarperCollins, 2015).

26 Bostrom, Nick, "Existential Risks: Analyzing Human Extinction Scenarios and Related Hazards," *Journal of Evolution and Technology*, Vol. 9, No. 1 (2002), pp. 1–30.

27 Carstensen, Laura L.; Fredrickson, Barbara L., "Influence of HIV Status and Age on Cognitive Representations of Others," *Health Psychology*, Vol. 17, No. 6 (1998), pp. 494–503.

28 Motsenok, Marina; Kogut, Tehila; Ritov, Ilana, "Perceived Physical Vulnerability Promotes Prosocial Behavior," *Personality and Social Psychology Bulletin*, Vol. 48, No. 2 (2022), pp. 254–267.

29 Cuddy, Amy J.C.; Fiske, Susan T.; Glick, Peter, "The BIAS Map: Behaviors from Intergroup Affect and Stereotypes," *Journal of Personality and Social Psychology*, Vol. 92, No. 4 (April 2007), pp. 631–648.

30 Cuddy, Amy J.C.; Fiske, Susan T.; Kwan, Virginia S.Y.; Glick, Peter; Demoulin, Stéphanie; Leyens, Jacques-Philippe; Ziegler, René, "Stereotype Content Model Across Cultures: Towards Universal Similarities and Some Differences," *British Journal of Social Psychology*, Vol. 48, No. 1 (March 2009), pp. 1–33.

31 "Phantom Thread," directed by Paul Thomas Anderson, was released by Focus Features in 2017.

32 Cohen, Dov; Shin, Faith; Liu, Xi, "Meanings and Functions of Money in Different Cultural Milieus," *Annual Review of Psychology*, Vol. 70 (January 2019), pp. 475–497.

33 Merkin, Daphne, "The Rich in Fiction," *The New Yorker* (September 12, 2015); found at www.newyorker.com/culture/culture-desk/the-rich-in-fiction.

34 Fiske, Susan T., "Envy Up, Scorn Down: How Comparison Divides Us," *American Psychologist*, Vol. 65, No. 8 (November 2010), pp. 698–706. Grewal, Daisy, "How Wealth Reduces Compassion," *Scientific American* (April 12, 2012); found at www.scientificamerican.com/article/how-wealth-reduces-compassion.

35 Korndorfer, Martin; Egloff, Boris; Schmukle, Stefan, "A Large Scale Test of the Effect of Social Class on Prosocial Behavior," *PLoS One* (Public Library of Science), Vol. 10, No. 7 (2015), pp. 1–48.

36 Zhou, Xinyue; Vohs, Kathleen D.; Baumeister, Roy F., "The Symbolic Power of Money: Reminders of Money Alter Social Distress and Physical Pain," *Psychological Science*, Vol. 20, No. 6 (May 2009), pp. 700–706.

37 Mukherjee, Sumitava; Manjaly, Jaison A.; Nargundkar, Maithilee, "Money Makes You Reveal More," *Frontiers in Psychology*, Vol. 4 (November 11, 2013), p. 839.

38 Vohs, Kathleen D.; Mead, Nicole L.; Goode, Miranda R., "The Psychological Consequences of Money," *Science*, Vol. 314 (November 17, 2006), pp. 1154–1156.

39 Piers, A.; Krus, J.; Dooley, E.; Wallace, H., "Effects of Money Priming and Imagined Wealth on Need to Belong," on an easel board presented at the annual meeting of the Society for Personality and Social Psychology, Austin, TX, February 2014.

40 Vohs, Kathleen D.; Mead, Nicole L.; Goode, Miranda R., "The Psychological Consequences of Money," *Science*, Vol. 314 (November 17, 2006), pp. 1154–1156.

41 Mogilner, Cassie, "The Pursuit of Happiness: Time, Money, and Social Connection," *Psychological Science*, Vol. 21, No. 9 (August 31, 2010), pp. 1348–1354.

42 Vohs, Kathleen D., "Money Priming Can Change People's Thoughts, Feelings, Motivations, and Behaviors: An Update on 10 Years of Experiments," *Journal of Experimental Psychology: General*, Vol. 144, No. 4 (November 2015), p. e86.

43 Vohs, Kathleen D.; Mead, Nicole L.; Goode, Miranda R., "The Psychological Consequences of Money," *Science*, Vol. 314 (November 17, 2006), pp. 1154–1156. See also Kraus, Michael W.; Keltner, Dacher, "Signs of Socioeconomic Status: A Thin-Slicing Approach," *Psychological Science*, Vol. 20, No. 1 (January 2009), pp. 99–106; Schwartz, Shalom H., "Value Orientations: Measurement, Antecedents and Consequences Across Nations," in Jowell, Roger; Roberts, Caroline; Fitzgerald, Rory; Eva, Gillian (eds.), *Measuring Attitudes Cross-Nationally: Lessons from the European Social Survey* (London: SAGE Publications, 2007), pp. 169–203; Stellar, Jennifer E.; Manzo, Vida M.; Kraus, Michael W.; Keltner, Dacher, "Class and Compassion: Socioeconomic Factors Predict Responses to Suffering," *Emotion*, Vol. 12, No. 3 (June 2012), pp. 449–459.

44 Milyavsky, Maxim; Kruglanski, Arie W.; Gelfand, Michele; Chernikova, Marina; Ellenberg, Molly; Pierro, Antonio, "People Who Need People (and Some Who Think They Don't): On Compensatory Personal and Social Means of Goal Pursuit," *Psychological Inquiry*, Vol. 33, No. 1 (January 2022), pp. 1–22.

2

KNOWING HOW YOU QUEST

How many times a day, on average, do you look at yourself in the mirror? How fussy are you about your haircut? How often during the week do you step on the scale to check your weight? How concerned are you about your fitness? About your diet? About your annual check-up? The point is that people are often very aware of aspects of their physicality. They know how they currently look and how different that is from the ideal in their mind. They are also typically aware of the state of their health and try to take care of themselves with advice from experts, or they follow an exercise regimen aimed at augmenting their strength or sculpting their muscles.

Yet, while people's familiarity with their bodies is often adequate, they appear to have much less knowledge about their own minds. This is the topic – people's ignorance about the way their personality functions – to which we turn next. Fitting with this book's overall theme, we focus particularly on people's self-knowledge (or its absence) about their cravings for mattering and Significance.

DOI: 10.4324/9781003410706-2

Thus Spoke the Oracle!

The first of the three Delphic maxims inscribed in the forecourt of the Temple of Apollo in Delphi was, "Know thyself."[1] This aphorism has been widely cited by ancient Greeks including the playwright Aeschylus, as well as Socrates and his students, the philosopher Plato and the historian Xenophon.

Inspired by 25 centuries of wisdom, we hope you share our enthusiasm for self-knowledge, and our chief concern here is the role of the Quest for Significance (QFS) in your life. As part of the story, you will have the opportunity to assess the strength of your personal QFS. But first, let us consider the issue of self-knowledge more generally.

Obstacles to Self-Knowledge

Despite the wise admonitions of the ancient Greeks, self-awareness is in short supply for most people. By circumstance and often choice, we are directed outwardly rather than inwardly. We look at and form impressions of events and people around us, rather than analyzing our own motivations and reactions. We think that our responses to the world are "objective"; that we feel the way we feel because the world is the way it is. This is called "naïve realism" and is often erroneous.

In fact, Sigmund Freud's interpretation of how our brains work assumes that much of what people do or feel is driven by experiences in their early childhood of which they are blissfully unaware. Psychoanalysis is a journey aimed at discovering the irrational source of our inner conflicts and gaining a deeper understanding of why we feel the way we do about things.

Rigorous psychological research has amply documented how most people are oblivious to what causes even their most mundane reactions. Participants in one study[2] watched different videotaped interviews with the same individual, allegedly a college instructor, who spoke with a foreign accent. In one version of the video, this person behaved in a warm and friendly manner; but in the other version, the teacher seemed cold and distant. Participants who saw the "warm" interviewee formed a positive overall impression of this individual and rated their appearance, mannerisms, and accent as appealing. Participants who watched the "cold" interviewee formed a negative impression and rated the very same attributes as annoying. The participants were completely unaware of what affected their ratings – reporting, in fact, that their like or dislike of the instructor had no effect on how they had scored the person's specific attributes. They were, of course, wrong.

In another study,[3] individuals who suffered from insomnia were asked to keep records of the time they had gone to bed and the time they had fallen asleep. Participants in one group were given a placebo pill, to be taken 15 minutes before they went to bed. They were told that the pill would have an arousing effect: rapid heart rate, some unsteady breathing, bodily warmth, and alertness – all of which are symptoms associated with insomnia. Subjects in a second group were told that the pill would be relaxing: a lowered heart rate, calmer breathing, slightly lower body temperature, and a reduction in alertness. Can you guess which participants were able to fall asleep more quickly?

The researchers expected that the first group would suffer insomnia, as usual, but would figure it was caused by the pill – so they would not worry about it and would fall asleep with comparative ease. The second group, however, would be disappointed that the relaxation pill was not helping them fall asleep – and so would be anxious, worried, and awake for longer. The researchers were right! Participants in the first group reported drifting off to sleep 28% more quickly on the nights with the pill, whereas the second group complained that it took 42% longer than usual on those nights. Despite Delphic maxims, these test subjects had absolutely no idea how they had been influenced by a pill containing nothing.

Yet another study[4] involved asking people to judge which of several articles of clothing was of the best quality. One group was shown four different nightgowns, arrayed left to right; the other took a good look at similarly arranged four pairs of nylon stockings. Unbeknownst to the participants, all the items in each category (that is, nightgowns and stockings) were of the same quality. Participants made their choices and were asked for their reasons. It turned out that all the items that were on the far right side were over-chosen as the best by most participants. Nobody mentioned that the position of the item had any impact on them, and when asked explicitly if the position influenced them, they all strongly denied it – and appeared surprised by the question!

People are also notoriously bad at what psychologists call "affective forecasting," predicting how they would feel in specific future situations. They overestimate the degree and duration of happiness they would experience in reaction to positive events, as well as the pain and suffering they would feel in response to negative events. In one study,[5] fans of sports teams went overboard in predicting how happy they would be after their favorite team won the game, and they overestimated how long the feelings of happiness would last. In another study,[6] women predicted how they would feel if they were asked sexually inappropriate questions by a job interviewer. Most predicted that they would primarily feel anger, more than feeling afraid; but in reality, fear turned out to be the dominant, most intense emotion.

Interestingly, if we try to think hard about our reactions and decisions, that kind of focus often will not improve them – and sometimes might make them worse, leading to regret. This is so because we usually focus on "reasonable," socially appropriate choices, basically choosing with our "head" rather than with our "heart." King Edward VIII, who chose with his heart, never said he regretted abdicating the throne of England in 1936 so he could marry the American divorcee Wallis Simpson; indeed, theirs is considered a great, if controversial, love story. More recently, Prince Harry violated royal norms by marrying a mixed-race American actress. Choosing Meghan Markle and then moving with her to America meant that he was unapologetically following his heart.

In one study that demonstrates the counterproductive effects of over-thinking, participants who were college students were presented with five art posters and allowed to choose one to take home.[7] Two of the posters were reproductions of famous Impressionist paintings and were generally very popular with the student population. The remaining three were less generally popular with students: contemporary, kitschy posters, for instance, showing a cat perched on a rope with the caption, "Gimme a Break." Half of the subjects were asked to analyze their reactions to the posters. The other half were not. The results of this study were striking. Subjects who did not analyze the reasons for their preferences overwhelmingly preferred the Impressionist paintings. In contrast, participants who did think about their reasons were a lot more likely to choose one of the contemporary posters – yet later they were less satisfied with the art they had chosen.

Secretly Questing for Significance?

Knowing what we now know about how people do not understand their own motivations, there is good reason to believe that people are quite oblivious to their desire for Significance. They might be quick to see it in other people, but often they will deny that they also crave Significance and are doing all they can to matter and to be noticed.

Although having high self-esteem is generally considered a good thing, and we often wish to instill it in our children, chasing Significance as such is considered inappropriate, conceited, and boastful. People who obviously engage in the chase are pejoratively referred to as "egomaniacs," "full of themselves," and "arrogant." Because most people like to think of them-selves in positive terms, they hope to be viewed as modest and humble – not prestige pursuers who are desperate for Significance at any cost.

There is another reason why acknowledging that your Quest for Significance may be difficult: because striving too much for anything is frowned upon in our talent-worshipping culture. Significance, the critics seem to feel, should come about effortlessly as just desserts for one's obvi-ous greatness – rather than something obtained through investing tons of energy and stubborn efforts. Descriptions of people as "eager beavers" or "social climbers" who "try too hard" show that there is often a lack of admiration (if not outright disdain) toward people who strive hard to make their own luck and to author their own success story.

And yet, it is obvious that expecting innate talent to be immediately recognized and rewarded is like believing in mythology. The lives of great artists like Mozart and Modigliani, who died in poverty, or scientists such as Galileo, who had to recant his views under duress and spent his last years under house arrest, clearly demonstrate that instant Significance is a myth.

People in the know frequently declare that every great athletic achieve-ment, musical virtuosity, or earth-shattering scientific discovery came after years of arduous training, effort, and virtual rivers of "blood, sweat, and tears." Far from being something unseemly and shameful, then, the quest we call QFS is a necessary ingredient in success, achievement, and any out-standing contribution to society that brings a person Significance. But at the same time, if pushed to extremes, QFS can be counterproductive and cause distress and palpable suffering.

You may well be interested in finding out for yourself just how much Significance you desire – and what are the elements of your ambition. Knowing oneself can be very helpful, as the ancient Greeks tried to tell us. Self-knowledge is particularly useful when it is about aspects of our psyche that give our lives meaning, define our ultimate purpose, make us feel good or bad about ourselves, shape our relations with others, and determine whom we love and whom we hate and why. Indeed, we hope to demonstrate to you in the following chapters that people's yearning for Significance and mattering is a central aspect of our psyche and that it determines much of our thoughts, feelings, and actions.

If you can somehow quantify how important Significance is to you, how strongly you react to challenges to your dignity, how badly you feel when "put down" by others, and what arouses your envy, empathy, or admiration, then you might identify guidelines for navigating your life more successfully. This part of "knowing thyself" may suggest to you which situations could be beneficial and which ones to avoid, which invitations to accept and which to turn down, which friends to choose or to eschew, and which goals to commit to or reject.

You might find out, for instance, that you are lower on ambition than you would like to be; and you might wonder if there is a way for you to become more ambitious. (There is!) On the other hand, you might discover that you are more ambitious than is good for you and that your oversized ambitions cause you stress and worry. Again, there are ways in which the Quest for Significance can be toned down, and a later part of this book tells you how.

But the first step in this process is to assess the strength of your QFS, so that you know where you stand on this critical aspect of your personality. To that end, we now present an ambitiousness scale, which comes with instructions for self-administering it. Doing so will allow you to gauge your attitude toward Significance and mattering, and to estimate the degree to which they play a role in your life.

The Ambitiousness Scale

The Ambitiousness Scale, developed by Italian psychologist Elena Resta and her colleagues at the University of Rome,[8] is a questionnaire that includes ten simple statements pertaining to the way individuals see themselves. The scale has been tested in numerous contexts and has been shown to be reliable and valid.

Administering the scale to yourself is easy – although it does require you to think about what is truly important to you. You are simply asked to state your degree of agreement or disagreement with each of the ten items, by choosing a number from 1 to 5. The way the scale is scored, 1 denotes complete disagreement with the item, 5 denotes total agreement, and numbers between 1 and 5 express intermediate degrees of agreement or disagreement. So, for example, one of the items states: "I aspire to do something special." If you completely agree with that, you would score it 5; if you feel you disagree completely, you would give it a 1; and if you agree but not fully, you might give it a 2, 3, or 4 depending on how you feel about that item.

Here are the ten statements you should consider:

1. I am ambitious.
2. One of my goals is to do something that leaves a mark.
3. I aim to succeed.
4. I aspire to do something special.
5. I never stop trying to overcome my limits.
6. I always aim higher than I know I can.
7. I always try to stand out in what I do.
8. I aim to do or have something enviable.
9. I aim to hold positions of prestige and responsibility.
10. Attaining recognition, respect, and consideration for what I do is very important to me.

Simple arithmetic reveals that the lowest score possible is 10, and the highest is 50. Scores between 10 and 35 mean you have relatively low ambition, while scoring over 35 means you have an above-average degree of ambition.[9] In subsequent chapters, we tell you more about possibly modifying your degree of ambitiousness if you so desire, amping it up or toning it down as the case may be.

But for now, consider some research aimed at finding out how highly ambitious and less ambitious people differ in various aspects of their personalities. Try to think about how these descriptions might apply to you, and if you already calculated your ambitiousness score, whether the results of these studies fit with what you know about yourself.

What Are Ambitious People Like?

Are you highly interested in getting things you desire and achieving your goals? Or are you often more concerned about avoiding things you dread? Research has been done into how people balance what seem like positive and negative priorities. Professor Tory Higgins, director of the Motivation Science Center at Columbia University, created the Regulatory Focus Theory, which labels the divergent impulses as *promotion* and *prevention*.[10]

Prevention-focused individuals are concerned with not losing. They get upset when they expect that their current situation might change for the worse: for instance, that they are going to be abandoned by their loved ones, fired from their job, or they might fail in some important domain of endeavor. When these possibilities appear real, prevention-oriented individuals become anxious and antsy. They mobilize all their energies to prevent the calamity from happening and to safeguard the status quo from deteriorating.

Promotion-oriented individuals are of a different species. They are not particularly concerned about losing. It is not that they like to lose – nobody does. But they are willing to take the risk of losing for a shot at winning. Rather than defending the current status quo, they dream of improving it. They want to climb to a higher level, whether that is in their career, athletic prowess, social status, or any other dimension of human striving.

Their goals are growth, advancement, and accomplishment, whereas the prevention types prioritize concerns about safety, security, and responsibility.

You might be able to guess how the two different motivational orientations relate to ambition. If you guessed that people who are highly ambitious are more promotion- rather than prevention-focused, you would be right; this is exactly what the research finds.

We want to be clear that neither promotion focus nor prevention focus is the "right" or "wrong" approach for people; and for that matter, we declare neutrality on whether high or low ambitions are best for any particular person. Every one of these orientations has advantages and disadvantages, pluses and minuses. Almost any course in life you choose will involve trade-offs. And while you might think, therefore, that moderation (in all things) is the answer, moderation typically gives you only moderate pleasures. Extreme action – going for broke or pouring all your energy into a project – can give you ecstasy, albeit at the risk of agony.[11]

Are You a Locomotor or an Assessor?

Research has identified two categories of people with contrasting dimensions of personality that are relevant to ambition and the Quest for

Significance. You will find, if you think about it, that you can label yourself and almost everyone around you as either a "locomotor" or an "assessor."[12]

People who are high on the locomotion dimension are impatient "go-getters." They are quick to set goals for themselves and simply itch to get going. They hope to enjoy smooth progress toward their objectives and are upset when other people or events knock a project off its tracks. They hate traffic jams, are upset when misunderstandings hamper the flow of communication, and strongly prefer a sense of steady movement. They seem happy with a long taxi ride, so long as the highway is clear. Moreover, locomotors strangely hate for the ride to end on arrival at their destination.

Do you see these qualities in yourself? How much of a locomotor do you think you are?

Or perhaps you are more of an assessor? "Assessment" refers to the tendency of some people to examine every single option and be worried about possible mistakes and wrong decisions. Assessors therefore spend a lot of their time weighing and thinking before taking any action – and even after that, they keep re-examining it and often regret their decisions in light of new considerations.

For instance, assessors tend to agonize over their shopping choices and often return items that they purchased. In contrast, locomotors quickly decide what items they want to purchase, and they rarely return anything or look back.

Again, neither locomotion nor assessment is all "good" or all "bad." In fact, elements of both orientations are needed for the successful pursuit of a person's goals. Someone who is an excessive locomotor is likely to make a lot of mistakes and get into many jams caused by impulsive actions that have not been sufficiently thought out. A person who is very strongly an assessor will likely be unable to initiate action and will fall victim to "paralysis by (over)analysis." Assessors tend to overthink their choices and decisions.

People who are highly ambitious are particularly strong at locomotion, while they score as moderate to low when it comes to assessment. In other words, ambitious people are people of action, eager to move on toward their desired objectives. They are less likely to be the kind of people who carefully weigh every option and take their time to make up their minds about something.

Achievement

If the Quest for Significance is largely a need to feel that your life matters, you naturally want to achieve something recognizable in the years from birth to death. So, it is no surprise that one of the best-known and most-researched dimensions of personality is known as the Need for Achievement.[13] This is usually related to a person's striving for success, typically defined in terms of career aspirations, as well as demonstrating competence and skills in various areas.

Psychologist David McClelland showed that countries and cultures differ in the importance placed on individual accomplishments. The predominant cultures in the United States and other developed Western nations are individualistic, marked by an often noisy clamoring for success. The name of the game is personal achievement.

One effect, perhaps unexpected but clearly evident, is that many immigrants have found it relatively easy to be accepted and integrated into their new host society – despite differences in accent, culinary tastes, and skin color – if those newcomers can attain widely recognized successes. Consider how Albert Einstein, Isaac Stern, Henry Kissinger, Zbigniew Brzezinski, and more recently Elon Musk, became leaders in America. On the other hand, individuals who fail to be identified with success – and groups that are held back by injustices such as slavery and racism – have been blocked from enjoying full acceptance. Only an exceptional few, who are at the top of their game (and that might be in sports or music, and money is usually the measuring stick), get on the TV talk shows and can afford the top restaurants.

Other cultures (in Asia, for instance) are more collectivistic and place less emphasis on individual initiative and success. In those countries, family background and class identity are much stronger determinants of social status than the achievements of one person. McClelland convincingly showed that the nature of the culture helped explain the level of technological prowess, innovation, and prosperity in various countries.

As you might surmise, the personal need for achievement should be strongly related to the Quest for Significance, and our research shows that it is. Yet, needing achievement is only part of QFS, because one can attain Significance in ways other than through achievement (which entails demonstrating skills and competence). Other routes include self-sacrifice for a

cause, even to the extent of martyrdom.[14] A person might also display courage in battle, demonstrate honesty by "speaking truth to power," or live up
to any societal value deemed to be of importance. Those values could be
material, moral, or aesthetic. They all bestow Significance on people whose
actions represent them.

The Search for Meaning

Psychologists have long been fascinated by a motivational dimension they
call the "search for meaning,"[15] defined as looking for "a life purpose, a
unique mission to strive for throughout their lives."[16] In Japanese culture,
people try to be aware of their *ikigai* – combining words for "life" and
"value." A purpose in life, for all humans, is not just a goal or objective. It
is something that gives you the sense that you matter, are a worthy person,
or in other words, have Significance.

High scorers on our scale of ambitiousness should also score highly
when it comes to mounting a strong search for meaning.[17] And they do.

In other words, people who are high on ambition care about who they
are and whether or not they matter socially, and they choose their life pursuits in a way that gives them a sense of Significance.

Moral Values

Adhering to morality and doing "the right thing" are among the key factors
that give people a sense of social worth and Significance. Accordingly, it
should be the case that people whose Quest for Significance is strong would
care about being "good," "fair," and "just." They want to feel that they possess moral traits that are generally cherished in society.

It is no wonder that research has found a correlation: Scoring high on
ambitiousness is linked with people's declaration that they care deeply
about being moral.[18] In addition to being driven by achievement and
displaying competence, ambitious individuals are often animated by the
desire to "do good."

Bill Gates, co-founder of Microsoft and among the world's richest people, is clearly a highly ambitious man. In 1999, at age 44, he and his then-
wife launched the Bill and Melinda Gates Foundation, which has dispensed
more than $65 billion in grants aimed at promoting healthcare, improving

education, spreading information technology, and combating extreme poverty in dozens of nations.

His friend Warren Buffett, hailed as a master of investments who amassed over $100 billion, pledged that 99% of it will go to philanthropy during his lifetime or at death. Elon Musk, however erratic and controversial he might be, launched his own charitable foundation in 2021 by donating almost $6 billion worth of Tesla shares. Musk declared that he was motivated by the desire to solve humanity's greatest problems, such as climate change, traffic congestion, and the need to colonize other planets in order to save humanity from extinction. Oprah Winfrey, whose hard work as an actress, talk show host, and movie producer led to a fortune of over $2 billion, styled herself as a highly public philanthropist.

These are highly ambitious people who achieved immense success, certainly by the simple measure of wealth. But they didn't stop there. They strived, with yet another dose of ambition, to be perceived as good, generous, and moral people – a key "feather" in their cap of Significance.

Does the Quest for Significance Make You Happy?

Now you have had the opportunity to score yourself on the Ambitiousness Scale and to discover the connection with your "promotion" or "prevention" orientation (always pursuing higher goals without fear of possible setbacks, or mostly trying to avoid losing anything so you might miss new opportunities). Perhaps you took a moment to identify whether you are more of a "locomotor" or an "assessor." You may have judged the strength of your need for achievement, your honest desire to be moral, and the overall search for your *ikigai* – your purpose in life.

But the big question that might interest you the most is whether ambition, or the Quest for Significance, is a good motivation to have. Whether for you or for society as a whole, does ambition make people happy?

The answer is that it depends. Professor Timothy Judge tracked the lives of 700 people over seven decades and found that the ambitious ones were generally no happier, and sometimes they were less happy than the less ambitious ones.[19] On average, however, ambition was positively related to success and achievement. So, being ambitious is likely to produce "social worth," as measured in terms of wealth, status, and station in life. You may wonder, then, why ambition does not deliver more happiness.

There are two reasons why. First, whereas ambition may be a necessary condition for success, it is not a sufficient condition. Lack of sufficient ability, or plain bad luck, can produce failure no matter how high your ambition. The legendary Don Quixote, created by novelist Miguel de Cervantes in the 17th century, comes to mind: Tilting at windmills meant he was too ambitious for his capabilities, hence ending up as the Knight of the Sad Countenance, disillusioned and dejected.

The second reason is that the Quest for Significance is frequently insatiable, so that regardless of your achievements, wealth, or fame, you might be aiming for more and initiating new projects with no guarantee of success. For instance, Elon Musk was not satisfied with his spectacular successes at Tesla, SpaceX, PayPal, and other future-oriented corporations. He paid more than $40 billion to acquire Twitter in 2022, courting a possible debacle, and then sought political influence by befriending an American president. Perhaps it will take a few decades to know whether the perpetually ambitious end up happy – and not just rich.

We should emphasize that while people are not identical in their Quest for Significance – and not equally ambitious – being deprived of some satisfactory level of Significance will almost always arouse a person's QFS. If you feel disenfranchised, ignored, or humiliated, you will want to get back to some kind of even keel for yourself, a level of Significance that is just enough for you.

And what is your satisfactory level of Significance? That often depends on to whom you are comparing yourself. A sociologist at Harvard, Samuel Stouffer, led a classic study of American soldiers and their attitudes just after World War II.[20] His team coined a phrase, "relative deprivation," to describe a puzzling observation. They found that members of the military police (MP), where promotions were rare, were happier with their lot than people serving in the highly ambitious US Air Force (USAF), where promotions were almost routine. Accordingly, the USAF personnel expected to be promoted frequently and were therefore frustrated when this did not happen, whereas the MPs did not expect their rank and salary to improve. So the military police were not particularly upset.

The concept of relative deprivation also applies to a finding by researchers that women in the United States became more unhappy, from the 1970s through 2009, despite the fact that their status in the workforce improved by many objective measures.[21] Based on questionnaires, women in the

1970s reported higher "well-being" than did men, but nearly 40 years later the men's responses indicated greater happiness.

The explanation for what the researchers called "the paradox" seems to be that in the 1970s, women were comparing themselves with other women, so they derived satisfaction from doing well by that measure. You might say now that they had low expectations back then, but the fact is that most felt they were doing okay. But by 2009, women compared themselves with men – certainly in the context of the American workplace – and the so-called "glass ceiling" restricting their promotions, clearly unequal pay, and frequent harassment all produced measurable unhappiness. In addition, traditional household chores and child rearing remained largely the women's responsibility – on top of all the demands of a job, where a host of circumstances hampered their ability to compete on an equal basis with men.

Perceived unfairness – or relative deprivation – frequently arouses a person's Quest for Significance. This QFS, when experienced by many, eventually expresses itself in social movements aiming to redress injustices. In America and elsewhere, we have seen that determined activism can lead to profound changes in societal norms.

Those issues are discussed in greater detail in subsequent chapters. However, before turning to them, we consider a different and quite fundamental question: What explains the fact that humans have such an overriding need for Significance and mattering, incomparably more than any other species in the phylogenetic universe? To address this question, we must consider how human nature became what it is; how we came to be the desperate Significance seekers that we are. Chapter 3 deals with the evolutionary roots of our quest.

Summary

The sage advice of Greek philosophers notwithstanding, self-knowledge is typically in short supply. People are often blissfully unaware of why they do what they do, and what basic motives underlie their choices, decisions, and actions. The reasons for their ignorance are several. They include assuming that our likes and preferences are "reasonable," that they reflect what we should like or prefer. Yet some of our yearnings may be socially undesirable; therefore, we may try to avoid admitting (even to ourselves) that they exist. Our Quest for Significance may be of just this kind, caring too much about how we are perceived by others, being what is pejoratively described as "social climbers," people who "try too hard."

Despite these misgivings, it may be better to face the truth about ourselves and navigate it, rather than bury our head in the proverbial sand. In the present context, this means confronting the size and content of our ambition, and realizing its benefits and possible drawbacks. In this chapter, we have offered you an opportunity to do so through the self-administered Ambitiousness Scale, and the depiction of attributes and inclinations to which ambition is related.

Notes

1 The other two maxims were "Nothing in excess" and, intriguingly, "Certainty brings insanity" – implying that keeping one's mind open, and the readiness to change it, are hallmarks of mental health.

2 Nisbett, Richard E.; Wilson, Timothy DeCamp, "The Halo Effect: Evidence for Unconscious Alteration of Judgments," *Journal of Personality and Social Psychology*, Vol. 35, No. 4 (1977), pp. 250–256.

3 Storms, Michael D.; Nisbett, Richard E., "Insomnia and the Attribution Process," *Journal of Personality and Social Psychology*, Vol. 16, No. 2 (1970), pp. 319–328.

4 Nisbett, Richard E.; Wilson, Timothy D., "Telling More than We Can Know: Verbal Reports on Mental Processes," *Psychological Review*, Vol. 84, No. 3 (1977), pp. 231–259.

5 Wilson, Timothy D.; Wheatley, Thalia Parker; Meyers, Jonathan M.; Gilbert, Daniel T., "Focalism: A Source of Durability Bias in Affective Forecasting," *Journal of Personality and Social Psychology*, Vol. 78, No. 5 (June 2000), pp. 821–836.

6 Woodzicka, Julie A.; LaFrance, Marianne, "Real Versus Imagined Gender Harassment," *Journal of Social Issues*, Vol. 57, No. 1 (2001), pp. 15–30.

7 Wilson, Timothy D.; Lisle, Daniel J.; Schooler, Jonathan W., "Introspecting About Reasons Can Reduce Post-Choice Satisfaction," *Journal of Personality and Social Psychology*, Vol. 56, No. 3 (March 1989), pp. 331–339.

8 Resta, Elena; Ellenberg, Molly; Kruglanski, Arie W.; Pierro, Antonio, "Marie Curie vs. Serena Williams: Ambition Leads to Extremism through Obsessive (but not Harmonious) Passion," *Motivation and Emotion*, Vol. 46 (March 2022), pp. 383–393.

9 For the 3,428 persons tested by the scale when it was new, the average score was 34, the average of the upper quartile of the distribution was 40, and the average of the lower quartile of the distribution was 29.

10 Edward Tory Higgins is one of the world's leading researchers on human motivation, and he suggests that promotion and prevention are strategies for self-regulation so people can align with their standards and goals. His books include *Focus:*

Use Different Ways of Seeing the World for Success and Influence (Plume, 2013), with co-author Heidi Grant Halvorson.

11 Kruglanski, Arie W.; Szumowska, Ewa; Kopetz, Catalina H.; Vallerand, Robert J.; Pierro, Antonio, "On the Psychology of Extremism: How Motivational Imbalance Breeds Intemperance," *Psychological Review*, Vol. 128, No. 2 (September 2020), pp. 264–289; and a book edited by Kruglanski, Kopetz, Szumowska, Ewa; *The Psychology of Extremism: A Motivational Perspective* (New York: Routledge, 2021).

12 Kruglanski, Arie W.; Pierro, Antonio; Higgins, E. Tory; Capozza, Dora, "On the Move: Mechanisms Underlying Motivational Primacy in Goal Pursuit," *Journal of Personality and Social Psychology*, Vol. 79, No. 5 (November 2000), pp. 793–815.

13 Harvard psychology professor David C. McClelland and his Need for Achievement theory were popularized by his book, *The Achieving Society* (New York: Free Press, 1961). He posited that people are motivated by needs for achievement, power, and affiliation.

14 Moskalenko, Sophia; McCauley, Clark, *The Marvel of Martyrdom: The Power of Self-Sacrifice in a Selfish World* (Oxford University Press, 2018).

15 Frankl, Viktor E., *Man's Search for Meaning: An Introduction to Logotherapy*, (New York: Washington Square Press, 1963). The first edition of Frankl's book was published in 1946.

16 Steger, Michael F., "Making Meaning in Life," *Psychological Inquiry*, Vol. 23, No. 4 (October 2012), p. 381.

17 Ibid.

18 Aquino, Karl; Reed, Americus, "The Self-Importance of Moral Identity," *Journal of Personality and Social Psychology*, Vol. 83, No. 6 (2002), pp. 1423–1440.

19 Judge, Timothy, "On the Value of Aiming High: The Causes and Consequences of Ambition," *The Journal of Applied Psychology*, Vol. 97, No. 4 (July 2012), pp. 758–775. A professor of management at Notre Dame's Mendoza College of Business, Judge told a university newspaper in March 2012, "Ambition may breed success, but not happiness," as found at edition.cnn.com/2012/03/09/business/ambition-route-to-the-top, which summarized Judge's research, "Why Ambition Could Make You Rich, But Not Happy."

20 Stouffer, Samuel A.; Suchman, Edward A.; Devinney, Leonard C.; Star, Shirley A.; Williams, Reginald M., "The American Soldier: Adjustment During Army Life," in Osborn, Frederick; Cottrell, Leonard S., Jr.; DeVinney, Leland C.; Hovland, Carl I.; Russell, John M.; Stouffer, Samuel A. (eds.) *Studies in Social Psychology in World War II* (Princeton: Princeton University Press, 1949), Vol. 1.

21 Stevenson, Betsey; Wolfers, Justin, "The Paradox of Declining Female Happiness," *National Bureau of Economic Research* (May 2009); found at www.nber.org/papers/w14969.

3

HOW THE QUEST EVOLVED

Human Nature and Significance Strivings

Have you ever noticed how all babies seem alike, how they smile alike, hold their heads alike, crawl alike, and try to walk alike? They do so because they are members of the same species. They are all little humans.

Later in life, differences between them will be illuminated by family history, culture, ethnicity, or religion, and the advantages or deficiencies that genetics gave them. But the similarities seen in the first months of a human's life attest to the fact that we share a fundamental commonality and are all individual members of the human race. And the Quest for Significance (QFS), our main focus in this book, is an integral part of our human nature.

The most ancient texts are replete with stories that illustrate human ambition and people's (often outsized) Quest for Significance. The Old Testament, for instance, recounts the story of Adam and Eve's defiant decision to eat the fruit from the Tree of Knowledge so that their "eyes shall

DOI: 10.4324/9781003410706-3

be opened, and [they] shall be as gods, knowing good and evil" (Genesis 3:5). The story of the Tower of Babel is also about ambition, as it recounts the Babylonians' intention to "build… a city and a tower, whose top may reach unto Heaven; and make a name for themselves" (Gen. 11:4). In both cases, however, the excessive ambition led to punishment. Adam and Eve's eating the fruit is considered the original sin for which they were banished from Paradise. And the Babylonians were punished for their uppity project by being scattered over a wide area and forced to speak different languages, resulting in confusion.

Twenty-five centuries ago, the Greek philosopher Heraclitus declared that there had been two types of creation. Men and gods were the products of intentional creation, whereas irrational brutes comprised a separate category of living creatures.[1] According to Heraclitus, only gods and men possessed souls.

Greek mythology also has much to say about ambition, and it too gives it a negative spin. As told by the Roman poet Ovid in the year 8 CE in his mammoth work *Metamorphoses*, Phaethon – son of the sun god Helios – craved recognition and constantly bragged to his friends. He got permission to drive Helios's chariot (meaning the sun) for one day, but he then proceeded to lose control of the horses, scorching the earth and turning Africa into a desert. Zeus intervened and struck down Phaethon with a lightning bolt.[2]

Another mythological tale warning against excessive Significance-seeking tells of Icarus and Daedalus, his father, escaping from imprisonment by King Midas with the aid of wings made of beeswax and feathers. Although cautioned by his father not to fly too close to the sun, Icarus, in his great ambition, ignores the admonition. The sun's rays melt the wax that holds the feathers together, the wings disintegrate, and Icarus falls into the sea and drowns.

Scholars in the Middle Ages habitually assigned Significance to human beings by highlighting that they possessed a soul and the ability to reason, denied to other living organisms. In the 13th century, a German friar who was a scientist and philosopher, Albertus Magnus – later canonized by the Vatican as the patron saint of scientists – wrote *De Animalibus*, a book that described humans as absolutely distinct from other animals, so that no comparisons could be valid, because humans possess the gift of reason and an immortal soul.[3] Animals, lacking rational thought, were assumed to be directed by their instincts and therefore unable to act freely.

Thomas Aquinas, also canonized as a saint, was a student of Albertus and supported his teacher's distinction between humans and animals. The rational soul, according to Aquinas, is divinely implanted in the human fetus at some time before birth. Therefore, the behavior of people depends upon reason, whereas other animals are governed by instinct. Four hundred years later, the renowned 17th-century philosopher René Descartes and his followers emphatically restated the human–brute dichotomy and proudly held up the view of humans as rational reasoners.

The ambition theme appears time and again in literary classics. Shakespeare's Macbeth admits to having a "vaulting ambition, which o'erleaps itself / And falls on the other" (Act 1, Scene 7). James Joyce's protagonist Dedalus in *A Portrait of the Artist as a Young Man* is all about ambition: Dedalus's desire to be great.

In modern American literature, F. Scott Fitzgerald's *The Great Gatsby* is about the lofty ambitions of Jay Gatsby. Arthur Miller's play, *Death of a Salesman*, portrays Willy Loman, whose frustrated ambition precipitates his demise. And in African literature, Chinua Achebe's acclaimed book, *Things Fall Apart*,[4] depicts the protagonist Okonkwo's misguided ambition that brings about his downfall, like a fatal flaw of character in a Greek tragedy.

You might wonder whether these famous literary characters have anything to do with reality, and whether any of it has anything to do with you. We suggest they do, because just like these fictional personages who yearn to stand out and be respected, you too are governed in your everyday pursuits by the ever-present Quest for Significance and mattering. It is hardly accidental that people's QFS, though not in that precise terminology, has been a topic of such great interest to observers of human nature from ancient times to the present day.

This issue of Significance and mattering has been – and is – a key concern for billions of people around the globe. It represents a fundamental human need that shapes the fates of nations and charts the course of world history. The Quest for Significance is no less than the "mother" of all social motivations.

The Quest Evolving

Why is the need for Significance and social worth of such overriding importance in human affairs? Charles Darwin's theory of evolution offers an answer. Darwin suggested that many features that living creatures exhibit were factors that helped their ancestors survive and procreate. Here is the logic: We are the way we are because our ancestors' attributes gave them an edge in a struggle for life in whatever circumstances confronted them. Those of our forebears who possessed given attributes survived; those who lacked them did not, hence those fortunate attributes were genetically transmitted to the survivors' offspring, including ourselves, the present-day humans.

So, the question is, what may have been the natural circumstances in which the need for Significance was advantageous – even to some of the earliest forms of men and women?

Anthropologists tell us that the first hominids, about 4 million years ago, whose remains have been found in various African locations, existed in a physical environment largely covered by rainforests. They ate fruits and nuts, walked on all fours, and lived in little groups that interacted with each other.

The rainforests began to die due to climate change, scientists believe, and hominids were no longer able to live in and among trees. The later hominids,[5] 2 million to 1 million years ago, had to survive on vast African plains known as the savanna. The savanna environment posed considerable challenges. First, forests were still needed to supply food, but trees were no longer so abundant and available.

Now, to secure food, there was a need to hunt for it. Also, because of food's relative scarcity, bands of hominids had to compete with rival hominid groups for good hunting grounds. The open expanses of the savanna also made it a challenge to escape or hide from predators such as lions, tigers, and cheetahs.

All those circumstances encouraged – under the Darwinian principle that only the fittest survived – further development of walking on two legs. Bipedality allowed the hominids a better view of the area around them, including animals to hunt and predators to avoid. In addition, bipedality freed our ancestors' hands. Now they could hold weapons for hunting and for self-defense.

In short, life on the savanna was more complicated and challenging than the hominids' prior existence in the forests. This promoted a particularly important element of human evolution: the start of hominid sociality. Individuals motivated to live together with others, and capable of doing so, were particularly likely to survive and procreate.

Because of the increased challenges of life on the open grasslands of Africa, it was advantageous for our ancestors to live in larger groups. Their survival and amazing success prove the validity of the idiom that there is strength in numbers. Hunting for large animals – such as zebras, antelopes, and other grass eaters – became more efficient when done in coordinated teams.

However, life in groups called for organization and cooperation. It required a division of labor in which different individuals fulfilled different functions – some might scout for food, others would go hunting, and a team would prepare and distribute the edibles – all of which created a new need for effective communication among group members.

Early hunter-gatherers in the savannas also practiced labor differentiation by gender, with females assuming relatively larger roles in nurturing the children, as well as engaging in the gathering of food items, while males were more engaged in hunting and defending the group against its enemies: other bellicose bands of hunter-gatherers and animal predators.[6]

Some anthropologists promote a persuasive hypothesis known as "the social brain." It holds that because social life became more complex on the savanna, individuals and families with larger brains coped a lot better. As Darwinism would suggest, they are the ones who would survive and thrive.

Do those anthropologists have any evidence? Yes. Discoveries of bones show that among hominids, as well as in other primates such as great apes, there is a correlation between the individual's brain size and the size of his group.[7]

Scientists also point to findings in our modern era that the size of an individual's social network is related to activity in certain brain regions: those involved in thinking about what other people are thinking. That accords with a facet of increased sociality that psychologists call the "theory of mind" – the ability to figure out the beliefs, emotions, and desires of oneself and of other people.[8]

In short, because of its many dangers and challenges, life on the savanna led the hominids to coalesce in larger groups. Members had increasingly varied interactions. It is likely that evolution favored more intelligent individuals who had larger brains.[9] This was not simply a matter of having to be smarter to hunt effectively for food. The finding that brain size is associated with the size of the mini-society shows that the main factor was socializing: having to get along and cooperate with other members of the group.

The "social brain" analysis is particularly fascinating when the focus turns to childbirth – and which babies survive the rigors of being born. As the brains of hominids became larger, on average, a typical vaginal birth became more difficult. The fetus had a larger head! Therefore, the survivors were the ones born prematurely – with heads that were not especially large. Those babies, in turn, required more care after they were born. The mother usually took that responsibility, and that made the average mother dependent on the father for food. That is an explanation for why, compared with other animal species, humans displayed a far higher incidence of pair bonding. Parents stayed together, nurturing their offspring.

Competition for sexual partners, coping with harassment by more powerful individuals, forming alliances and coalitions, maintaining loyalties, and reacting to betrayals are some of the problems that intense group life presents. Individuals need to be aware of third-party relationships, which is no easy cognitive task. Among others, this means refraining from attacking or exploiting another individual that has powerful allies, even when those allies are not physically present. These problems of group coordination were at least as challenging as foraging for food and defending against predators and enemies.

It is also interesting that though the social brain hypothesis speaks of primates in general, it especially applies to humans. For instance, one study[10] found that humans and great apes performed equally well on instrumental tasks such as efficiently moving objects; yet humans significantly outperformed apes on social tasks that involved cooperation or understanding others' perspectives. Compared with great apes, humans have much larger and more developed frontal lobes of their brains, the area that does the thinking about what others are thinking – the aforementioned "theory of mind."

But what does the development of the "social brain" have to do with the Quest for Significance and social worth? As we explain in what follows, quite a lot.

Sociality and Significance

As sociality developed, to truly thrive, our ancestors had to be highly attuned to other members of their group. They were likely aware of differences between members and oriented themselves to their tribe's hierarchy. Accordingly, they very likely cared a lot about what they meant to other members in the group and tried to improve their standing within the group's structure.

It is not that our ancestors, the early hominids, had anything like the social sensitivities that we have now. But the seeds of our highly evolved capabilities — and desires such as questing for Significance — can be found in the early era when our ancestors' social brain was developing.

Caring about what other members of the group think and striving to improve your social standing in their eyes is a key factor in the Quest for Significance. And it always has been. Archeologists have cataloged countless pieces of ancient pottery that show efforts by individuals to advance their social standing through public competitions in athletics or hunting. Those men on the antique pottery were seeking Significance, and so were women when portrayed as models of virtue and beauty.[11]

Even the pre-pottery hominids were concerned about their reputation within the tribe. There is ample evidence that our ancestors also tried to manage their image among members of their group. Those with a good reputation enjoyed greater access to food and desirable partners for procreation.

Surprisingly to some, the importance of reputation is not uniquely human. Animals also seem to care about it, at least to some degree. For example, male and female Siamese fighting fish assess other males' fighting ability by watching them fight, and then approach or avoid them accordingly.[12] The female of the bird species known as the Great Tit pays attention to the results of interactions between males and tends to approach the victorious ones for mating opportunities.[13] And the female Japanese quail avoids males she has seen acting too aggressively.[14]

Returning to a species related to our own, researchers found that primates that lose a fight are known to then become aggressive toward lower-ranking group members, possibly to show them that they are still formidable and not to be trifled with.[15]

As for humans, evolutionary researchers discuss two types of reputations that people strive to acquire: the image of a "cooperator" likely to go along and join with others to accomplish common tasks; or a reputation as an aggressor who will insist on getting their way, by force if necessary. Humans evaluate others based on whether they have the *ability* (to cooperate or to aggress) and whether they show a *tendency* to do so.[16] Whether consciously or unconsciously, people were shown to engage frequently in such evaluations.[17]

Humans have evolved to estimate their own strength and compare it to the reputed strength of possible competitors. Engaging in a conflict over resources can be worthwhile if they could win – but not if they would lose. For instance, trying to poach the sexual partner of a powerful individual is risky, whereas courting the spouse of a weaker individual or someone who is absent, unaware, and unable to retaliate is less so. It makes sense, then, that researchers find people tracking to what extent others are able, willing, and available to mete out some kind of punishment or reward; and they refrain from conflict with those who are high on those dimensions.[18]

People who acquire the reputation for being helpful and cooperative are treated better and are more likely to receive help, compared to individuals who are unhelpful and uncooperative. Social scientists call this phenomenon "indirect reciprocity."[19] In one study, participants got the chance to donate to others in a way that was publicly known. In a subsequent round of the experiment, the other members of the group were more likely to hand gifts to the participants who had been generous in the past, even when it was clear that those recipients would be unable to return the favor.[20]

Significance and mattering can be competitive, and humans have evolved to compete in building up their reputations. In humans as well as other species, choosing sexual partners, friends, or team members often leads to "market" competition, and almost everyone tries to project the image of being the "best" on whatever dimension of behavior seems salient and important to the group members.[21] That can be seen at fundraising events, where wealthy people attempt to outdo each other in donating or bidding up the prices at charity auctions. We could call that "competitive altruism" or "competitive helping," in which people do not just try to seem nice, but rather strive to seem *nicer* than anyone around them.[22]

There is evidence that people become more generous when their reputation might be enhanced. For example, in group experiments, participants give more money when their donations can be seen by others,[23] and they give the largest amounts when there is a high chance of interacting with those same observers in the future.[24] In short, acquiring the reputation of being a cooperative group member – taking into account the needs of fellow members and being willing to invest efforts on their behalf – results in earning the others' trust and reciprocation. The cooperative individual is bestowed with Significance: a sense of being appreciated and accorded social worth that further reinforces their cooperativeness.

Reputation for Aggression

Many people have had to cope with someone who has a bad reputation, for instance, a bully. Unfortunately, a person who intimidates others through threats of violence often gets their way and hence develops a feeling of dominance as their form of Significance.

Research attests that bullying is widespread in American schools, and the impact can be lethal. A report in 2002 found that in two-thirds of school shootings in the United States, the attackers had been bullied. They had obviously had enough, and attempting to kill their tormentors was a way to regain some Significance.[25]

Bullying occurs at all grade levels, but it is especially prevalent in middle and high schools. Yet, even out of school, notably in tough inner-city neighborhoods, people are often rude and pushy toward each other – with bullies identifying and picking on weaker individuals. Remarkably, this strife is also found in adult workplaces, where one employee labeled as weak will be exposed to offensive remarks, direct insults, persistent criticism, or even physical abuse. When a group of colleagues practically surrounds the victim with torment, that is known as "mobbing at work."[26]

One of the most common forms of bullying is sexual harassment, and in the United States, 81 percent of women and 43 percent of men reported experiencing some form of sexual harassment or assault in their lifetime.[27] There is no excuse for such aggressive, ugly behavior, but there is an explanation: the perpetrators are "proving" to themselves and to others that they are superior, that they can dominate others and get them to do what they wanted – hence manifesting power and Significance.

Aggression as a form of dominance has always been part of international relations. The 19th-century military theorist, General Carl von Clausewitz, is known for his aphorism that "war is a continuation of politics by other means." To him, politics was not motivated by the desire to serve others, but rather the pursuit of dominance over others.

The notion that aggression is a primitive way to affirm one's Significance and mattering is something that social thinkers and scientists of various backgrounds have long realized. The influential early 20th-century French philosopher Georges Sorel, who is generally labeled a revolutionary, commented in his book, *Reflections on Violence*: "History is based entirely on the adventures of warriors... [hence] the ardent desire to try one's strength in great battles... and to conquer glory at the peril of one's life."[28]

Hannah Arendt, the German-American political theorist of the 1950s and 1960s, also commented on "the enormous role violence has always played in human affairs."[29] Evolutionary scholars have highlighted a connection between Significance and having a reputation for aggression. Being perceived as "formidable," that is, as willing and able to inflict costs on others if your own interests are marred, has been and is a major way to matter, to garner the respect of others, and thus to feel worthy and significant.[30]

If you do not think that aggression is an admirable trait, you may be surprised to learn that it is most likely to manifest itself when other people are looking – providing what the social psychologists call "opportunities for reputation."[31] For instance, men react more aggressively to challenges in front of an audience, compared with when no one else is present.

Other research, in fact, shows that if people can avoid being aggressive without "losing face," they are more likely to back down rather than engage in hostile confrontations.[32] It has also been shown that people who strongly crave status and Significance are more likely to engage in aggressive encounters.[33]

We have discussed how a person's reputation – whether it is for being cooperative or being aggressive – provides a sense of mattering and Significance. Yet, these two routes to Significance are very different in other ways. Aggression-driven Significance is based on fear and coercion. The bullies are typically hated, and they are overthrown when the opportunity arises. For instance, during the Nazi occupation of European countries in

World War II, there were resistance movements in each occupied country in which people were willing to risk their lives to oust the occupiers. Major European underground militias appeared across the continent: in Poland, Yugoslavia, the Czech Republic, Albania, France, the Netherlands, Belgium, and Norway, among others.

But when a person has a reputation for cooperating, armed squads of defiant heroes are unlikely to rise up against that person. No, indeed, building a reputation by being cooperative creates a positive attitude toward oneself. People of that kind are sought after and courted, rather than avoided.

So, all things considered, it seems a better idea to acquire a reputation as a great cooperator rather than as an aggressive tyrant. Alas, being a tyrant gives a person a sense of control over others, which many people who pursue that power seem to enjoy as a mark of dominance and Significance.

Costly Signaling

Reputation, as we have been emphasizing, represents a person's social worth. The key is how you are perceived. That is why acquiring a good reputation – giving you a sense of mattering in your social milieu – depends on other people. Even if you are proud of yourself, it is important to signal your excellence to an audience.

Evolutionary scholars have identified a strategy that people follow to enhance their worth in the eyes of others. The methodology is known as "costly signaling."[34] It refers to animals (including humans) sending signals about reputable personal characteristics by displaying behaviors generally perceived as somewhat painful. For example, a worker who arrives at the office before everyone else, and is also the last to leave at night, is signaling their great devotion to the job. That, assuming their behavior is noticed, should enhance their reputation as an outstanding employee. But it is probably costly to their physical well-being.

Similarly, workers who manage to carry out tasks that require a great deal of effort – for instance, recruiting a large pool of clients for a business – signal their ability or motivation to excel at the job with which they were entrusted. That, of course, builds up their reputation. Completing a task thoroughly and well conveys one or both of these messages: that the person can do things that may be difficult for others, or that the individual is willing to sacrifice things that others might not be prepared to sacrifice, out of a commendable commitment to the job.

Anthropologists have found countless signs that bolstering a person's own image has been part of human behavior since its beginnings. In ancient societies, an effective pathway to build a reputation was by hunting – finding animals, keeping up with the fast ones, and killing them. The core motivation was to "show off" and demonstrate one's importance to the tribe.

Picking berries and fruits for the tribe should merit some degree of praise. But that is nothing like hunting. Being out there with a bow and arrow, or perhaps just a knife, is risky and unpredictable. Without doubt, the extra excitement adds to the hunter's reputation. He (more likely than she, in ancient times) is demonstrating strength, skill, quick instincts, and acumen. That greatly increases the hunter's social worth and Significance to others.

An extra benefit is the meat. A successful hunter comes back to the tribe with so much food that he cannot possibly eat it all himself. The result can be a feast for the entire tribe, which is great for the entire group while definitely elevating the hunter's reputation.

Yet another positive aspect of hunting is that it prompted the development of tools. Foraging for food became more efficient, to be sure, but the key to tool-making was that it required a great deal of cooperation. Members of the tribe would sharpen their sticks and stones, and then in the field, they would experiment in the trial-and-error process of discovering what works best. The bottom line is that hunting – motivated partly by the Quest for Significance and male "show-offism" – was an important factor in human evolution and in people displaying the traits that they possess today.

A far more sedate human activity – in fact, unique to humans in the known universe of animals – is the creation of art. It has also been a way of acquiring Significance and a good reputation. We might think, in our time, of the pleasures of seeing visual arts or hearing music. Yet, even in prehistoric times, early humans valued sketches, paintings, and other visual depictions. Chances are high that not everyone was equally talented at producing art, so there was an area in which the better artists would gain more Significance. The effort to turn their experiences into something lasting – cave drawings, for instance – facilitated communication and promoted the earliest forms of education. Art might depict how a hunt is carried out, thus evoking common memories and expressing common values. This was part of human cognitive development, and it reflected and articulated the increased complexity and richness of the human experience.

Producing art qualifies as a form of costly signaling because it must have required great effort to acquire the materials, to sculpt something meaningful, or to draw a hunting scene for days or weeks. The artist was demonstrating the willingness to do something costly for the sake of other members' aesthetic pleasure, and that fact alone showed that their Quest for Significance was underway.

Because creating art was a rare skill – appreciated and admired by others in the tribe – the artist was signaling his or her social worth, becoming a significant person in the eyes of their society. One modern-day study of mating preferences, carried out in 37 cultures worldwide, found that being "creative and artistic" was the sixth most important trait to females and the seventh most important trait to males, out of 13 qualities related to sexual attractiveness.[35] More directly relevant to costly signaling, those who expended greater effort in creating art for public spaces[36] reported a greater number of sexual partners.

We have learned that evolution was not only a matter of standing on two feet or advancing from grunts to speech. At every stage of humankind, evolution included developing the motivation to matter and be significant. That, in turn, prompted early humans to invest resources in pursuits that went beyond simply getting fed. Hunting and art were fine examples of how to build a sense of mattering, and acquiring Significance.

Summary

The evidence is strong that the desire to have Significance, and to matter in the eyes of others around us, is an important part of human nature, an inseparable aspect of our sociality. In a real sense, to care about one's social worth is what it means to be human. The evidence for human ambition, the desire to impress others, and to "show off" is plentiful in ancient narratives and modern literature alike. Signs of those traits have been found by archeologists and anthropologists who studied the earliest human forms. Moreover, the desire to score high in Significance provided the impetus for human inventiveness and, in this way, was a major force propelling the development of human culture, art, science, and technology.

In subsequent chapters, we show more specifically how the craving for social worth applies to many concerns in our lives, and how it governs our relations with others. Understanding the mechanism of Significance's impact on those around us could help us navigate through society and do so happily and successfully.

Notes

1 Graham, Daniel W., "Heraclitus: Flux, Order, and Knowledge," in Curd, P.; Graham, D.W. (eds.), *The Oxford Handbook of Presocratic Philosophy* (New York: Oxford University Press, 2008), pp. 169–188.
2 The story of Phaethon is widely told, for instance – including Ovid's role in dis-seminating the tale – at www.britannica.com/topic/Phaethon-Greek-mythology.
3 Magnus, Albertus, *Man and the Beasts: De Animalibus* (Books 22–26) (translated by J.J. Scanlan), Center for Medieval and Early Renaissance Studies (Binghamton, New York: 1987).
4 Achebe, Chinua, *Things Fall Apart* (New York: Everyman Books, 1995), first pub-lished to great acclaim for the Nigerian author's debut novel in 1958.
5 The early pre-humans included the species scientists call *Homo erectus*, which lived until around 100,000 years ago and overlapped with our species, *Homo sapiens*, which apparently first arose in Africa around 300,000 years ago. Anthropologists who wrote about this include Eleanor Scerri, "Human Evolution: Secrets of Early Ancestors Could be Unlocked by African Rainforests" (2018); found at theconvers ation.com/human-evolution-secrets-of-early-ancestors-could-be-unlocked-by-a frican-rainforests-101636; and Zeresenay Alemseged of the University of Chicago, who has written of hominins – a group referring to today's humans and their most direct evolutionary ancestors. See Thompson, J.C.; Carvalho, S.; Marean, C.W.; Alemseged, Z., "Origins of the Human Predatory Pattern: The Transition to Large-Animal Exploitation by Early Hominins," *Current Anthropology*, Vol. 60, No. 1 (2019), pp. 1–23.
6 Pinker, Steven, *The Better Angels of Our Nature: Why Violence Has Declined* (New York: Penguin, 2012).
7 Jolly, Alison, "Lemur Social Behavior and Primate Intelligence," *Science*, Vol. 153, No. 3735 (July 1966), pp. 501–506. Also, Brothers, Leslie, "The Neural Basis of Primate Social Communication," *Motivation and Emotion*, Vol. 14 (1990), pp. 81–91.
8 Kwak, Sungil; Joo, Wooyoung; Youm, Yong-Yeol; Chey, Joon, "Social Brain Volume is Associated with In-Degree Social Network Size Among Older Adults," *Proceedings of the Royal Society B: Biological Sciences*, Vol. 285, No. 1873 (January 2018). That study involved "68 elderly residents of a rural village in South Korea."

9   Dunbar, Robin; Shultz, Susanne, "Bondedness and Sociality," *Behavior*, Vol. 144, No. 6 (2007), pp. 775–803.

10 Herrmann, Esther; Call, Josep; Hernández-Lloreda, María Victoria; Hare, Brian; Tomasello, Michael, "Humans Have Evolved Specialized Skills of Social Cognition: The Cultural Intelligence Hypothesis," *Science*, Vol. 317, No. 5843 (2007), pp. 1360–1366.

11 Nicholson, Nigel, "How Hardwired Is Human Behavior?" *Harvard Business Review* (July–August 1998); found at hbr.org/1998/07/how-hardwired-is-human-behavior.

12 Doutrelant, Claire; McGregor, Peter, "Eavesdropping and Mate Choice in Female Fighting Fish," *Behaviour*, Vol. 137, No. 12 (2000), pp. 1655–1668. See also: McGregor, Peter K.; Peake, Thomas M., "Communication Networks: Social Environments for Receiving and Signalling Behaviour," *Acta Ethologica* (Springer Verlag: Heidelberg, Germany), Vol. 2 (2000), pp. 71–81. Also Oliveira, R.F.; McGregor, P.K.; Latruffe, C., "Know Thine Enemy: Fighting Fish Gather Information from Observing Conspecific Interactions," *Proceedings of the Royal Society of London, Series B: Biological Sciences*, Vol. 265, No. 1401 (1998), pp. 1045–1049.

13 Otter, Kathryn; McGregor, Peter K.; Terry, Anna M.R.; Burford, Fiona R.; Peake, Thomas M.; Dabelsteen, Torben, "Do Female Great Tits (Parus Major) Assess Males by Eavesdropping? A Field Study…," *Proceedings of the Royal Society of London, Series B: Biological Sciences*, Vol. 266, No. 1426 (1999), pp. 1305–1309. Also: Otter, Kathryn A.; Stewart, Ian R.K.; McGregor, Peter K.; Terry, Anna M.R.; Dabelsteen, Torben; Burke, Terry, "Extra-Pair Paternity Among Great Tits (Parus major) Following Manipulation of Male Signals," *Journal of Avian Biology*, Vol. 32, No. 4 (2001), pp. 338–344.

14 Ophir, Alexander G.; Persaud, Keneisha N.; Galef Jr, Bennett G., "Avoidance of Relatively Aggressive Male Japanese Quail (Coturnix Japonica) by Sexually Experienced Conspecific Females," *Journal of Comparative Psychology*, Vol. 119, No. 1 (2005), pp. 3–7.

15 Kazim, Ali J.N.; Aureli, Filippo, "Redirection of Aggression: Multiparty Signalling within a Network?" in McGregor, Peter K. (ed.), *Animal Communication Networks* (Cambridge: Cambridge University Press, 2005), pp. 191–218.

16 Barclay, Pat, "Strategies for Cooperation in Biological Markets, Especially for Humans," *Evolution and Human Behavior*, Vol. 34, No. 3 (2013), pp. 164–175.

17 Alvergne, Alexandra; Lummaa, Virpi, "Does the Contraceptive Pill Alter Mate Choice in Humans?" *Trends in Ecology & Evolution*, Vol. 25, No. 3 (2010), pp. 171–179.

18 Daly, Martin; Wilson, Margo, "Evolutionary Social Psychology and Family Homicide," *Science*, Vol. 242 (1988), pp. 519–524; Also see Sell, Aaron; Cosmides, Leda; Tooby, John; Sznycer, Daniel; Von Rueden, Christopher; Gurven, Michael, "Human Adaptations for the Visual Assessment of Strength and Fighting Ability from the Body and Face," *Proceedings of the Royal Society B: Biological Sciences*, Vol. 276, No. 1656 (2008), pp. 575–584.

19 Nowak, M.A.; Sigmund, K., "Evolution of Indirect Reciprocity," *Nature*, Vol. 437, No. 7063 (2005), pp. 1291–1298.

20 Wedekind, C.; Milinski, M., "Cooperation through Image Scoring in Humans," *Science*, Vol. 288, No. 5467 (2000), pp. 850–852.

21 Noë, R.; Hammerstein, P., "Biological Markets: Supply and Demand Determine the Effect of Partner Choice in Cooperation, Mutualism and Mating," *Behavioral Ecology and Sociobiology*, Vol. 35 (1994), pp. 1–11.; Noë, R.; Hammerstein, P., "Biological Markets," *Trends in Ecology & Evolution*, Vol. 10, No. 8 (1995), pp. 336–339.

22 Barclay, Pat, "Trustworthiness and Competitive Altruism Can Also Solve the 'Tragedy of the Commons,'" *Evolution and Human Behavior*, Vol. 25, No. 4 (2004), pp. 209–220; also Barclay, P., "Competitive Helping Increases with the Size of Biological Markets and Invades Defection," *Journal of Theoretical Biology*, Vol. 281, No. 1 (2011), pp. 47–55; Barclay, P., "Strategies for Cooperation in Biological Markets, Especially for Humans," *Evolution and Human Behavior*, Vol. 34, No. 3 (2013), pp. 164–175.

23 Hardy, Charlie L.; Van Vugt, Mark, "Nice Guys Finish First: The Competitive Altruism Hypothesis," *Personality and Social Psychology Bulletin*, Vol. 32, No. 10 (2006), pp. 1402–1413; also Rege, Mari; Telle, Kjetil, "The Impact of Social Approval and Framing on Cooperation in Public Good Situations," *Journal of Public Economics*, Vol. 88, No. 7–8 (2004), pp. 1625–1644.

24 Barclay, P., "Trustworthiness and Competitive Altruism...," *Evolution and Human Behavior*, Vol. 25, No. 4 (2004), pp. 209–220; Barclay, P.; Willer, R., "Partner Choice Creates Competitive Altruism in Humans," *Proceedings of the Royal Society B: Biological Sciences*, Vol. 274, No. 10 (March 2007), pp. 749–753; also Sylwester, Karolina & Roberts, Gilbert, "Cooperators Benefit through Reputation-Based Partner Choice in Economic Games," *Biology Letters* (October 2010) found at pubmed.ncbi.nlm.nih.gov/20410026.

25 Sampson, Rana, "Bullying in Schools," in *ASU Center for Problem-Oriented Policing* (ASU Watts College: 2002); found at popcenter.asu.edu/content/bullying-schools-0.

26 Zapf, Dieter; Einarsen, S., "Bullying in the Workplace: Recent Trends in Research and Practice," *European Journal of Work and Organizational Psychology*, Vol. 10, No. 4 (2001), pp. 369–373.

27 National Sexual Violence Resource Center publishes research findings at www.nsvrc.org/statistics.

28 Sorel, Georges, *Réflexions sur la Violence* (Paris: Marcel Rivière et Cie, 1908), p. 188.

29 Arendt, Hannah, *On Violence* (Boston: Houghton Mifflin Harcourt, 1970), p. 4.

30 Daly, Martin; Wilson, Margo, "Evolutionary Social Psychology and Family Homicide," *Science*, Vol. 242, No. 4878 (1988), pp. 519–524.

31 Benard, Stephen, "Reputation Systems, Aggression, and Deterrence in Social Interaction," *Social Science Research*, Vol. 42, No. 1, (January 2013), pp. 230–245; Daly, Martin; Wilson, Margo, "Evolutionary Social Psychology and Family Homicide," *Science*, Vol. 242, No. 4878 (1988), pp. 519–524; Felson, R.B., "Aggression as Impression Management," *Social Psychology*, Vol. 41, No. 3 (1978), pp. 205–213; Frank, Robert H., *Passions Within Reason: The Strategic Role of the Emotions* (New York: WW Norton & Co., 1988).

32 Daly, Martin; Wilson, Margo, "Evolutionary Social Psychology and Family Homicide," *Science*, Vol. 242, No. 4878 (1988), pp. 519–524; Felson, R.B., "Aggression as Impression Management," *Social Psychology*, Vol. 41, No. 3 (1978), pp. 205–213.

33 Griskevicius, Vladas; Tybur, Joshua M.; Gangestad, Steven W.; Perea, Emily F.; Shapiro, Janet R.; Kenrick, Douglas T., "Aggress to Impress: Hostility as an Evolved Context-Dependent Strategy," *Journal of Personality and Social Psychology*, Vol. 96, No. 5 (2009), pp. 980–994.

34 McAndrew, Francis T., "Costly Signaling Theory," in Shackelford, Todd K.; Weekes-Shackelford, Viviana A. (eds.), *Encyclopedia of Evolutionary Psychological Science* (New York: Springer, 2021), pp. 1525–1532.

35 Buss, David M.; Barnes, Michael, "Preferences in Human Mate Selection," *Journal of Personality and Social Psychology*, Vol. 50, No. 3 (1986), pp. 559–570.

36 Beaussart, Melanie L.; Kaufman, Scott B.; Kaufman, James C., "Creative Activity, Personality, Mental Illness, and Short-Term Mating Success," *Journal of Creative Behavior*, Vol. 46 (2012), pp. 151–167. Also: Clegg, H.; Nettle, D.; Miell, D., "Status and Mating Success Amongst Visual Artists," *Frontiers in Psychology*, Vol. 2 (2011), p. 310. Also: Lange, B.P.; Euler, H.A., "Writers Have Groupies, Too: High Quality Literature Production and Mating Success," *Evolutionary Behavior Sciences* (American Psychological Association, 2014), Vol. 8, Issue 1, pp. 20–30.

4

THE SHAPERS OF OUR AMBITION

The afternoon of March 15 in the year 44 BCE marked one of the most infamous assassinations in history: the murder of the Roman dictator, Julius Caesar, by a conspiracy of 60 Roman senators. As related 165 years later by Gaius Suetonius Tranquillus, the Roman Empire equivalent of our modern-day presidential historians,[1] Caesar tried to get away after the first thrusts of the knives, but he was blinded by his own blood and tripped and fell. The assassins stabbed him some more – 23 thrusts, no less.

The reason for the plot against Caesar was that he had recently been named "dictator in perpetuity" of the Roman Republic, and the senators feared that he planned to become a king, overthrow the Senate, and rule as a tyrant. His assassination is thus a story of ambition, or at least alleged ambition, because the assassins feared that they would lose much of their Significance – their social worth in Rome's hierarchy – if Caesar truly did disband the Senate. As the slain leader's friend, military hero Mark Antony, famously declared in Shakespeare's 1600 play, *Julius Caesar*: "If it were so

DOI: 10.4324/9781003410706-4

[meaning, if Caesar really was ambitious], it was a grievous fault, and grievously hath Caesar answered it."[2]

And yet the Roman people admired Caesar. They were outraged by the murder and, spurred on by Mark Antony, demanded the conspirators' blood. They did not mind Caesar's climb to power and his ambition. Their love for Caesar is often explained by his initiatives to reduce debt, arrange jobs for the poor, and generally improve the lives of Roman citizens. Strikingly, his will transferred his villa, its fabulous gardens, his art gallery, and practically all his wealth to the public.

However, beyond the material gifts, Caesar consistently showed Romans that he cared about them, that in his eyes they mattered. And because his own glory and social worth were so immense, his caring for the people of Rome bestowed upon them a special and immensely exalted type of Significance.

Intriguingly then, the Roman people loved Caesar precisely because of his power and status. Being cared for and loved by someone as great and significant as Caesar conferred uniquely powerful Significance on the recipients of this love, the people of Rome. We have more to say about how Significance "trickles down" from the high and mighty person (for example, an admired leader) to those receiving the love (the followers or subjects), and how it makes them feel great and important.

For now, notice how issues of Significance permeate the story of Caesar's assassination: The reason for killing him was his unbridled quest for greatness and social worth, which threatened the Significance that the conspirators felt. In turn, the outrage expressed by the people of Rome was partly because his death removed their own source of Significance.

Why Do People Differ in Their Significance Quest?

Genetics. Some people, like Julius Caesar, have a truly "oversized" drive for Significance. They are more brazenly ambitious and explicitly Significance-seeking than others. You can probably think of differences among your friends, colleagues, and acquaintances in how ambitious they are. Some may seem to be consumed with prestige, awards, and attainments. They cannot stop thinking of, worshipping, and talking about people who are doing well, are successful, and admired.

Willy Loman, the tragic, Significance-bereft character in Arthur Miller's *Death of a Salesman*, goes on and on incessantly about his brother Ben who fell into wealth quickly – and hence Significance – having discovered diamonds in the jungles of Africa on one of his expeditions at the age of 21.

The obviously named Alexander the Great, Catherine the Great, Napoleon, Hitler, and Putin are historical figures whose insatiable megalomania left an indelible mark on world history. On the softer and more productive side of this spectrum in our here and now are people like Elon Musk, Jeff Bezos, Sir Richard Branson, and, of course, anyone who runs for president of the United States.

However, not everyone needs constant demonstrations of their social worth on such a grandiose scale, and indeed it truly is not an option for most people. Most of us are satisfied to be appreciated by people we care about, our loved ones, our friends, and our colleagues. Most of us have limits to our ambition imposed by our circumstances. In the words of Bruce Springsteen's hit song, "Badlands": "Poor man wanna be rich, Rich man wanna be king, And a king ain't satisfied 'Til he rules everything."

Above all, however, people do not like to be disrespected, to be treated as if they do not matter. And when a person *does* like to be abused in such a way, that is often seen as a sign of hazardous psychological dysfunction and a mental health crisis.

What explains those immense differences between people in the degree of Significance they would consider sufficient? One factor that we already alluded to in Chapter 3 is evolution. There is such a thing as human nature, psychologically speaking. In the same way that humans generally display a core set of physiological attributes – such as two lungs, one stomach, one pancreas, two ears, and two eyes – human beings share a core of psychological features. Those aspects we have in common relate to how we reason, what we feel, what motivates us, and how we perceive the world.[3]

However, these commonalities are not absolute. Different humans can differ in the degree to which a given psychological feature (such as intelligence or aggressiveness) is manifested in a particular individual and how dominant it is in driving this person's behavior. As is the case with any species, humans share a common gene pool, but there is definitely quite a degree of variation among individuals. This applies to the Quest for Significance (QFS) as well.

Genetics, then, is one factor that explains why individuals differ in their ambitiousness and strength of desire to have social worth and to matter.[4]

How unique are we, as we pursue our QFS? We have learned that no two individuals are genetically the same. Even "identical twins" – that is, monozygotic twins born of a single egg fertilized by a single sperm cell – can differ when it comes to their genes. In a study published in 2021, Icelandic scientists who examined the DNA of 381 monozygotic twin pairs discovered that on average, so-called identical twins differed by 5.2 mutations, with 39 pairs differing by more than 100 mutations, while 38 pairs did not differ at all in their DNA.[5]

As complicated as those statistics may seem, their gist shatters the long-held belief that there are no physical differences between identical twins. These differences can be substantial; for instance, one twin might have autism or suffer from some other chronic health condition, while the other might not.[6] Moreover, people's genetic make-up can change with the passage of time due to environmental influences – meaning that monozygotic twins can drift away from each other and end up with substantially disparate DNAs.[7]

Culture

Genetic makeup is hardly the only determinant of what kind of people we turn out to be, and how our differences affect our Quests for Significance. Another major factor shaping our personalities is the environment in which we find ourselves. A widely known Minnesota study of identical twins raised in different households attributed about 70 percent of the research participants' IQ to genetic factors, and around 30 percent to environmental influences.[8]

A particularly influential factor in shaping people's personality is culture. One recent case study describes a pair of South Korean identical twins, referred to as S and U, born in 1974.[9] Due to accidental circumstances, the twins were separated at age 2. One twin, S, grew up in South Korea, while the other, U, grew up with foster parents in the United States. At age 44, the twins were reunited, and a study was done to compare them on various psychological characteristics.

Specifically, the twins took a battery of tests. These comprised a general ability assessment, a self-esteem survey, a personality questionnaire, a job satisfaction survey, and a measure of whether the person is more of an "individualist" or a "collectivist."

Although there were some similarities between the twins' responses, there were also considerable differences. Their general ability scores were quite different – U scored 84, while S scored 100. Of greatest interest, U, in keeping with the individualistic American norms by which she had been raised, perceived herself as independent and believed that all members of a collective are equal in status. In contrast, S, raised in South Korea, had views consistent with that nation's collectivistic culture. She perceived herself as part of a collective and was willing to accept hierarchy and inequality within that societal unit.

Culture, then, is a major factor beyond genetics that determines our attitudes, the goals we set for ourselves, and our behavior. As the leading evolutionary biologist E.O. Wilson put it, "No serious scholar would think that human behavior is controlled the way animal instinct is, without the intervention of culture."[10]

But what is culture? That word refers to the characteristics and knowledge of a particular group of people. You can speak of not only the culture of a society or a group of societies (such as Western nations or Asian countries), but also the culture of an organization or a workplace. The term "culture" can cover many meanings. It includes what we believe in, what we eat and how we prepare it, our clothing, what we consider beautiful or ugly, our manners, our relationships with others, and a host of other things. Cultures differ from each other in all those ways. A culture could, even without using these precise words, promote the Quest for Significance as a major concern – or treat it as a less central issue to worry about, way down the list below the sheer struggle for survival and subsistence.

Cultures also differ on what they consider Significance, which behaviors and activities confer social worth and merit the appreciation and esteem of people. Such appreciation and esteem thoroughly depend on *values* the given group of people (the society, nation, organization, etc.) care about and cherish. Warrior cultures value physical courage and fighting ability,[11] merchant cultures value business acumen, academic cultures value abstract reasoning and experimental rigor, and so on.

To feel good about yourself, to consider yourself worthy and significant, you need to represent, affirm, or exhibit some degree of commitment to your group's values. So, to feel significant in a warrior culture, you need to be known as a courageous and skillful fighter; in an artistic culture, you must demonstrate creativity and unique talent; and in an athletic culture, you must shine in your physical prowess to be admired.

Cultural Evolution

It is common for cultures to evolve as they encounter various conditions – anything from drought to years of war – and attempt to adapt to them. These changes shape the mentality of people in that culture. For instance, in an environment where a group of people is in frequent contact with its enemies and detractors (think of Ukrainians near Russia, or the often violent friction between Israelis and Palestinians), fighting ability, courage, and leadership may be especially valued. In a community situated near a seacoast, navigational ability and a knack for exploration will likely acquire value.

A fascinating cross-cultural study with data from 33 nations has shown that various external challenges – such as a history of territorial conflict, a scarcity of resources, disease, and various environmental threats – contributed to the development of "tight" norms and rules. Societies where these challenges were prevalent, such as Singapore, Japan, or Germany, have come to love order; and those nations are known for punishing individuals who deviate from agreed-upon ways of doing things.[12] In Singapore, for example, spitting on a street earns you a fine of up to a thousand dollars, and smuggling illicit drugs is punishable by death. In parts of Germany, residents of apartments observe a "sweeping week" in which they assume responsibility for cleaning up areas around their buildings.

In contrast, cultures whose history did not involve major threats evolve norms and customs that are "loose" by comparison. Citizens in "loose" countries such as Canada, New Zealand, or Brazil have gained a reputation for littering, creating noise pollution, and ignoring any commitments to punctuality.

The Ambitious Society

The characteristics of a culture and its values often depend on members of that culture, which naturally leads to age-old questions of nature or nurture: Are the people predisposed to certain behaviors, thanks to their genetic endowment? Or have they been shaped by experiences? One explanation for Americans' well-known drive for success is that America is a land of immigrants – not just an interesting mix of backgrounds, but people who had enough initiative and ambition to leave their countries of origin in search of a better future for themselves and their children.

A landmark psychological analysis of cultural differences in ambition was published in 1961 by Harvard University professor David McClelland, already referred to in Chapter 2. He was out to solve a challenging economic puzzle: the vast differences in the wealth and economic growth of different nations. Why was it, for example, that 7 percent of the world's population in North America enjoyed 43 percent of the world's wealth (at that time), whereas 55 percent of the world's people were in Asia, yet they had only 16 percent of the world's wealth? Why was the per capita income in the United States nearly 15 times higher than in Mexico, five times more than in Argentina, and twice that in the United Kingdom? Why indeed?

To McClelland, a psychologist and expert on human motivation, the solution to the puzzle had to be anchored in the psychology of the people in those regions and nations. The vast economic differences must be explicable by examining what motivates the residents of different nations and the strength of their ambition. He identified a motivational factor he called the Need for Achievement, which in some places might be high among the denizens of a location and in other places low. He defined that need as the desire for success in the attainment of socially appreciated outcomes, stemming from "desires for social approval, power, or knowledge."[13] Obviously, that aligns closely with our analysis of an environment characterized by individuals' strivings for Significance and social worth.

McClelland was influenced in his thinking by Sigmund Freud, the legendary psychiatrist who laid the groundwork for modern psychoanalysis. Freud suggested that human motives often operate on the unconscious level, so that people do not actually know why they act in a given way, say the things they say, or do the things they do.[14] For instance, a person may think they bought a car because of its good gasoline mileage or its repair record, whereas in fact they did so because of its sexy appearance, or "head-turning quotient." To measure individuals' need for achievement, McClelland devised a specific method. He first sought to arouse that need in research participants by asking them to perform a series of tasks that would measure their intelligence and were known to "demonstrate whether the person is suited to be a leader."[15]

After these tasks were completed, participants' need for achievement was measured by asking them to write short stories – mostly about their work situation (a context highly charged with the achievement theme) – in response to pictures flashed on a screen for a few seconds. McClelland labeled those stories "fantasies," and his researchers searched through them for themes of seeking achievement: standards of excellence, doing well, and the desire to do well. The number of such achievement-oriented themes in one's writing was then treated as that person's "need for achievement" score.

Research by McClelland and other scientists showed that people with high scores in the need for achievement – as opposed to low scorers – have better memories of tasks still to be completed, volunteer more for psychology experiments, are more active in college and community activities, and learn faster to excel in achievement tasks.

One particularly interesting study[16] found that high-need-for-achievement mothers of eight-year-old boys expected their sons to be remarkably independent: to know their way around the city, be active and energetic, do well in competitions, make their own friends, and try hard at whatever they were undertaking. This was very different from the restrictive child-rearing practices – not trying to foster self-reliance – of mothers with a low "need for achievement." They did not want their sons to play with children unless approved by parents and, in general, discouraged their sons from making important decisions on their own.

Using methods of assessing the "need for achievement" motive, McClelland and his team compiled scores for tribal cultures, well outside modern urban centers or the halls of academe. Researchers identified 12 folk tales in each of 50 cultures being assessed – above all, looking for themes of achieving success in those popular stories that spanned the globe from Africa to Asia to Oceania and North and South America. Every tribe was given a score, and McClelland correlated the scores with the percentage of adult males engaged in full-time entrepreneurial activity. That was his measure of economic growth. The hypothesis was that cultures telling stories about achievement would have more individuals willing to take financial risks and invest in a business. Indeed, this research found a significant correlation between a tribe's need for achievement (as found in cultural folklore) and economic growth, lending empirical support to McClelland's insight.

Impressively, McClelland replicated his findings about tribal cultures when he turned to 23 modern, developed nations. Here, he came up with "need for achievement" scores based on children's stories prevalent in the various nations. His index of economic growth was the amount of electricity produced in each country. Again, in an impressive support of his hypothesis, McClelland and his team did find a strong correlation between the strength of achievement themes in the kids' stories in 1925 and the country's economic growth in the 25 years that followed.

The studies by McClelland strongly suggest that the need for achievement – representing individual's desire for Significance and mattering – is typically instilled in children through parental attitudes and expectations, as well as fairy tales the children are brought up on. All of this ends up contributing to their culture's economic growth.

Yet, it is also true that a strong link between people's Quest for Significance and economic growth depends on societal values. In cultures that subscribe to materialistic values and appreciate people who do well economically, we could expect that people who crave Significance and social worth would invest their efforts in economic activity. But in societies with values that are spiritual, intellectual, or artistic, you would not expect a relationship between QFS and the economy. Think about the "mad scientist" and the "starving artist" as models for having high interest in Significance, but channeling their quest in non-economic directions.

David McClelland and his colleagues made a fascinating discovery: Personal psychological factors, like the need for achievement or the Quest for Significance, can have a huge impact on macro-level trends such as a country's economic development. Later, we explore how QFS can fuel political movements that shape history. It is not just about leaders who start wars or conquer lands; it is also about everyday people whose daily actions help build their nation's economy. The British philosopher John Stuart Mill declared, "All social phenomena are rooted in human nature."[17] The way that the ubiquitous Significance quest influences economies and politics bears testimony to his wisdom.

Parenting and Family Dynamics

In addition to genetics and culture, life circumstances and family dynamics also shape the depth of people's personal ambition and the strength of their craving for Significance. Stereotypes, though undesirable, seem to be confirmed by findings that Americans of Jewish and Asian backgrounds strongly encourage striving for excellence, and reactions by cultural commentators have included blasting so-called Tiger Moms as too pushy.

Of course, every family should have the right to decide what it wants to emphasize in raising its offspring. America's Congress passed legislation in 2015 that included a "Free-Range Kids and Parents" provision. The most discussed aspect was permitting children to ride bicycles or walk to school at whatever age their parents deemed appropriate. Until then, parts of the country had laws that, for safety's sake, banned children from going to school on their own. Now parents can exercise discretion, but if they do grant their children a sense of greater independence, the result will generally be an enhanced ability for them to cope with and overcome challenges. When young people have a "can-do" attitude, they typically set high goals for themselves. If allowed to aim for the stars, their natural Quest for Significance will only be enhanced.

Parenting, Jewish Style

A good place to look at how parenting affects children's QFS is the oft-stereotyped child-rearing practice prevalent in Jewish communities around the world. Although Jews are only a tiny minority of the world's population (around 0.2%), 170 of 850 Nobel Prize winners are Jewish, as are 21 percent of Ivy League university students, 37 percent of Academy Award–winning directors, and half of Pulitzer Prize winners for non-fiction.[18] We posit that the results stem from the Jewish parenting style, which can build children's confidence. Jewish kids are frequently encouraged to express their own opinions, distrust authority, and engage in debate.

Another factor relevant to ambition is the Jewish sense of community. Perhaps because of suffering religious persecution over the millennia, Jewish families have a reputation for encouraging their children to be aware of society's many ills and try to combat injustice. That traditional goal is known by the Hebrew phrase, Tikkun Olam, which means "Repairing the World."

In addition to transmitting positive societal values, Jewish parents typically make no secret of their admiration for people with a prestigious "professional" standing in the community; thus, whether tacitly or out loud, they may be urging their children to consider being a doctor, a lawyer, or a scientist. That broad-brush facet of Jewish life in most Western countries may be traced back to medieval Europe, where until 500 years ago Jews were not allowed to own land or many businesses. Their ambitiousness and instinct for survival tended to be channeled into professions that required extensive education, and in modern society, those are highly valued.[19]

Parenting, "Tiger" Style

The Jewish style of parenting is hardly the only one meant to encourage ambition. In the wake of Yale law professor Amy Chua's book, *Battle Hymn of the Tiger Mother*,[20] much discussion was devoted to Tiger parenting, supposedly very common among families whose elders had moved from Asian countries to the United States or Britain. Tiger parents were reputed to be very strict, discouraging time "wasted" on too much fun, with relentless encouragement of children to achieve success in socially valued activities such as academics, music, and some sports.

According to Chua, Tiger parents focused on their children's grades, awards, and potential income. They completely identified with their kids' future potential and measured their own Significance by the successes and failures of the younger generation. Chua also highlighted punishments, often in the form of instilling guilt when the child fails to meet the parents' expectations.

Does Tiger parenting work? Does it develop ambition in the child? Does it lead to the sense of Significance that makes those kids feel good about themselves? Like Chua, a Chinese-American author named Leslie Hsu Oh wrote about her own family's Tiger parenting and answered those questions in the affirmative.[21] Her own success is undeniable. Oh gained admission to every college she applied to, graduated from Harvard, went on to earn two master's degrees, became an official White House "Champion of Change," and founded an award-winning non-profit.

The achievements attained by Chua, Oh, and millions of others raised in Asian immigrant families might suggest that Tiger parenting is effective in instilling ambition and yielding success. Unfortunately, systematic research on the consequences of Tiger parenting suggests the opposite. Studies have found an association of such parenting with depression and anxiety, and for many children, it led to less successful academic performance.[22,23] One study found that adolescents in so-called Tiger households yearned for less restrictive support, and they frequently felt alienated from their parents.[24] It appears that whatever its benefits, the Tiger style is a mixed bag at best. By holding the child to impossibly high standards, the parents are making their child feel inadequate. Paradoxically, that may be lowering the young person's motivation for Significance because of the lowered expectancy of meeting the impossible standards to which they are held.

That is a lesson worth remembering: If a person's Significance relies on some elusive or impossible standard, then he or she ends up with the pain of feeling a lack of Significance most of the time, and ultimately might give up on striving for Significance altogether.

Promotion- and Prevention-Driven Parenting

As mentioned in Chapter 2, Professor Tory Higgins of Columbia University identified two motivational orientations shaped by different parenting styles: promotion and prevention foci.[25] Promotion-focused individuals aim for the good things they can achieve, dreaming of fame and fortune and seizing opportunities to make these dreams a reality. In contrast, prevention-focused individuals are more concerned with avoiding potential disasters. They prioritize safety over ambition, and they are content to steer clear of the pitfalls they fear.

How do these orientations develop? According to Higgins, parenting plays a crucial role. When parents reward successes but withdraw affection in response to failures, they foster a promotion focus. This creates individuals who are eager and excited by their achievements, such as good grades or athletic accomplishments, but feel sad and dejected when they fail. On the other hand, punishing failures and remaining neutral or unresponsive to successes cultivates a prevention focus. These individuals experience anxiety and agitation when they fail or anticipate failure, and they feel relief when they avoid it.

Interestingly, prevention-focused people do not respond to success with exuberance; instead, they feel a calm comfort from avoiding failure. Tiger parenting, with its emphasis on punishment and constraint, is likely to induce a prevention focus. These individuals strive not to disappoint and to meet the high standards set by their parents, whose voices they internalize long into adulthood. Their ambition is driven by anxiety and fear of failure, unlike promotion-focused individuals whose ambition is fueled by antici-pating success. Supportive parenting that celebrates children's successes and takes failures in its stride is more likely to create ambitious, promotion-oriented individuals who dream of success, aim for the stars, and feel a healthy and uplifting measure of Significance.

Helicopter Parenting

Because of their close relationship, parents and children can significantly impact each other's sense of mattering in life. Children can feel proud or ashamed of their parents, just as parents can feel about their children. Sometimes, parents' vicarious pursuit of Significance through their chil-dren's achievements can be excessive and harmful to the child's psycho-logical and social development. This overinvolvement, often referred to as "helicopter parenting," was coined by Dr Haim Ginott in his 1969 book, *Between Parent and Teenager*.[26] The term originated from teens who described their parents as hovering over them like helicopters.

An example of this is when parents become overly involved in their children's athletics or arts, making their children's successes or failures the parents' primary source of social worth. This can turn activities meant to foster the child's development and well-being into significant sources of stress, ultimately hindering their effective functioning in various domains.[27] The detrimental effects of helicopter parenting include lowered self-confidence and self-esteem, undeveloped coping skills, and increased anxiety in children.[28]

Summary

Even though the desire to matter and be significant is a universal charac-teristic of humans, people differ nonetheless in their appetite for glory. Some, like Julius Caesar, Vladimir Putin, or Elon Musk, have an almost unquenchable thirst for admiration. They aim to leave a lasting legacy and be remembered as pioneers of positive change, whether for their commu-nity, nation, religion, or humanity as a whole. These individuals seem to seek recognition from billions of people, across centuries still to come. On the other hand, many people are perfectly happy being appreciated by just their family and friends.

These differences in the Quest for Significance stem from a mix of personal temperament, genetics, cultural background, and family upbringing. Some upbringing styles boost people's confidence in their ability to succeed, viewing failure as just a step on the path to learning and achieving Significance. Then there are some upbringing styles that focus on the negative aspects of failure, promoting a cautious approach to life and a preference for maintaining the status quo.

These varied upbringing styles shape how people pursue Significance, the risks they are willing to take, and their level of satisfaction with the recognition they receive from others.

Notes

1 Suetonius, *The Lives of the Twelve Caesars*, translated by J.C. Rolfe (London: William Heinemann, 1913–1914). Details of the assassination of the first Julius Caesar are in Suetonius's book, which he wrote in 121 CE, in a chapter titled "Divus Julius," pp. 80–82, in the volume published by Heinemann.

2 William Shakespeare, Julius Caesar, Act 3, Scene 2, Lines 82–83.

3 Tooby, John; Cosmides, Leda, "On the Universality of Human Nature and the Uniqueness of the Individual: The Role of Genetics and Adaptation," *Journal of Personality*, Vol. 58, No. 1 (1990), pp. 17–67; Tooby, John; Cosmides, Leda, "The Psychological Foundations of Culture," in Barkow, Jerome H.; Cosmides, Leda; Tooby, John (eds.), *The Adapted Mind: Evolutionary Psychology and the Generation of Culture* (New York: Oxford University Press, 1992), pp. 19–136.

4 Hopwood, Christopher J.; Donnellan, M. Brent; Blonigen, Daniel M.; Krueger, Robert F.; McGue, Matt; Iacono, William G.; Burt, S. Alexandra, "Genetic and Environmental Influences on Personality Trait Stability and Growth During the Transition to Adulthood: A Three-Wave Longitudinal Study," *Journal of Personality and Social Psychology*, Vol. 100, No. 3 (2011), pp. 545–556.

5 Jónsson, Hákon; Magnúsdóttir, Erna; Eggertsson, Hannes P.; Stefánsson, Ólafur A.; Árnadóttir, Guðný A.; Eiríksson, Ögmundur; Stefánsson, Kári, "Differences Between Germline Genomes of Monozygotic Twins," *Nature Genetics*, Vol. 53 (January 7, 2021), pp. 27–34.

6 A British newspaper report from January 8, 2021, found at www.telegraph.co.uk /news/2021/01/08/identical-twins-dont-always-have-identical-genetics-study -finds.

7 Jarry, J., "Identical Twins are Not Identical," *McGill Office for Science and Society* (January 21, 2021); found at www.mcgill.ca/oss/article/general-science/identical-twins -are-not-identical.

8 Bouchard, Thomas J. Jr., Lykken, David T., McGue, Matthew, Segal, Nancy L., Tellegen, Auke, "Sources of Human Psychological Differences: The Minnesota

Study of Twins Reared Apart," *Science*, Vol. 250, No. 4978 (January 12, 1990), pp. 223–228.

9 Segal, Nancy L.; Hur, Yoon-Mi, "Personality Traits, Mental Abilities and Other Individual Differences: Monozygotic Female Twins Raised Apart in South Korea and the United States," *Personality and Individual Differences*, Vol. 194 (2022), p. 111643.

10 Wilson, Edward O., *The Origins of Creativity* (New York: Liveright Publishing, 2017).

11 Futterman, Adam, "5 Fierce Warrior Cultures," *Discover Magazine* (November 4, 2021); found at www.discovermagazine.com/the-sciences/five-fierce-warrior-cultures.

12 Gelfand, Michele J.; Raver, Jana L.; Nishii, Lisa; Leslie, Lisa M.; Lun, Janetta; Lim, Benjamin C.; Yamaguchi, Susumu, "Differences Between Tight and Loose Cultures: A 33-Nation Study," *Science*, Vol. 332, No. 6033 (2011), pp. 1100–1104.

13 McClelland, David C., *The Achieving Society* (New York: Simon and Schuster, 1961).

14 Nisbett, Richard E.; Wilson, Timothy DeCamp, "Telling More than We Can Know: Verbal Reports on Mental Processes," *Psychological Review*, Vol. 84, No. 3 (1977), pp. 231–259.

15 McClelland, David C., *The Achieving Society* (New York: Simon and Schuster, 1961).

16 Winterbottom, Marian Ruth, "The Relation of Childhood Training in Independence to Achievement Motivation," (PhD dissertation, University of Michigan, 1953).

17 Mill, John Stuart, *A System of Logic, Ratiocinative and Inductive* (London: J.W. Parker, 1843).

18 Aziz, Alan, "Why Are There So Many Jewish Nobel Winners?" *The Jewish Chronicle* (London: December 8, 2022); Weissman, Sara, "Jewish Student Enrollment Declines at Many Ivies," *Inside Higher Ed* (May 8, 2023); "List of Jewish Academy Award Winners and Nominees," *Wikipedia*, 2023.

19 Berenbaum, Michael, "Anti-Semitism in Medieval Europe," in *Encyclopaedia Britannica* (Chicago: Encyclopaedia Britannica, 2024); "History of European Jews in the Middle Ages," *Wikipedia*, 2024; Wachtel, David, *The Jews in the Medieval Period* (London: Sotheby's, 2013).

20 Chua, Amy, *Battle Hymn of the Tiger Mother* (New York: Bloomsbury Publishing, 2011).

21 Oh, Leslie Hsu, "5 Things We Can All Learn from Tiger Parents," *Parents Magazine* (December 20, 2019); found at www.lesliehsuoh.com/parents-5-things-we-can-all-learn-from-tiger-parents.

22 Kim, Su Yeong; Wang, Yijie; Orozco-Lapray, Diana; Shen, Yishan; Murtuza, Murtaza, "Does 'Tiger Parenting' Exist? Parenting Profiles of Chinese Americans and Adolescent Developmental Outcomes," *Asian American Journal of Psychology*, Vol. 4, No. 1 (2013), pp. 7–18.

23 Tam, Hoi Lam; Kwok, Sylvia Y. C. L.; Ling, Chi Ching; Li, Chi Iok Kuan, "The Moderating Effects of Positive Psychological Strengths on the Relationship between Tiger Parenting and Child Anxiety," *Children and Youth Services Review*, Vol. 24 (11/2018), pp. 207–215.

24 Kim, Su Yeong, "Defining Tiger Parenting in Chinese Americans," *Human Development*, Vol. 56, No. 4 (2013), pp. 217–222.

25 Higgins, E. Tory, "Promotion and Prevention: Regulatory Focus as a Motivational Principle," in Zanna, M.P. (ed.), *Advances in Experimental Social Psychology* (New York: Academic Press, 1998), Vol. 30, pp. 1–46.

26 Ginott, Haim, *Between Parent and Teenager* (New York: Macmillan, 1969).

27 Ogilvie, Bruce, "The Child Athlete: Psychological Implications of Participation in Sport," *The Annals of the American Academy of Political and Social Science*, Vol. 445 (1/1979), pp. 47–58.

28 Bayless, Kate, "Helicopter Parenting and 5 Ways it Impacts Kids," *Parents Magazine* (October 12, 2022); found at www.parents.com/parenting/better-parenting/what-is-helicopter-parenting.

5

NEEDING AND GETTING SIGNIFICANCE

From Cradle to Grave

A baby is crying in its crib or, to borrow Shakespeare's terms, it is mewling and puking.[1] What does the infant want? Attention from its parents, of course, which is essential for its survival. When parents care for the baby's needs, they implicitly convey to the child that it matters to these important figures in its tiny social universe.

The infant's crying is not yet a Quest for Significance (QFS). It is motivated by physical discomfort, such as hunger, thirst, wetness, or cold. Crying is the baby's instinctive response to discomfort. However, the attentive response it elicits from others begins to portray such attention as rewarding and pacifying. This instills in the infant a sense of security and safety and, in an unarticulated way, the sense that its needs will be cared for and, therefore, that it counts.

A true Quest for Significance develops later in life, around age four or five, when children develop the ability to understand that other people's thoughts may differ from their own. This is known as the Theory of Mind.[2]

DOI: 10.4324/9781003410706-5

With this new perceptiveness, the child becomes aware that others' evaluations of them may differ from their own self-concept, and that they may need to measure up to some standard of worth. This realization marks the beginning of the child's concern about how they are evaluated by others,[3] introducing their interest in social value and sowing the seeds of their desiring Significance.

Indeed, concerns about Significance loom large throughout our lives, from the cradle to the grave. This is evident in slogans such as "dying with dignity," which motivates support for euthanasia. Our striving for Significance shapes our career paths, colors our loves and hates, and accompanies us like a shadow in all our comings and goings.

Life's Mundane Setbacks

Think about your everyday joys and disappointments: how many of them, large or small, important or unimportant, have to do with your social worth, mattering, and Significance. A smile from a stranger implies that, however superficially, they approve of you; whereas an unreturned greeting or unanswered email can be jarring and hurtful because it seems to suggest that you do not matter to the other person, so insignificant are you as to not even warrant a reply.

A set of studies by Kipling Williams, a professor at Purdue University, vividly demonstrates how seemingly trivial slights from others can feel like serious losses of Significance. An incident that happened to Williams years ago triggered his interest in exclusion: being inexplicably ignored by others, and the profound feeling of hurt it can evoke. As Williams poignantly recounts:

> One afternoon in the mid-1980s I was sitting in a park on a blanket beside my dog when a Frisbee rolled up and hit me in the back. I turned around and spotted two guys standing a short distance away with hopeful looks. After standing to return their Frisbee, I moved to sit back down, when, to my surprise, the two strangers threw the disk back to me – an invitation. We formed a triangle on the grass, beginning a spontaneous game of three-way toss. But minutes later, for no discernible reason, they stopped throwing the Frisbee to me. At first, it was sort of funny, but when it became clear that they were

not going to include me again, I felt foolish, awkward, and hurt. I felt ostracized.[4]

In the decades that followed, Williams carried out an extensive set of studies that demonstrated just how painful seemingly trivial slights can be. In this research paradigm, called Cyberball, the three-way Frisbee fun is replicated on a screen. Three avatars, one representing the research participant, are throwing a ball to one another evenly, until at some point the avatar belonging to the participant is tossed no more balls. The emotional impact of this situation is remarkable. The excluded participants experienced lowered self-esteem; and, as revealed in their answers to questions, they had less belief in the meaning of their lives or their power to control their lives.

To be sure, feelings of exclusion and being slighted are common in real life outside the laboratory. In a diary study, which required people to record their experiences and reactions every day, Americans reported an average of one such event per day.

Undermining one's sense of Significance through exclusion is so deeply ingrained that it can be triggered by circumstances where the exclusion seems unrelated to one's personal qualities. For example, people can feel bad and rejected even when playing the Cyberball game with an "excluding" computer. The slight is truly "nothing personal."

The sense of rejection can also occur when the rejecting individuals are despised by the person, such as being excluded by the Ku Klux Klan and feeling bad about it, even though you hate the KKK's racism. You even feel bad when the game is configured in such a way that you get money each time the Frisbee isn't tossed to you, suggesting that a little cash cannot overcome the social pain of exclusion!

Of course, the slights in real life can be much more severe than not being tossed a ball by unknown others. Not hearing back about job applications or manuscripts submitted, being fired from a job, or having romantic advances rejected can be devastating. These experiences seemingly convey one's worthlessness and insignificance on dimensions that are central to one's sense of self. Such rejections can deeply impact an individual's self-esteem and sense of Significance, highlighting the profound effect that social exclusion and rejection can have on our psychological well-being.

Involuntary Celibates (Incels)

Incels make up an online community of men who consider themselves "involuntarily celibate," rejected by women because of their unattractive physical appearance or quirks in their behavior. These men are deeply aggrieved by the perceived insult to their masculinity – and they blame feminism – and some occasionally are driven to vengeful violence.[5] As one example of this phenomenon, in a horrific incident in Isla Vista, California, in May 2014, a 22-year-old killed 6 people and wounded 14 others – by gunshots, stabbings, and vehicle ramming – before shooting himself in the head. While pausing between attacks, he uploaded a video titled "Elliot Rodger's Retribution" and a 137-page manifesto, "My Twisted World," expressing hatred toward women for rejecting him and toward romantically successful men because he envied them.[6] He obviously believed that his own inner agonies merited wide public attention: a violent demand for a bit of Significance as he shattered so many people's lives.

Although rejections and disappointments are hard to avoid in life, most people's lives also include positive events that make them feel good about themselves. Typically, these are events that affect a person's sense of Significance. Spending time with people who accept, value, and love you nearly unconditionally is a definite boost. So are having a manuscript or proposal accepted, some prediction you made coming true, your affection reciprocated, and feeling that you did a good job.

Individual and Social Sources of Significance

Individual accomplishments and accolades are only a part of the story. Feeling good or bad about yourself – your sense of social worth – depends not only on what you *do*, but also on who you are in a society. Some social categories a person belongs to, such as race, gender, ethnicity, religion, or social class, are accorded high prestige (for instance, being an upper middle–class white Anglo-Saxon Christian male in America); others (for example, being a working-class African-American Muslim female) are accorded less prestige. Your category's social worth rubs off on you. You may not feel as secure about your social worth if you belong to a less prestigious group; events affecting your group's prestige (for example, your favorite team's victories and defeats) also affect how worthy you feel and how you are regarded. Psychologists refer to derived pride or shame, triggered by the successes or failures of others, as "basking in reflected glory." They even created an acronym for that, BIRGING.[7]

In a well-known study that demonstrates BIRGING, Robert Cialdini, a social psychologist at Arizona State University, showed that students had a greater tendency to wear apparel with the university's colors and name after the university football team won a game. In a second experiment, participants used the pronoun "we" to associate themselves with their university when describing a game in which their team won as compared to when their team lost. This tendency to use the pronoun "we" when describing a winning game was noticeably stronger after the participants experienced failure on a quiz, which had temporarily lowered their sense of Significance. Those students needed a dose of pride; their Quest for Significance was aroused.

A similar increase in the tendency to use the "we" pronoun was observed in yet another study by Cialdini in 1976, in which participants were told to talk about a winning game after talking for a while about a losing game. Recalling their team's loss must have lowered their sense of Significance, because the students obviously attempted to elevate it by associating themselves more emphatically (via the "we" pronoun) with the winning team.

In another social psychology experiment conducted almost half a century later,[8] participants were asked to write an essay recalling either a personal failure or a personal success. Afterward, their national identification as Americans was assessed. Interestingly, those who wrote about their failures reported a markedly stronger identification as Americans compared to those who wrote about their successes. In other words, when participants' sense of personal Significance was lowered by recalling a failure, they clung more strongly to the successful and powerful group identity of being American to compensate for the loss of Significance.

There are times when personal achievements boost one's sense of pride and importance, while social identity can have the opposite effect and drag down one's sense of Significance. Many highly accomplished European Jews in the 19th and 20th centuries attempted to assimilate into the cultures of the countries in which they resided and to de-emphasize, if not completely shed, their (low prestige) Jewish identity. They typically had accepted, reluctantly, that wider society looked down on them, so they were made to feel less significant than their individual attributes and attainments would have warranted.

Another example, not so different as one might think, is the choice made by brilliant female writers to publish their work under male names. Think of George Sand,[9] the Bronte sisters, J.K. Rowling, and others. It seems that they wanted to avoid the stigma of society's gender bias, which would attempt to force low Significance on women, no matter how creative.

In short, an individual's Significance can be heightened or lowered by personal successes or failures, but it will also be affected by the prestige or disdain attached to the person's social identity. Many people face unfair challenges of this kind, and not all have the strength or persistence – when personal or social sources of satisfaction fail them – to tap alternative sources for their Significance needs.

Activating the Significance Quest

We do not *incessantly* ruminate about our reputation and mattering. No one quests for Significance 24/7. When in a "resting state," we may just cruise along, busy with our everyday tasks, and not give much thought to our Significance and "mattering." The Quest for Significance is real, but often in the background like a simmering pot.

But it does not take much to bring it to boiling point that spurs action. Events that represent failures, possibilities, triumphs, and disappointments immediately wake up our need for Significance from its slumber and thrust it into the center of our attention. QFS may be awakened in two major ways: sensing an opportunity to gain new Significance, or reacting to a stinging loss of Significance.

Opportunity for Significance Gain

Spotting possible opportunities for a gain in Significance is a natural feeling we experience repeatedly throughout life. Children are often complimented by being called "so grown-up" and are eager to attain the Significance that adulthood confers. They dream of becoming policemen, firemen, or pilots – figures that, in their imagination, are heroic and prestigious. Stories about humanitarians, martyrs, and selfless saints inspire them to fantasize about embarking on professions of service that offer ample opportunities to acquire Significance: enlisting in the army, becoming a life-saving physician, or perhaps a psychiatrist whose wisdom unravels the mysteries of their patients' souls.

Opportunities for Significance can sometimes arise from events that demand immediate intervention. For example, seeing a friend in need offers a chance to be altruistic, while seeing a child in danger provides an opportunity to be heroic.

However, not all opportunities for Significance are rooted in generosity and kindness. Some, like a Ponzi scheme orchestrated by an unscrupulous scoundrel, are based on selfish greed. These schemes promise quick riches and the allure of becoming significant overnight. Striking shady deals, or "selling your soul to the devil" to gain a prestigious appointment or win an election, are temptations some may succumb to for the prize of Significance.

In a more destructive realm, the exhortation to become a suicide bomber for the promise of martyrdom and immortality – "living forever" in the reverence of a revolutionary or terrorist group – has led thousands of people to sacrifice their lives for a cause that promises Significance.

QFS and the continual temptation of new gains in social worth explain why today's billionaires, such as Elon Musk, Jeff Bezos, and Richard Branson, started competing to venture into space. With a net worth of around $200 billion, Bezos would gain no noticeable increment in social worth by making an additional billion or even $50 billion. However, the Amazon.com founder can achieve far more in the Significance market by being the first (or second) tourist in space or by sponsoring a human expedition to another planet. That achievement would be special, and very few people could afford to do it.

The same goes for people who find new value or purpose in their all-consuming business start-ups, in activist causes such as protesting the deaths of black men at the hands of white police officers, or even in storming Capitol Hill in Washington, DC, when angered by politics on January 6, 2021. Many changes or inflection points in life – for good and for ill – are windows of opportunity for Significance.

The Sting of Significance Loss

It is not only boom times that inspire people to new quests. Sometimes it is a crash – a precipitous loss of Significance that delivers a profound psychological blow and is the trigger for rushing to make a splashy come-back. Psychologists speak of "social pain" occasioned by Significance loss, and that can be felt as acutely as physical pain. Indeed, research demon-strates that the very same brain structures are activated by both types of pain.

A sharp experience of social pain from losing Significance can be trig-gered by seemingly trivial incidents in which one feels slighted and ignored. Reactions to feeling "excluded" were at the center of a noteworthy study at Purdue University, as participants felt pain from being left out − even when they were being excluded by a total stranger they did not need to care about.[10]

There are many ways of experiencing exclusion. Failing at a task, suf-fering romantic rejection, or being discriminated against because of race, gender, religion, or ethnicity − all can be circumstances causing social pain.[11] This wound typically motivates a person to seek ways to alleviate it by initiating what the individual sees as a Significance-restoring action. The action taken can be positive or negative, constructive or destructive, pro-social or anti-social.

Restoring Lost Significance

On the constructive side, Significance-restoring efforts can provide impe-tus for new directions or pursuits that people otherwise would never have considered. Michael Bloomberg famously created his business information company after being fired by an investment bank. George W. Bush decided he should run for Texas governor after realizing his party-boy lifestyle was pathetic and empty (hence undermining his Significance). We all are aware of more humble examples from our own lives and the media: the former corporate strivers who "burned out" and found new meaning on a goat farm; the couch potato who pushed aside his video games and crunchy snacks and enlisted in the air force to find new pride; or someone like the all-but-atheist sister who now sings in a church choir.

Clearly, some people can embody comeback stories when they suffer blows to their sense of Significance. Sadly, some never recover.

In recent years, increasing numbers of young Americans have commit-ted suicide after being humiliated online. One of those was Hope Witsell, a 13-year-old at Shields Middle School in Ruskin, Florida. She had "sexted" a topless picture of herself to her boyfriend. The photo found its way onto the phone of another girl, who proceeded to send it to students across several schools in the area. The photo went viral, and Hope became the target of vicious bullying. She was cruelly vilified on a MySpace page called the "Shields Middle School Burn Book," and a "Hope Hater" page was filled with horrible slurs. After several months of such torment, the teen could bear it no more. One evening, her mother discovered Hope's body hanged on scarves from her canopy bed.

Other tragic stories abound. Indeed, bullying by extreme humiliation, both online and off-line, has reached epidemic proportions in America's schools – causing immense suffering and misery to millions of youngsters who experience Significance loss with seemingly no hope of recovery.

Take a large step back and look at our rapidly modernizing, hyperconnected societies. We see a Significance crisis that threatens the rising generations we will depend on for productive work and wise leadership. Hoping to penetrate the foggy world of unhappy youth, the New York Times reached out to 13-year-olds, "an age when self-esteem is at its most fragile," seeking to interview thousands on how they were impacted by the Covid pandemic and by increasingly living life through their mobile phones. Among the Times's questions in 2022: "Does social media make you feel good or bad about yourself?" One girl who harbored suicidal thoughts told a reporter that just one hurtful online remark could make her feel as though she had no friends – and no hope.[12]

Loss of Significance is hardly restricted to the teenage years. In their 2020 book Deaths of Despair, Princeton economists Ann Case and Angus Deaton analyzed the rapidly rising suicide rates among working-class white Americans. While the authors use different terms, their explanation of this troubling trend is the sharp decline in Significance felt by millions of American workers.

As Case and Deaton put it,

> Simple falling [of] material standards cannot by itself account for what has happened. …jobs that come with the lower wages do not bring the sense of pride that can come with being part of a successful enterprise… Jobs are not just the source of money;… it is the loss of meaning, of dignity, of pride, and of self-respect …that brings on despair, not just or even primarily the loss of money.[13]

These crises of Significance can be hard, more taxing than some can bear. As Linda Loman sternly admonishes in the final monologue of Arthur Miller's *Death of a Salesman*, eulogizing her fallen husband Willy: "Attention must be paid!"

Reclaiming the Significance of Our Social Identity

Often, our feelings of insignificance and worthlessness have to do with our social identity that suffers from prejudices, discriminations, and inequities that mar our society. When that happens, members of the disparaged group may join together and form a social movement aimed at elevating the worth of their compromised identity. The civil rights movement, the Black Lives Matter movement, the feminist movement – but also Fascism, Communism, and National Socialism in other nations – are typically fueled by a sense of insignificance experienced by members of a given category of people: women, African Americans, members of the working class, or denizens of a given nation. People who feel disrespected because of their social identity want to restore their dignity, and leaders can whip them up with pledges to elevate their social standing.

Many white Americans felt their privileged position was being eroded, so they responded to a Trumpian message that promised to restore them as top dogs. It seems obvious that a campaign promise to make America great again was mostly about making certain Americans *feel* great again.

A person's loss of Significance on a given dimension, such as failure on an important task or a moral lapse, can be compensated for by attaining Significance on another valued dimension. For instance, several Palestinian women volunteered for suicide missions after they had suffered some kind of stigma in their lives: due to infertility, divorce, or an extramarital affair. Similarly, a teenager who blew himself up at an Israeli military checkpoint had been diagnosed with HIV, and AIDS patients were totally stigmatized in traditional Palestinian society.[14] All these individuals suffered from a serious Significance loss because of failing to live up to a given societal value (fertility, marriage, fidelity) and strove to regain it by serving a different value, willing to kill and die for the cause of Palestinian nationhood.

Consider also a pair of self-radicalized terrorists in the United States: the Tsarnaev brothers, Dzokhar and Tamerlan, who planted bombs at the finish line of the Boston Marathon in April 2013. They killed three spectators and wounded 260. The Tsarnaevs were young immigrants from the for-mer Soviet republic of Kyrgyzstan. The elder brother, Tamerlan, was poorly assimilated, with no American friends, parents on the verge of divorce, no job, depending on his wife for money, and in a constant feud with his more successful uncles who branded the brothers as "losers." What he certainly lost was Significance. He tried to become a good boxer, but those dreams of glory led nowhere. He chose a more attainable path by trying to be a hero or a martyr, guided by the extremist Muslim and anti-American ideology that he adopted, and he dragged his little brother into the plot.[15]

In a survey we conducted among members of a terrorist organiza-tion who had been arrested in Sri Lanka, we found three measurable factors that had led them to violence: the frequency of their feeling insignificant, as members of the Tamil minority that felt oppressed by the Sinhalese majority; the degree to which they felt anger in the few weeks before they attempted an attack; and the degree to which they felt shame in that period.[16] In other words, a loss of Significance, as reflected in feelings of shame and anger, may provide a big push toward bloodshed for a valued cause that would redeem their social worth and remove the shame.

One circumstance in which strong Significance loss may occur, particu-larly pertinent to young unmarried men in a traditional culture, is when they entertain (what to them are) "sinful" thoughts on forbidden matters. In one study that tested this idea experimentally,[17] religious participants were exposed to sexual stimuli (scantily dressed women in a Victoria's Secret ad) assumed to arouse forbidden thoughts and hence sexual guilt, or neutral stimuli (pictures of toasters). The researchers then assessed the participants' attitudes toward martyrdom for an (undefined) social cause. This was measured by reacting to statements such as, "I would be willing to renounce all my personal wealth for a highly important cause," and, "Under the right circumstances, I would sacrifice my life for an important cause."

Participants who were devoutly religious, who were exposed to sexual stimuli, reported much stronger sexual guilt than other sub-groups. More relevant to a Quest for Significance, they also affirmed a greater openness to self-sacrifice for a cause. That is how guilty (hence bereft of Significance) they felt.

Significance by Dominance

It is striking how often people attempt to restore their lost Significance through aggression against others and occasionally against themselves (in cases of suicide or self-immolation). As we noted earlier, aggression is a primitive, hence highly compelling, way to affirm your Significance. You mattered not only because you took action but you harmed and thus affected the lives and property of others. It was a negative and destructive path, but you left your mark.

Throughout history, leaders have often exploited feelings of humiliation and anger to incite their followers into aggressive actions. According to the *New York Times*, only 268 of the past 3,400 years (8%) have been marked by complete peace, and 108 million people died in wars during the 20th century alone.[18] As we already recounted in Chapter 1, the invasion of Ukraine by Russia in 2022 and the war that ensued were strongly influenced by the outsized Significance quest of one man, Russian President Vladimir Putin.

In 2005, Putin proclaimed that the disintegration of the Soviet Union was "the greatest geopolitical catastrophe of the century." He saw it as a profound loss of national Significance, a precipitous fall from greatness. He often felt that the United States was rubbing it in. While Air Force One was refueling at Moscow's airport in 2006, President George W. Bush refused to visit Putin at the opulent Kremlin, forcing Russia's leader to drive to an airport terminal for a meeting. In 2014, President Barack Obama also seemed to belittle Russia by calling it a mere "regional power." These affronts to Putin's social identity fanned the flame of his yearning for Significance and defined his mission to restore Russia's greatness. He proceeded then to do so in the primitive and direct way of using aggression and brute force.[19] Even while sustaining huge losses of troops in Ukraine, Putin seemed resolved not to let his opportunity to build Significance slip away.

Putin's 2014 annexation of Crimea, ignoring Ukraine's territorial claim, was met with massive support among the Russian public, with polls indicating a huge boost in his popularity. There was no reason to suspect that invading the heart of Ukraine in 2022 would be different. The war became very difficult for Russia, and Western sanctions attempted to cripple the country's economy. But Putin found support in China, North Korea, India, and Iran. To admit defeat or seek compromise would mean a tremendous loss of Significance, and that would be contrary to Putin's essence.

Make Love Not War

As noted, aggression is primordial and primitive, besides being devastating and destructive. So we are happy to note that it is hardly the only way to restore or gain Significance. In Chapter 6, we show other paths based on narratives that help people feel their lives matter. And here, we would like to propose that love, the very opposite of aggression, is a powerful way to feel significant.

From infancy onward, love bestowed on an individual communicates that they matter. Receiving loving attention from their parents in the earliest months of the child's life makes the little human feel secure and safe,[20,21] infusing them with the sense that they are a "big deal," the "center of the universe." In short, the message to the child is that their life truly matters. They are significant.

Romantic love is also greatly fortified by granting, sharing, or creating Significance: the feeling − or truly the certainty − that you are limitlessly important to each other.

Whether conscious or not, we often fall in love to boost our sense of Significance and mattering. There are two intertwined ways in which a partner's love can make us feel significant: the "merit" effect and the "appreciation" effect.

The merit effect is about the partner's perceived social worth, which reflects on us. This worth can come from their good looks, social status, popularity, accomplishments, or anything else that society values. As philosopher Harry G. Frankfurt put it:

> Love is often understood as being, most basically, a response to the perceived worth of the beloved. We are moved to love something, on this account, by an appreciation of what we take to be its exceptional inherent value. The appeal of that value is what captivates us and turns us into lovers.[22]

In other words, having a partner who is powerful, rich, or beautiful can make us feel significant by association.

The appreciation effect, on the other hand, comes from the direct Significance-boosting positivity that a warm, loving partner provides. This represents Significance through admiration. The ideal love partner is someone who excels in both areas: someone you admire and who admires you in return; someone worthy to whom you are special and highly significant. Conversely, if a partner falls short in either the "cheerleading" or the "trophy" dimensions, the chances of falling in love with them are slim.

You will not fall in love with someone you see as lacking minimal acceptable social value, nor with someone who obviously does not and will not ever love you back.[23,24] Similarly, your love will decline and "wither on the vine" if, during the relationship, you conclude that your partner is largely devoid of value or has no love to offer.

But if there is even a slight chance that a person is going to reciprocate your love, and if in addition they are of great merit, you might fall in love with them anyway – despite the lack of certainty that they will be firmly committed to you. The same holds true if they are offering a great deal of love but score only so-so when it comes to merit value.

These calculations are rarely made consciously and intentionally. Yet, what we are seeing is a form of mathematics that usually adds up in predictable ways. The "merit" and "appreciation" characteristics of a love partner compensate for each other. A lower level of expected love is compensated for by a high merit value; and a lower degree of merit value in your would-be partner is compensated for by the level of expected love and adoration from that person.

When Love Ends

When love ends, the person's most intimate Significance-acquiring mini-network is dissolved. Being widowed puts a person in that situation, usually without either partner desiring to break up. Much research has looked into people's reactions to the death of a spouse, especially after many decades of marriage. These events almost always induce a sharp loss of Significance, and men are more vulnerable to that than women.

A study conducted in 1992 looked at the dates of husbands' and wives' deaths relative to each other.[25] The researchers harvested the data from cemeteries, engraved on tombstones. They found that men were likely to die much sooner after their wives' passing, compared with women dying after their husbands' deaths. The explanation given by the authors was that, throughout their lives, women – but less often men – typically cultivate a support network of other women. Those networks provide social sustenance and make the widow feel that she matters, thus protecting her sense of Significance at a time of bereavement.

Loving the Leader

The "merit" and "appreciation" factors apply not only to romantic love but also to loving your nation's or group's leader. In Chapter 4, we described how the Roman people in 44 BCE adored Julius Caesar and wanted him to be a loving and beneficent king because being loved by a person of such supreme merit would bestow palpable Significance on the populace he professed to care about.

Support for monarchy or dictatorships is typically motivated by an adoration of a loving despot, a person of supreme power whose merit (whether authentic or not) rubs off on those whom the leader purports to respect and love. The public derives Significance from that relationship.

A similar psychological process accounts for religious fervor, the adoration of a God believed to care about the flock of the faithful. The common religious slogan, "Jesus loves you," is meant to build up believers' sense of worth and invite their affection and devotion to Jesus. It feels so good – meaning that our lives matter – to have faith that a holy one is looking down on us with adoration.

Hate and Love as Paths to Significance

The renowned psychiatrist and father of psychoanalysis, Sigmund Freud, famously discussed the instincts of death (Thanatos) and love (Eros) as two opposing forces that shape human behavior. The love instinct builds families, tribes, and societies, while the death instinct seeks to destroy. Interestingly, both the potential for destruction, akin to Freud's Thanatos, and the potential for love, akin to Eros, serve to gratify our sense of social worth or mattering. They are, in essence, two servants of the same master, fulfilling the same function of delivering Significance.

This is why unrequited love can turn into hate, as the desire to destroy the other takes over. As the 17th-century English playwright William Congreve famously said, "Hell hath no fury like a woman scorned" – and the same applies to a scorned man, as research on "incels" demonstrates.

In addition, the psychological concept of "identification with the aggressor" (and the related notion of Stockholm Syndrome) suggests that when one cannot overcome an aggressor by violent means, one may instead identify with and develop affection toward them. This is an example of "joining them if you can't beat them."

These psychological phenomena support the seemingly counterintuitive idea that aggression and love are two interchangeable ways of feeling worthy and significant.

Summary

The Quest for Significance and mattering is a constant in people's lives from early childhood, the time when they desperately crave attention from their parents (or other adult caretakers), all the way to their last moments on Earth, where dying with dignity becomes their major concern. In between these endpoints, our days are replete with small joys and moments of sadness – all determined by outcomes and events that make us feel significant and cared for, or those that make us feel excluded, ostracized, ignored, hence neglected, and insignificant.

The quest that drives the world is sparked either by losses of Significance or by opportunities to gain it. Often, the pursuit of Significance is achieved through aggressive means, based on the belief that human relations are competitive and the world is divided into "winners" (those who attain Significance) and "losers" (those who have lost it or never had much).

However, love – the force that unites people, builds societies, and promotes contentment – offers a genuine, alternative path to Significance where everyone can be a "winner." Loving and hating – or just putting people down – are diametrically opposed emotions; yet they are two means to the same end, two servants of the same master: the universal human Quest for Significance.

Notes

1 In William Shakespeare's *As You Like It*, the famous Seven Ages of Man soliloquy begins, "All the world's a stage."

2 Wellman, Henry M., "Developing a Theory of Mind," in Goswami, Usha (ed.), *The Wiley-Blackwell Handbook of Childhood Cognitive Development*, 2nd ed., (Malden, MA: Wiley-Blackwell, 2011), pp. 258–284.

3 Moskalenko, Sophia, "Down the Yellow Brick Road: How Socialization Through Early Narratives Shapes the Quest for Significance," in Kruglanski, Arie W.; Prilleltensky, Isaac; Raviv, Alon (eds.), *Quest for Significance and Mattering, Frontiers in Social Psychology* (Abingdon, Oxfordshire: Routledge, 2024).

4 Williams, Kipling D., "The Pain of Exclusion," *Scientific American Mind*, Vol. 21, No. 6 (2011), pp. 30–37.

5 Moskalenko, Sophia; Fernández-Garayzábal González, Juncal; Kates, Naama; Morton, Jesse, "Incel Ideology, Radicalization and Mental Health: A Survey Study," *The Journal of Intelligence, Conflict, and Warfare*, Vol. 4, No. 3 (2022), pp. 1–29.

6 "Man in Santa Barbara Rampage Sought Ways to Silently Kill," *Associated Press* (February 19, 2015); Manavis, Sarah, "Incel Ideology Has Entered the Mainstream," *New Statesman* (October 6, 2023); Fugardi, Rachael, "Nine Years after Deadly 'Incel' Attack, Threat of Male Supremacism Is Growing," *Southern Poverty Law Center* (May 23, 2023).

7 Cialdini, Robert Beno; Borden, Richard J.; Thorne, Alan; Walker, Marcus R.; Freeman, Stephen; Sloan, Linda R., "Basking in Reflected Glory: Three (Football) Field Studies," *Journal of Personality and Social Psychology*, Vol. 34, No. 3 (1976), pp. 366–375.

8 Kruglanski, Arie W.; Orehek, Edward, "The Role of the Quest for Personal Significance in Motivating Terrorism," in Forgas, Joseph Paul; Kruglanski, Arie W.; Williams, Kipling D. (eds.), *The Psychology of Social Conflict and Aggression* (New York: Psychology Press, 2011), pp. 153–164.

9 Her real name was Amantine Lucile Aurore Dupin, and she wrote notable books in French in the 1830s and 1840s.

10 Williams, Kipling D., "The Pain of Exclusion," *Scientific American Mind*, Vol. 21, No. 6 (2011), pp. 30–37.

11 Eisenberger, Naomi I., "The Pain of Social Disconnection: Examining the Shared Neural Underpinnings of Physical and Social Pain," *Nature Reviews Neuroscience*, Vol. 13, No. 6 (2012), pp. 421–434.

12 "'It's Life or Death': U.S. Teenagers Face a Mental Health Crisis," *New York Times* (April 24, 2022). The reporter, Matt Richtel, commented on CNN: "There's been a change in the adolescent brain and a change in the environment, so what we used to call teen angst has turned into dangerous pathology." The online invitation to 13-year-olds to be interviewed is at https://www.nytimes.com/2022/04/25/well/family/call-for-13-year-olds.html

13 Case, Ann; Deaton, Angus, *Deaths of Despair and the Future of Capitalism* (Princeton, NJ: Princeton University Press, 2020).

14 Pedahzur, Ami, *Suicide Terrorism* (Cambridge: Polity, 2005).

15 A note captured at the location where Dzokhar was finally apprehended indicates that he perceived his brother as a martyr and a hero and that he too craved similar recognition; see Speckhard, Anne, "The Boston Marathon Bombers: The Lethal Cocktail That Turned Troubled Youth to Terrorism," *Perspectives on Terrorism*, Vol. 7, No. 3 (2013), pp. 64–78.

16 The prisoners had been guerrilla fighters or merely recruited would-be suicide bombers for the Liberation Tigers of Tamil Eelam (LTTE), interviewed by author Kruglanski and others. See: Webber, David; Chernikova, Marina; Kruglanski, Arie W.; Gelfand, Michele J.; Hettiarachchi, Malkanthi; Gunaratna, Rohan; Lafreniere, Marc Andre; Belanger, Jocelyn J., "Deradicalizing Detained Terrorists," *Political Psychology*, Vol. 39, No. 3 (2018), pp. 539–556.

17 Bélanger, Jocelyn J.; Kruglanski, Arie W.; Kessels, Ursula, "On Sin and Sacrifice: How Intrinsic Religiosity and Sexual-Guilt Create Support for Martyrdom," *Psychological Research on Urban Society*, Vol. 2, No. 2 (2019), pp. 65–75.

18 Hedges, Chris, "What Every Person Should Know About War," *The New York Times* (July 6, 2003).

19 Sonne, Paul; Dixon, Robyn, "Wielding the Threat of War, a New, More Aggressive Putin Steps Forward," *The Washington Post* (February 20, 2022).

20 Bowlby, John, *Attachment and Loss: Volume 1. Attachment* (New York: Random House, 1969).

21 Ainsworth, Mary D.S.; Bell, Sylvia M., "Attachment, Exploration, and Separation: Illustrated by the Behavior of One-Year-Olds in a Strange Situation," *Child Development*, Vol. 41 (1970), pp. 49–67.

22 Frankfurt, Harry G., *The Reasons of Love* (Princeton, NJ: Princeton University Press, 2006).

23 Baumeister, Roy F.; Wotman, Sara R., *Breaking Hearts: The Two Sides of Unrequited Love* (New York: Guilford Press, 1994).

24 Baumeister, Roy F.; Wotman, Sara R.; Stillwell, Arlene M., "Unrequited Love: On Heartbreak, Anger, Guilt, Scriptlessness, and Humiliation," *Journal of Personality and Social Psychology*, Vol. 64, No. 3 (1993), pp. 377–394.

25 Stroebe, Margaret; Gergen, Mary M.; Gergen, Kenneth J.; Stroebe, Wolfgang, "Broken Hearts or Broken Bonds?" in Klass, Dennis; Silverman, Phyllis R.; Nickman, Steven L. (eds.), *Continuing Bonds: New Understandings of Grief*, (Washington, DC: Taylor & Francis, 1996), pp. 31–44; also Stroebe, Margaret; Stroebe, Wolfgang; Schut, Henk, "Gender Differences in Adjustment to Bereavement: An Empirical and Theoretical Review," *Review of General Psychology*, Vol. 5, No. 1 (2001), pp. 62–83.

6

NARRATIVES OF SIGNIFICANCE

The United States had its first massacre of the year 2023 on January 4. A man in Enoch, Utah, murdered seven members of his family and then took his own life. On that day and the next, there were mass shootings – meaning at least four victims dead or wounded – in Maryland, Virginia, Louisiana, and Florida. Sadly, that was just a normal Wednesday and Thursday in the United States. The nation went on to report more than 600 mass shootings that year.[1]

By the end of January 2023, California alone had experienced three such tragedies. In Goshen, a gunman killed six people, including a baby, in what police described as gang violence. Days later, 11 people were shot dead at a dance studio in the town of Monterey Park. Just two days after that, seven people were murdered at farms near Half Moon Bay.

As police, hospitals, and coroners dealt with the aftermath, Americans expressed their shock. Some offered "thoughts and prayers," while others called for gun-control legislation. But everyone wondered what drives these violent outbursts. What were the shooters' motives?

DOI: 10.4324/9781003410706-6

The Motive Question

Understanding motives is crucial to comprehending human behavior. People do not act randomly; they do things to gain something or to avoid losing something. But is the "thing" they want or want to keep what *really* drives them to take another person's life? Maybe not.

Take, for example, a shooter who kills innocent victims after losing his job. Is frustration over his setback enough to explain his actions? After all, not everyone who gets frustrated goes on a shooting spree. So, why did this individual do it?

Suppose it turns out that the shooter had marital problems or faced romantic rejection. Again, it is unclear how this explains his actions, given that most people with such issues do not resort to violence.

Moreover, we could ask why people care so much about keeping their job and about romantic rejection that they would kill someone – often a stranger. These questions invite an even more general question: What is the core reason to strongly hate being fired or being turned away while wooing?

Experts on human motivation contend that all people share the same set of basic needs, and everything people do, try to attain, or avoid is in the service of satisfying one or more of those basic needs.

The need for Significance and mattering is one such pre-eminent basic need that all people have.

Now, here is the interesting part: Whereas the set of basic needs is common to all humans, the means of satisfying them differ greatly among people depending on their culture, its worldview, and its norms. Being "fired from a job" may undermine the sense of Significance of an employee in contemporary society, but the concept may mean little to a high school student, a member of an aboriginal tribe in the South Pacific, or a monk in a Buddhist monastery. That does not mean that a pupil, a tribe member, and a Buddhist monk do not have a need to feel significant. They most certainly do; but they do not satisfy it by guarding their place on an employer's payroll.

Here is another noteworthy point: People can be exposed to different cultures or subcultures, and therefore learn various ways to satisfy the same basic needs. Take, for example, the universal need for Significance.

This need can be met not only by holding a respectable job and supporting one's family, but also by creating something beautiful and artistic.

Consider J.K. Rowling at the start of her writing career. She was a divorced, unemployed single mom without much public recognition. Yet, she invented an entire fantasy world for a book she was writing, which must have given her a great deal of satisfaction and feelings of Significance. The book's subsequent success – and the phenomenal popularity of the Harry Potter series – allowed her to feel even more significant through its immense popularity, making her the second richest woman in Britain, after Queen Elizabeth II.

To satisfy the question of "what was the motive?" we should identify the underlying basic need served by the action and explain what led the person to choose this way of fulfilling that need.

Simply awakening a basic need is not enough for behavior to happen. You must also know how to satisfy that need. This knowledge is contained within cultural narratives shared within the individual's community. For instance, feeling hungry isn't enough to make you eat. You must know how to go about satisfying that hunger. If you are a city dweller in the 21st century, this narrative might include "eating out" or "ordering in," whereas if you were a member of a hunter-gatherer tribe, the narrative might include "going on a hunt," and so on.

Narratives of Significance

A Significance-promising narrative identifies social values such as courage, beauty, wisdom, creativity, moral purity, wealth, or superior performance in a particular domain. These attributes can enhance an individual's social worth, as recognized by a community that upholds these values. By embodying or representing these values – whether through beauty, courage, wisdom, accomplishment, or wealth – an individual gains Significance in the eyes of their community.

In essence, personal Significance and social worth "trickle down" from the values cherished by one's group (society, community, culture) to the individual who demonstrates commitment to or personifies those values. These values and the ways of embodying them are communicated through narratives that are embraced by both the individual and their community.

But where do these narratives originate? In a 2018 book, social psychologists Sophia Moskalenko and Clark McCauley explained that children's fairy tales often highlight the values that confer Significance within a culture.[2] Cinderella, the heroine of an iconic fairy tale, is cheerful, friendly, and hard-working. Snow White is affectionate and loving. Both are presented as positive ideals for little girls to identify with. The implication of these stories is that modeling oneself to resemble those positive protagonists is valued and appreciated, and that helps make the child a good person with plenty of social worth.

On the other side of the coin, the wicked stepmothers who torture these beloved characters are portrayed as selfish and cruel. They serve as negative models, representing behaviors that detract from a person's societal worth.[3]

Some fairy tales, particularly German ones like "Rumpelstiltskin" and "Hansel and Gretel," emphasize the societal worth gained from being smart and conscientious, while also highlighting the loss of worth from being lazy and dense. In contrast, French fairy tales such as "Bluebeard," "Beauty and the Beast," and "Cinderella" underscore the courage to stand up against oppression and the aesthetic value of beauty. "Peter Pan," with its thrilling adventurousness and irreverent rule-breaking, carries the values of courage and non-conformism.

Through these tales, cultural worldviews and values are imprinted on people from childhood. They portray both behavioral models that represent social worth and Significance, as well as those that detract from Significance, which people would do well to avoid.

Some fairy tales focus on self-sacrifice for a cause. Moskalenko and McCauley recounted the Grimm brothers' story, "Six Swans," which tells of a sister's suffering on behalf of her brothers who had been turned into swans by an evil witch. To remove the curse, the sister must weave each brother a shirt from stinging nettles, without uttering a word for six years. Accused of witchcraft, she is nearly burned at the stake but is saved when she (almost) completes the shirts in time. This tale, along with Oscar Wilde's "The Happy Prince," where both the prince and a little bird sacrifice their lives to help the poor, introduces the idea of martyrdom for a moral cause as something of supreme social value, bestowing great Significance on those who are prepared to take that action.

Hark back to the psychological project examining "the achieving society" by David McClelland and his colleagues, which we discussed in

Chapter 5. They collected and analyzed children's stories from 23 countries between 1920 and 1929. They found that the economic growth of a nation decades later (in 1950) was predicted by the number of achievement themes in children's stories earlier on (in 1929). That supports the idea that fairy tales are narratives that shape children's character and instill in them the values they later try to affirm in their behavior. While McClelland's team studied a particular set of values related to achievement, other values such as morality, courage, power, and generosity are similarly conveyed to children through fairy tales. These values strongly influence their behavior as adults, including notions of what traits and actions merit the bestowal of Significance.

Two Kinds of Significance-Lending Narratives

A person can acquire social worth by embracing one or both of two types of values: individualistic values, such as great personal attainments in business, science, the arts, athletics, great looks, or wealth; and collectivistic values, such as patriotism, generosity, honesty, and cooperativeness. Different cultures emphasize these values differently. Western cultures, represented by European nations, North America, and Australia, tend to be more individualistic. In contrast, Eastern cultures, such as China, Japan, and India, tend to be more collectivistic.

These cultural differences are not absolute. Individualistic and collectivistic values coexist within each culture, albeit in different proportions. They offer members of those cultures alternative ways to pursue Significance. Sometimes, when one of those ways fails or is impossible to attain, individuals pursue Significance via a different route.

Collectivistic shift. There is evidence that if someone suffers personal failure, they will move toward collectivistic attitudes, meaning a stronger orientation toward their group and its values. In an internet survey of 12 Arab countries, Pakistan, and Indonesia, carried out by the University of Maryland's START Center,[4] participants who reported a lower level of success in life – presumably suffering Significance loss – tended to self-identify more strongly as members of collectives (their nation or religion) rather than as individuals.

This does not mean that being religious or nationalistic is generally correlated with being a failure. What it does suggest is that people who feel their lives are not going well, and who therefore experience insignificance, are more disposed to embrace a collectivistic ideology (whether nationalistic, social, or religious) that promises Significance to anyone who faithfully follows its dictates.

In Chapter 5, we reported on the study that found people who wrote an essay describing their personal failures (which would lower their sense of Significance) showed later that they identified strongly as Americans, compared with participants who had written about their own successes. That is further support for the notion that lowered personal Significance results in a collectivistic shift.[5]

When people become accustomed to gaining Significance through collectivistic means, their ability to achieve it individually may weaken or atrophy. As an example, the collapse of Communist regimes in the late 20th century led to a loss of personal coping skills among citizens who had relied on the state for life's necessities. When countries such as Poland, East Germany, and Romania transitioned from Communism to individualistic, market-oriented economies, many people found themselves struggling. One study found that Bulgarian students experienced higher levels of personal helplessness after the transition to capitalism, compared to Swedish students who did not go through such a change.[6] Another study found that older adolescents – compared with younger children – in post-Communist countries were less likely to believe that anyone who worked hard could make a good living, presumably because the older youth had spent more time under the Communist regime.[7]

Narrative Shortcuts to Significance

Get-rich-quick schemes. People's behaviors often reveal a strong desire to achieve Significance quickly and with minimal effort. In money-driven capitalist societies, "get-rich-quick" schemes have always been enticing. On December 11, 2008, federal agents arrested Bernie Madoff for orchestrating the largest Ponzi scheme in history, defrauding thousands of investors of nearly $65 billion. The following year, Madoff was sentenced to 150 years in prison. How did he justify moving money from account to account to make it look like investments were growing? Madoff blamed the greed of his customers.[8] He died in custody in 2021 at the age of 83.

Our focus here is not on Madoff, but rather on his investors. How could so many sophisticated people fall prey to such a massive scheme that went on for decades? Two aspects of Madoff's scheme provide the answer, both related to people's need for Significance. First, Madoff promised extraordinarily high returns on investments. In our materialistic society, wealth is one of the surest ways to achieve social worth and Significance. Getting rich (or richer) quickly makes you "worth" much more, both economically and socially. This is capitalism. Money matters.

The second aspect is the image of exclusivity that investing with Madoff entailed. To cultivate that appearance, Madoff initially turned clients away, and in the early days of his fund's operation, the minimum acceptable investment was in the tens or hundreds of millions of dollars. That exclusivity, signifying great Significance, attracted A-list actors like John Malkovich and Kevin Bacon, among others. Madoff's fraud went undetected for decades because his clients wanted to believe in the Significance-enhancing narrative he was offering.

Madoff's fraud was the largest Ponzi scheme in modern history, but it was hardly the first. In the 19th century, Scottish adventurer Gregor MacGregor claimed he had discovered a new, wonderfully fertile land called Poyais, where rivers contained chunks of pure gold and the water was of the purest quality. From his London office, MacGregor convinced investors and would-be settlers to give him their money. He even wrote a book under the pseudonym Thomas Strangways to convince potential investors of his claims. In this way, MacGregor raised nearly £200,000, or £3.6 billion in today's money, for land that was purely a figment of his imagination.[9]

Phony investment schemes, like those orchestrated by Madoff and MacGregor, are just one type of get-rich-quick narrative. Another common scheme is the "advance fee" scam, where individuals are enticed to pay a small amount of money (often labeled as a "handling and shipping fee") for a much larger promised sum that never materializes. The "rug pull" scheme involves getting investors excited about something worthless, prompting them to invest. As the stock price rises, the scheme's originator sells off their stock at its peak, leaving others' investments in ruins. These and other get-rich-quick schemes offer a tempting shortcut to Significance through promised wealth.

Luxury goods. Whether you amassed wealth quickly or at a more leisurely pace, luxury possessions like top-class automobiles and expensive watches are an obvious way to showcase your accomplishments – projecting your Significance and seeking admiration from others. The global luxury goods market continues to grow, from $284 billion in 2023 to a projected $392 billion by 2030, outpacing the growth rate of America's overall economy.[10]

Somewhat similar to the fake shortcuts to wealth promised by various Ponzi schemes, the streets of major cities are filled with stands offering cheap knock-offs of luxury brands: fake Louis Vuitton bags, Rolex watches, and Gucci eyeglasses that, in many cases, are nearly indistinguishable from the originals. These items offer affordable, albeit inauthentic, prestige.

Simple Significance-enhancing narratives exist in other domains, too. Why spend years sweating in a gym when you can expedite your muscular development and sculpt a great physique with steroids or through liposuction? Why not boost your athletic performance with various performance-enhancing drugs? Perhaps start taking new medications that reduce your appetite so you can easily shun sweets? Why not overcome the limitations of your physical appearance with plastic surgery that makes you beautiful overnight? Billions of dollars are spent annually by people on these various strategies offered as expressways to Significance.

Significance through violence. Violence-justifying narratives also play a role. Humans are a violent species, and the potential for aggression against others is deeply ingrained in human nature. We are not alone, though. In the animal kingdom, especially among male mammals,[11] aggression is a pre-eminent path to dominance. Among us two-legged creatures, a loss of Significance has the potential to bring out our so-called animal instincts. Our minds can be easily clouded by thoughts of aggression and revenge. Cultural narratives can legitimize or delegitimize our aggressive tendencies.

Because the violent destruction of other people is an especially quick and direct route to dominance and Significance, it is quite tempting for ambitious young men to embark on that malignant path. However, violence is typically prohibited by cultural norms, and the injunction not to kill is a common feature of most religions.

That is why violence, especially if it becomes a societal norm, needs to be culturally sanctioned or justified. This is often accomplished by presenting violence as a last resort in defense of a supreme value (for example, the survival of one's people, freedom, democracy, or the honor of one's religion) whose importance trumps the prohibition of violence. Consider the assassination of a health insurance executive in New York City in 2024, apparently intended as a cry for justice in insurance coverage – wherein again a killer chose the quick, primordial method of murder as a path to Significance, striving to be a hero for the masses who feel cheated.

The tactic of suicide bombing – employed for decades by terrorist organizations such as Al Qaeda, ISIS, Hamas, and Sri Lanka's Liberation Tigers of Tamil Eelam – relies on the idea that for the suicide bomber, this act is a gateway to unparalleled Significance as a martyr for a cause.

We think of Marwan Abu Abeida, who was interviewed in 2005 as a suicide-bomber-in-training by Bobby Ghosh, a TIME magazine reporter. Abu Abeida joined Abu Musab al Zarqawi's insurgent group, Tawhid, which later became ISIS. After months of distinguishing himself as a foot soldier in Al Zarqawi's outfit, he volunteered to become a suicide bomber. Following a long wait, he was selected and allowed to train for this mission. By his account, this was the happiest day of his life. From that point onward, he lived and breathed for the task he had chosen. Abu Abeida believed he was preparing to meet and be blessed by Allah, and his accomplishment would be measured by the number of infidels he would kill.[12]

A 2023 report by the United States Secret Service, examining a wave of mass shootings in America from 2016 to 2020, found that in most cases, attackers had a personal grievance of some kind, often targeting their workplace and coworkers. In a quarter of the shootings, the perpetrators tried to justify their attacks by citing conspiracy theories or expressing hatred toward women, Jews, or government authorities. The vast majority of shooters were men, many of whom exhibited incel-like misogyny. These individuals resorted to violence, targeting those they blamed for their loss of Significance. They sought to overcome their humiliation, embracing narratives whereby violence was a legitimate – perhaps the only – way to reassert their power and restore their sense of social worth.[13]

Attaining Significance and Dignity

Do people who follow a Significance-promising narrative actually feel significant? While suicide bombers who have completed their missions are not around to share their feelings, others can. Research shows that if you embrace a narrative (which could be a terrorist or extremist ideology) in a personal way – believing that the values you are fighting for are important to you – you will be willing to sacrifice a lot for the cause. You might even give your life, and just knowing that gives you a sense of Significance.

Among various groups of social activists interviewed for a study – members of a radical left-wing political party, democracy advocates, feminists, environmental activists, and supporters of some hero's hunger strike – those who saw the cause as personally important were more motivated to devote time and resources to activism. They felt proud to do so, reflecting their sense of personal Significance.[14]

A study in Poland compared the determination of protesters who engaged in radical actions versus those who took more moderate approaches, such as marching with signs. In May 2017, the government began logging the forest, allegedly to prevent damage caused by the spruce bark beetle. In response, environmental activists set up a protest camp and pursued radical actions aimed at blocking the logging, such as chaining themselves to the tree-cutting machinery.

The protest garnered support from environmental activists across Poland, who organized demonstrations, donated money, and advocated for the cause in front of European Union authorities. The study found that those who engaged in more radical actions were more committed to the cause and experienced a greater sense of Significance from their actions, compared with those who participated in more moderate protests.[15] In other words, the greater the commitment to a worthy cause, the stronger the feelings of Significance you gain from your actions on behalf of the cause.

Self-Affirmation

A sense of Significance comes from believing that you have served or represented an important societal value. This value radiates to those who show commitment to it. In other words, you feel good, worthy, and significant if you do something good, worthy, or significant. So, if you want to feel good about yourself, try to identify a value that you cherish and carry out actions that demonstrate your commitment to it. Alternatively, you might recall instances in which you showed commitment to this value in the past. This idea is at the core of the "self-affirmation" theory in social psychology.[16]

Originally developed by Professor Claude Steele of Stanford University, this theory assumes that "people are motivated to maintain the integrity of the self …defined as the sense that, on the whole, one is a good and appropriate person… given the cultural norms and demands within that culture."[17]

In many studies based on observations and data, participants' self-concept is typically challenged in some way. This is done by having a participant encounter someone who either strongly disagrees with them or holds a negative stereotype about their gender, religion, or ethnicity. Either before or after such a confrontation, the participant is given an opportunity to affirm an important value by declaring a strong belief in something. The typical finding is that, following self-affirmation, individuals become less defensive and more open-minded when faced with challenging or offensive information.

Imagine a woman overhearing someone making a snide remark about women's inability to drive, their lack of commitment to work, or their supposed weakness. Or picture a Jew hearing a comment about Jewish greed or a Jewish plot to dominate the world. Think of an American hearing about alleged American arrogance, brashness, and materialism. Even if these allegations are untrue, they can be deeply offensive and hurtful. The idea that someone, even a stranger, holds such a negative view of the social category you belong to can sting and diminish your sense of social worth.

However, if you are given a chance to remind yourself of the values you are committed to – an opportunity to "self-affirm" – this can remove the sense of insignificance evoked by the insulting remark and restore your stable sense of self. Interestingly, regaining your balance in this way also makes you less defensive and more open to considering views and opinions that may differ from your own.

In one study, the goal was to have pro-choice participants calmly discuss abortion policies with a pro-life advocate.[18] First, they were tasked with writing an essay about a personal value that was important to them (such as having a sense of humor or improving relationships with their friends). Then, a self-affirming group was created in which half the participants were told to describe three or four personal experiences where they embraced that value and how it made them feel good about themselves. As for the other half of the participants, in the so-called "threat condition," they were asked to write about an instance when they failed to live up to their cherished value or it had somehow failed them.

The results showed that those who had the self-affirmation opportunity were less defensive and less closed-minded. They made more concessions when debating the abortion issue, compared with those in the threat condition. The self-affirmed later evaluated their adversary more positively, as more objective and trustworthy. By comparison, those whose favorite value had not been self-affirmed were critical and skeptical.

Notice the implication of these findings for the Dale Carnegie ideal of "winning friends and influencing people." They suggest that if you want someone to be open to your views and to appreciate your perspective on things, even if different from their own, it may help to affirm that the other person has worth in your eyes. To be effective, this affirmation should, of course, be genuine rather than fake.

Surely this is a useful strategy for getting along better and getting what you want from someone. Develop a sense of respect and appreciation for others that invites reciprocal respect, and you will breed openness to your opinions and arguments.

It turns out that such openness to persuasion is not merely limited to respecting or tolerating the views of others. It can actually change people's subsequent decisions and behavior! In a study conducted with sexually active undergraduates,[19] participants were shown an AIDS educational video that warned of the virus dangers from unprotected sex. Half received a self-affirmation, focused on some values that were important to them, prior to watching the video; the other half did not. The latter participants were defensive and resisted the information in the video. In other words, their perception that there was only a tiny risk of AIDS did not change.

Participants in the self-affirmation condition reacted very differently. Of the non-affirmed participants, only 25 percent purchased condoms after viewing the video, whereas in the self-affirmed group, 50 percent did. Moreover, the affirmed participants were more likely (at 78%) to take an AIDS educational brochure, whereas the non-affirmed ones did so to an appreciably lesser extent (at 54%).

Ideals for Significance

Politics is a great example of how narratives can energize Significance in surprising ways. For instance, everyone knows that politicians crave power, influence, and importance, while the idealistic youths who follow them act out of selfless concern for the good of others. However, what most people fail to realize is that ideals like freedom, democracy, human rights, or equity are not the ultimate goals for idealists. Instead, they are a means to an underlying desire: to feel worthy and significant among like-minded others.

Ideals represent values, and for those seeking a way to matter, attachment to ideals, activism, and even idealistic self-denial are paths to Significance. Social scientists have conducted studies of political activists to understand what makes them tick. Young politicians often have no Significance to lose but much to gain from their idealism. However, as these idealists grow into seasoned politicians – members of Congress, mayors, governors, senior judges – their Significance becomes tied to their social status and position in society.

This often clashes with their ideals. Doing "the right thing" might mean losing votes or campaign donations and jeopardizing a prestigious position, leading to a major loss of Significance. As the saying goes, "If you aren't an idealist in your twenties, you haven't got a heart; and if you are an idealist in your forties, you haven't got a brain." Pragmatism often starts to outweigh idealism in midlife because a person has Significance to lose by following idealism with abandon and ignoring the possible consequences.

So, people are idealists because it makes them feel good about themselves; and seasoned politicians probably are not, because it might threaten their sense of Significance. Does this mean that fiery idealism and deal-making pragmatism are equivalent, just because both are ways of feeling that you matter? You can push the question further and ask whether a person ready to sacrifice their life for their humanitarian cause is equivalent to someone who derives Significance through greed and exploitation. They are not, morally speaking. Most people would prefer an altruistic hero over an exploitative tycoon.

The end does not always justify the means, and we are free to judge the different means to the same end differently and assign them different moral values.

Moreover, while a person can be respected both for having power and for doing good deeds, the way people feel toward the powerful and the altruistic can vastly differ. People may fear the powerful and have no qualms about turning on them when an opportunity arises. However, those who gain respect through good deeds evoke feelings of affection and are more likely to inspire loyalty and authentic commitment from others.

The politics of power are fraught with intrigue, backstabbing, and plots against rulers. No one understood this better than the Florentine philosopher and diplomat Niccolo Machiavelli, who lived in the 15th and 16th centuries and witnessed the violent struggle for power and dominance among Italian families such as the Medicis and the Borgias. Machiavelli believed that it was better for a ruler to be widely feared than loved, and he declared that exercising brute force or deceit is a legitimate tool in a ruler's toolkit. He portrayed violence as useful for eliminating political rivals, whipping resistant populations into obedience, and purging the community of other would-be usurpers who might plot to wrest the reins of power from the ruler.

Yet, there is a psychological price to be paid for the unmitigated reliance on violence as a source of power and Significance. Modern-day dictators – Adolf Hitler, Mao Zedong, Josef Stalin, and Pol Pot – who sought to maintain complete control through the imprisonment and murder of all who seemed to resist them, suffered perennial anxiety and dread of being violently overthrown. Saddam Hussein displayed a level of paranoia so great that he had multiple meals prepared for him across Iraq each day to ensure that no one knew where he was eating. He even went as far as to employ surgically altered body doubles. The North Korean dictators, Kim Jong-il and his son Kim Jong-un, exhibited such an excessive fear of assassination that they traveled on an armor-plated train.

Stalin, the Soviet dictator, was known for authorizing great purges against people suspected of opposing his rule. In the purge of 1936, on Stalin's orders, the NKVD (People's Commissariat for Internal Affairs), the Soviet secret police, removed the entire central party leadership, government officials, and regional party bosses. The purges spread to the Red Army and the military high command. But that was not the end. Stalin's paranoia led him to suspect threats everywhere, including certain ethnic minorities, such as the Volga Germans, who were forcibly deported and subjected to repression. At Stalin's behest, the NKVD used imprisonment, torture, violent interrogation, and arbitrary executions on a massive scale to enhance his control over people through fear.

Stalin's paranoia, though perhaps exaggerated, was not totally baseless, as there were at least four verified plots on his life. This number pales in comparison to plots against Hitler, which numbered 42, according to historians.[20] Benito Mussolini also faced several assassination attempts.[21] Other dictators had good reasons to look over their shoulder and to suspect that plots were continuously being spun against them.

In short, the Machiavellian recipe for power and Significance attained through the spreading of fear has a serious downside: the constant worry about the possibility of betrayal and of a violent coup aimed at toppling the leader.

Violent Narratives in the Here and Now

The times we live in are fraught with uncertainty.[22] Globalization has left masses of people feeling bewildered and left behind. The financial crisis of 2008 and the slow and sluggish recovery compounded the confusion. Massive migration was spotlighted in 2015 as a "refugee crisis" in Europe, contributing further to people's sense of instability and danger. That catapulted to power conservative political parties whose main attraction was their anti-immigrant attitudes. Finally, the unsettling Covid-19 pandemic and the surreal period of sheltering, masking, and restrictions elevated the sense of uncertainty and perplexity to a new high.

But it is not the uncertainty alone that has been so troubling to so many. It is a loss of Significance that the uncertainty connotes. For many, not knowing what will happen suggests the worst will likely happen – that multinational corporations will leave you in an economic lurch, that you will not be able to support your family and send your kids to college, and that foreigners will take over your country and make you a stranger in your own land.

The loss of Significance that people around the globe have been experiencing makes them vulnerable to a particular brand of narratives; ones that acknowledge their fears and anxieties and blame some agent or entity for nefarious plots and actions aimed at humiliating and diminishing them. An important aspect of those narratives has been a call to arms against the party or parties allegedly responsible for these evil machinations. In recent years, there has been a proliferation of conspiracy theories identifying an assortment of culprits as the enemy that must be violently confronted and whose satanic plans must be aggressively thwarted.

In the West, at least, most of these narratives emerged on the far-right end of the political spectrum. Their pet enemies have been the Jews, the Muslims, the Asians (particularly during the Covid-19 pandemic), the

Democrats, and the government assumed to collude with those evil forces to take away from White Anglo-Saxon Americans what is rightfully theirs.

One of the most bizarre conspiracy theories – that, nonetheless, is taken seriously by hundreds of thousands of online devotees – is that an inter-dimensional race of reptilians has assumed human form and is plotting to take over the world. The author of this conspiracy theory is David Icke, a former soccer player and TV sportscaster in Britain. Icke published, largely on his own, over 20 books and has delivered speeches on his ideas in over 25 countries. For instance, during a book tour for his 2010 title, *Human Race Get Off Your Knees: The Lion Sleeps No More*, no fewer than 2,100 attended his talk in New York City. His similar lecture in Melbourne brought in close to $90,000 worth of ticket sales.

In his writings, Icke develops what some call New Age conspiracies that allegedly endorse antisemitism. As for the reptilian beings, he calls them the Archons and the Anunnaki, who create fear among humans because the aliens feed on the "negative energy" that is emitted. Also, according to Icke, there is a clandestine Babylonian Brotherhood that plots the establishment of a global fascist state ushering in a New World Order, where truth has no place and all humans are enslaved.

His recommended solution to all this is for people to fill their hearts with love and wake up to realize how they have been manipulated by evil forces. In 2003, Icke asserted that 43 American presidents were reptilian–human hybrids, along with three British and two Canadian prime ministers, not to mention Egyptian pharaohs and Sumerian kings. Wealthy reptilian families were said to include the Rothschilds and the Rockefellers, as well as the entire British royal family.[23]

You might seriously wonder how anyone can believe or even consider Icke's outlandish theories. But from a psychological perspective, the real question is what do these theories offer Icke's audiences that motivates them to take the claims seriously? In fact, they offer quite a lot. First, to be privy to a truth so scandalous and shocking makes a person feel very special, one of a select few "in the know." Secondly, Icke's theories offer an explanation of sorts for the fears and anxieties that so many people have been experiencing. Finally, he offers a blueprint for action and Significance: defeating the evil reptiles through love.

The science of psychology reveals that people's judgments and beliefs are strongly guided by their motivations. Because conspiracy narratives make people feel significant and special and extend hope for a better future, they tend to be taken seriously by Significance-deprived audiences exposed to them.

Summary

People's behavior is motivated. That much, just about everyone knows. What is less widely realized, though, is how motivation works. As we explained earlier, all human behavior is ultimately traceable to basic human needs. Whereas those needs are universal, the means of serving them are highly varied and depend on cultural narratives as to how those needs may be satisfied. The need for Significance and mattering, our main topic here, is satisfied through narratives that embody cultural values and ways of respecting those values. Narratives of this kind are typically imprinted in members of a culture in their childhood through myths, stories, and fairy tales that present positive or negative role models who either personify or negate the culture's values.

Particularly when people's Significance is lowered by negative life circumstances, they are susceptible to narratives that offer to raise their dignity and sense of mattering. Writing, as we do, near the end of the first quarter of the 21st century, we see vast populations around the world feeling unsettled, left behind, or discriminated against. Disseminated by social media at lightning speed, conspiracy narratives purport to identify the alleged culprits responsible for proliferating misery. The results can be seen in a widespread loss of confidence in traditional media and government procedures, and the election of self-described disruptors who claimed they would make their nations great again.

In our private lives, and on the world stage, the challenge is to find ways that can enhance our Significance as a win-win project, rather than through a bitter, competitive zero-sum game.

Notes

1 The Gun Violence Archive listed 604 mass shootings in the United States in 2023, defining them as incidents in which at least four people (excluding the armed attacker) were shot.
2 Moskalenko, Sophia; McCauley, Clark, *The Marvel of Martyrdom: The Power of Self-Sacrifice in a Selfish World* (Oxford: Oxford University Press, 2018).

3 See also Moskalenko, Sophia; Kruglanski, Arie W.; Prilleltensky, Isaac; Raviv, Alon, "Down the Yellow Brick Road: How Socialization Through Early Narratives Shapes the Quest for Significance," in Kruglanski, Arie W.; Prilleltensky, Isaac; Raviv, Alon (eds.), *Quest for Significance and Mattering* (Abingdon, Oxfordshire: Frontiers in Social Psychology, Routledge, 2024).

4 The institution's full name is the National Center for the Study of Terrorism and the Response to Terrorism, and the senior author of this book, Professor Kruglanski, is the co-director of START and a founding co-principal investigator.

5 Kruglanski, Arie W.; Orehek, Edward, "The Role of the Quest for Personal Significance in Motivating Terrorism," in Forgas, Joseph P.; Kruglanski, Arie W.; Williams, Kipling D. (eds.), *The Psychology of Social Conflict and Aggression* (New York: Psychology Press, 2011), pp. 153–164.

6 Ådnanes, Marian, "Social Transitions and Anomie Among Post-Communist Bulgarian Youth," *Young* [a SAGE Publications journal], Vol. 15, No. 1 (2007), pp. 49–69.

7 Macek, Petr; Flanagan, Constance; Gallay, Leslie; Kostron, Livia; Botcheva, Liliana; Csapo, Bela, "Postcommunist Societies in Times of Transition: Perceptions of Change Among Adolescents in Central and Eastern Europe," *Journal of Social Issues*, Vol. 54, No. 3 (1998), pp. 547–561.

8 Madoff, Bernard, interviewed by M.J. Lee, "Madoff: Politics, Remorse, Wall Street," *Politico*, Vol. 3 (2014); found at www.politico.com/story/2014/03/bernie -madoff-interview-104838.

9 Escamilla, Bianca, "The Craziest Scam? Gregor MacGregor Creates His Own Country," *Encyclopedia Britannica* (undated); found at www.britannica.com/story/the -craziest-scam-gregor-macgregor-creates-his-own-country.

10 "Luxury Goods Market Size, Growth, Trends," *Fortune Business Insights* (2023); found at www.fortunebusinessinsights.com/luxury-goods-market-103866.

11 Wrangham, Richard W.; Peterson, Dale, *Demonic Males: Apes and the Origins of Human Violence* (New York: Houghton Mifflin Harcourt, 1996).

12 Kruglanski, Arie W.; Bélanger, Jocelyn J.; Gunaratna, Rohan, *The Three Pillars of Radicalization: Needs, Narratives, and Networks* (New York: Oxford University Press, 2019).

13 Ainsley, Julia, "One-Quarter of Mass Attackers Driven by Conspiracy Theories or Hateful Ideologies, Secret Service Report Says," *NBC News* (January 25, 2023); found at www.nbcnews.com/news/us-news/one-quarter-mass-attackers-conspir-acy-theories-hate-rcna6729.

14 Jasko, Katarzyna; Szastok, Marta; Grzymala-Moszczynska, Joanna; Maj, Marta; Kruglanski, Arie W., "Rebel with a Cause: Personal Significance from Political Activism Predicts Willingness to Self-Sacrifice," *Journal of Social Issues*, Vol. 75, No. 1 (2019), pp. 314–349.

15 Szulecka, Julia; Szulecki, Kacper, "Polish Environmental Movement 1980–2017: (De)Legitimization, Politics & Ecological Crises," *Social Science Research Network*, Vol. 11 (2017); found at https://ssrn.com/abstract=3075126.

16 Steele, Claude M., "The Psychology of Self-Affirmation: Sustaining the Integrity of the Self," in Berkowitz, Leonard (ed.), *Advances in Experimental Social Psychology*, Vol. 21 (New York: Academic Press, 1988), pp. 261–302.

17 Sherman, David K.; Cohen, Geoffrey L., "The Psychology of Self-Defense: Self-Affirmation Theory," in Zanna, Mark P., *Advances in Experimental Social Psychology*, Vol. 38 (New York: Academic Press, 2006), pp. 183–242.

18 Cohen, Geoffrey L.; Sherman, David K.; Bastardi, Anthony; Hsu, Lillian; McGoey, Michelle; Ross, Lee, "Bridging the Partisan Divide: Self-Affirmation Reduces Ideological Closed-Mindedness and Inflexibility in Negotiation," *Journal of Personality and Social Psychology*, Vol. 93, No. 3 (2007), pp. 415–430.

19 Sherman, David A.; Nelson, Lisa D.; Steele, Claude M., "Do Messages About Health Risks Threaten the Self? Increasing the Acceptance of Threatening Health Messages via Self-Affirmation," *Personality and Social Psychology Bulletin*, Vol. 26, No. 9 (2000), pp. 1046–1058.

20 "Killing Hitler: The Many Assassination Attempts on Adolf Hitler," *History* (undated); found at www.history.co.uk/article/killing-hitler-the-many-assassination-attempts-on-adolf-hitler.

21 Ben-Ghiat, Ruth, "Mussolini, Trump, and What Assassination Attempts Really Do," *Politico* (August 3, 2024).

22 Kruglanski, Arie W., *Uncertain: How to Turn Your Biggest Fear into Your Greatest Power* (London: Penguin, 2023).

23 Barkun, Michael, *A Culture of Conspiracy: Apocalyptic Visions in Contemporary America* (Oakland: University of California Press, 2003).

7

NETWORKS FOR SIGNIFICANCE

Three N's remind us of the key factors in Significance being so important in human behavior. The first is the *Need* that people have, in this case the motivation we call the Quest for Significance (QFS), which we introduced in Chapter 1. We wrote how satisfying that need is guided by *Narratives* that people accept, as discussed in Chapter 6. And now the third N refers to the *Networks* that connect people around those common narratives as they make choices meant to enhance their Significance – and try to avoid a Significance loss.

Connectedness

These days, as you look around, you see people everywhere gazing at their smartphones. Hardly anyone seems to be occupied with their private thoughts, inaccessible to others. Instead, everyone is socially interacting, networking, making contacts, touching base, and sending and

DOI: 10.4324/9781003410706-7

receiving not-so-necessary messages and video clips. Does that build anyone's Significance?

Humans are known as an "ultra-social" species because, compared with all other mammals, we are more cooperative, competitive, and interactive with each other.[1] Our reality, meaning the way we see the world, is shaped by the way other people see it. Our reality is a "shared reality"[2] – a set of beliefs and values that we hold in common with others. But who are they? It is no secret, after all, that our contemporary society is badly fragmented and polarized. Day in and day out, we learn about vehement disagreements among members of our society on almost any topic: politics, art, science, you name it.

Yet, there are some people with whom we agree on the basics. Our "ingroups," as scholars call them, are the people whose opinions we respect and whose judgment we trust. They are people who, we hope, will have a positive opinion of us. That enhances our feelings of Significance and self-worth. If our ingroup clearly dislikes us, however, that gives us a sense of humiliation and Significance loss.

Does Size (of the Network) Matter?

How big is our ingroup? You might wonder how many people it takes to constitute a shared reality we can trust. The answer varies widely depending on the topic and the issue. For some issues, the entire culture to which we belong may constitute an ingroup. If we acted improperly at a funeral or dressed outlandishly by the standards of our surrounding culture, the obvious disapproval we would receive – even from complete strangers – would probably cause us shame and embarrassment. It does not have to be a small, intimate ingroup that makes us feel bad or good; subtracting from or adding to our Significance.

In other matters, much smaller groups are the ones whose evaluations of our actions, attributes, and outcomes determine our sense of self-worth. For a teenager, that group may be their classmates at school, whose tastes in music, dress, and hobbies define the standards for social worth. According to those standards, a teenager may earn the respect and admiration of their peers – being viewed as "hot" or "cool" – or, on the other hand, be smeared as a "nerd," a "dork," or whatever insult may be fashionable by the time you read this book.

Small ingroups might have very specific behaviors that impress or repulse their members. In an army, for example, a soldier turns for approval to his or her buddies in the platoon. They step up as the judges of courage, toughness, trustworthiness, and dependability in battle. These are the qualities that matter for the tasks and challenges that a military fighting force is likely to confront.

A very different example of a small ingroup, whose views determine the Significance of members' social worth, is a terrorist cell. Whether in the Middle East, or in Europe when it came to the Red Army Faction in Germany or the Italian Red Brigades of the 1970s and 1980s, their way of assessing the quality of a person would be tied to their radical beliefs, running counter to the general non-revolutionary culture in the country. Terrorists invariably believe that through violence, they will replace existing regimes with morally superior alternatives.

An even smaller ingroup would be a couple in an intense romantic relationship. This would typically be only two people, and they are wrapped up in their own sense of morality and appropriateness – perhaps even finding it binding and exciting to believe that it is just "the two of us against the world." Psychologists refer to the smallest of all ingroups as a "dyad."

Network Functions

Large or small, mainstream or fringe, our ingroup or social network serves two crucial functions. First, it defines for us what is real and good; its common worldview tells us what we should try to accomplish and how to do it. It holds for us what we call "epistemic authority," the degree to which we regard a person (such as a parent, a priest, a scientist, or a political leader) or institution (the government, the media, the Church, or science itself) as knowledgeable and trustworthy; therefore, we accept their norms and values.[3] The network validates the Significance narrative (discussed in Chapter 6) through its consensus about beliefs, values, and opinions.

Secondly, our social network rewards us by bestowing Significance upon us when we do what its narrative suggests; but it also punishes us by withdrawing appreciation when we don't obey the narrative, thus undermining our sense of social worth. The network wields immense power over its members, motivating their loyalty to its narratives and worldviews.

Members of your culture, for example, treat you with respect and dignity if you are of the "right" race, gender, social class, or religion. They also respect you if you achieve something that society values, such as in politics, sports, business, the arts, or academia. Conversely, if you fall short of society's norms in some respect or act inconsistently with its values, you are likely to experience rejection and scorn.

Changing Networks

Sometimes, you might lose your network or feel the need to abandon it because of circumstances that are forcing you to relocate to a different country, as in the case of immigrants or refugees. Often, this entails a precipitous loss of Significance, where the host community to which you have migrated (which represents your new network) does not recognize your social worth the way your old community used to.

The following true stories of individuals who lost their Significance through immigration illustrate this phenomenon[4]:

Boris R., a Lithuanian, was in his 40s when he immigrated with his wife and two teenage children to Canada. Prior to leaving Eastern Europe, Boris had a successful career as a managing director of a major electronics factory, earning a high salary along with a company car and a driver. However, after immigrating, he could not find anything comparable and was forced to work as a gasoline station attendant pumping fuel.

Iryna R., a Ukrainian with a PhD degree, immigrated to Germany in 1990 with her husband and teenage daughter. Prior to immigrating, she directed a high-powered medical research lab in Kyiv focused on hearing loss. However, after immigrating, the only job she could find was as a lab assistant, carrying out menial tasks such as rinsing beakers and stacking shelves.

Zhanna M, a Belarusian, immigrated to the United States with her husband and two teenage children. In her "before" life in Minsk, Zhanna was a chief chemist at a furniture factory. In the United States, the only job she could obtain was cleaning people's houses.

Boris, Iryna, and Zhanna all lost a considerable sense of social worth because they switched networks. Their skills and credentials that provided them with Significance in their "old country" simply did not apply to their new network, the host country to which they migrated.

It is in part because of such circumstances that first-generation immigrants often associate with others of their kind, rather than quickly assimilating into the networks of their host societies. The strongest explanation is that among their co-ethnics, they could retain their old social standing. Boris could still be treated as a successful entrepreneur rather than a gas station attendant. Iryna could be treated as a lab director rather than a lowly assistant, and Zhanna as a chief chemist rather than a domestic cleaner.

A move to a different network can have positive consequences. Cases include members of violent organizations who came back from the fringe through friendship or romantic relations with individuals from the mainstream. Christian Picciolini, formerly a leading figure in the white supremacist movement in America, recounted how – after he opened a record store to support his family – he met mainstream individuals whom he befriended, and how those relationships (his new network) ultimately made him leave the extremist milieu. As he wrote in his memoir:

> Surprisingly, my customer base was quite diverse. I began to meet gay and Jewish customers and increasingly found myself being genuinely civil to them, as well as other minorities. Our conversations were brief, guarded at first, but slowly we got to know each other through our shared interest in music. And they kept coming back. Through music we found some commonality, and I found myself thinking clearly 'These are good people. I do not want to hurt them.' We talked about bands, laughed, swapped stories about concerts we'd been to. Related to each other in ways I hadn't thought possible.[5]

Back from the Fringe

A similar and particularly interesting story is that of Derek Black, a man who at the age of 19 was a featured speaker at a racist conference attended by former heads of the Ku Klux Klan and prominent neo-Nazis. That was in Memphis, Tennessee, in late 2008, in reaction to the election of Barack Obama as America's first black president.

From early childhood, Derek had been raised on a diet of white supremacist ideas. Don Black, Derek's father, was the founder of Stormfront, the first and largest white nationalist internet site, boasting 300,000 users. His mother, Chloe, was a former wife of David Duke, a longtime leader of the

Ku Klux Klan and a persistent denier of the Holocaust, who had become Derek's godfather. Immersed in radical white supremacist worldviews, Derek was widely seen as the future of the movement, an anointed leader and the worthy heir to his "royal" parents.

In his speech at the conference, he talked about taking over the Republican Party and remaking it as "the White People's party." His eloquence brought the audience to their feet in thunderous applause as he issued a call to action and prophesized that, "Years from now, we will look back on this," and "The great intellectual move to save white people started today."[6]

Yet eight years later, Derek was expressing strong opposition to white supremacism. A longtime hater of Muslims, he now engaged in the study of Islam and other religions. He spoke about the importance and societal benefits of diversity, and he even declared that he was on Hilary Clinton's side in the 2016 presidential election.

What can explain this about-face – a once-rabid racist now turned into an enthusiastic supporter of racial tolerance and social justice? You might think it was the truth of liberal ideas that suddenly struck him, an "aha!" experience that made him realize the error of his ways, a light of revelation that instantaneously shone upon him. But no, the process of his conversion was much more gradual and less mystical than that. A major role was played by the social network in which Derek found himself. And here is how it all came about.

After graduating from high school and studying at a community college, Derek proceeded to study medieval European history at New College of Florida, a highly reputed liberal arts school with a strong history program. There, he encountered a student community with strongly liberal values, the opposite of the values he was brought up to embrace and uphold. At first, he tried to conceal his views from his fellow students, whom he liked and respected. But soon enough, his identity was revealed, and he became a pariah at the college, ostracized by his erstwhile friends who now came to view him as a fake and a traitor.

Matters took a different turn when Mathew Stevenson, an Orthodox Jew and fellow student, began inviting Derek to Sabbath dinners that Matthew cooked for his friends. Attending those meals and meeting other attendees of varied backgrounds, including Jews and people of color, led Derek to know and like them. Indirectly, too, he was gradually exposed to their liberal values and worldviews that treated people of all races, religious creeds, and ethnicities as equal and deserving of the same rights and privileges.

After months of feeling ostracized from a community of people he respected, Derek especially appreciated the acceptance he got from the Sabbath diners and from their host, Matthew. His deepening immersion in this network correspondingly increased his openness to his new friends' narrative and their moral outlook.

At first, Derek tried to hold on to his old white supremacist way of thinking, even as he was becoming increasingly committed to the liberal worldviews of his academic community. Finally, he realized the incompatibility of these two worldviews. In 2013, he sent a statement to the Southern Poverty Law Center, which monitors racists and extremists, in which he publicly renounced his former views. A few years later, he explained: "I wanted them to know that I understood what we believed, and I was systematically disbelieving each point."[7]

Embrace of the Network

We recently analyzed interviews with 42 former neo-Nazis in Germany who recounted the circumstances in which they had joined the movement.[8] It turns out that in many cases they were not initially attracted to the Nazi narrative, nor did they know much about it. What drew them to the movement was the network. Feeling low on Significance for various reasons, they had accepted an invitation to a party or a rock concert without knowing the sponsors or attendees of those events. At first, they did not exactly identify with the hateful lyrics shouted by right-wing extremists at the punk concerts they attended. Slowly but surely, however, most of them came to feel comfortable with their new friends and got used to their narratives. In their new milieu, they wanted to be liked and accepted, so they endorsed the views of their new comrades and internalized them as their own new opinions.

Persuading the Network

The impact of our networks on what we think and feel is immense. Nothing much happens in our minds that does not involve inputs from the group with which we identify. Messages directed at an individual alone typically fail to convince, especially if that person's network holds a different opinion.

A striking illustration of this is psychologist Kurt Lewin's famous research on changing the food-serving habits of American housewives during World War II. At that time, as much as 80 percent of US meat production was being sent overseas to feed American soldiers and allies.[9] This raised the cost of beef and, consequently, Americans ate less meat. To avoid protein deficiencies, the government wanted people to consider eating the cheaper and more readily available "organ meats": kidneys, brains, liver, hearts, and intestines. The problem was that, at the time, Americans viewed such meats as low class (that is, devoid of Significance) and disgusting, and hence families were reluctant to serve them at home.

Professor Lewin (generally recognized as the founding father of American social psychology) decided to use his expertise to overcome that obstacle and change Americans' negative attitude toward those despised meats.[10] His approach brilliantly recognized the importance of networks in persuasion. First, he realized that as far as food was concerned, it was typically the woman of the house who led the family network. She called the shots and determined the family diet. So, Lewin reasoned, it would be futile to try to convince the men, because in culinary matters they followed their wives' lead.

Secondly, he realized that directing persuasive arguments at women individually would also miss the mark. Why? Because even if, as individuals, the women were convinced by the arguments presented – that organ meats were nutritious and cheap – that new opinion would not last. On meeting with network friends, old norms and habits would quickly surface and cause a relapse to the original attitudes. What, then, was the solution? To engage the women in a group discussion, Lewin decided, the norms of the collective should be changed.

To test his ideas, Lewin recruited 85 Midwestern married women to participate in a research study and randomly assigned them to one of two experimental conditions. One was the "lecture group," where about 15 women at a time listened to a talk by a nutritionist on adding organ meats to the family diet. The nutritionist explained how to cook and serve these meats appealingly and work around their unpleasant color, texture, and appearance.

The other group was dubbed by Lewin the "group decision condition," where the nutritionist began by relating to women the same facts about organ meats and cooking techniques. In addition, the women actively participated in a discussion about how to change Americans' eating habits to cope with wartime food shortages. They were invited to air their criticisms and apprehensions. Then the nutritionist responded with persuasive counterarguments, including cooking tips for making organ meats taste better.

One week later, researchers interviewed each housewife. They discovered that 23 out of 44 participants (52%) in the "group decision" were now serving organ meats, while only 4 out of 41 in the "lecture group" audience (less than 10%) did. As Lewin had anticipated, the group discussion led the participants to change the group norms toward accepting the nutritionist's narrative. That format allowed the women to see how their fellow participants were altering their opinions, and that made it easier for them to do the same.

So, in forming our attitudes and opinions, we defer to our *networks*, which operate on *narratives* that suggest how a *need* (for Significance, as we have been discussing in this book) can be met. Those are the three N's that make behavior happen.

In the example above, it was the expert nutritionist, a credible espouser of a narrative, who showed women a path to Significance as good housewives and homemakers. But it took a network, the community of women, to "certify" the narrative and turn it into a shared reality. What followed was action, the inevitable consequence of effective persuasion and social influence.

It is worth emphasizing that the visceral need for Significance felt by every human being – and the narratives that define what the goals and methods should be to attain respect, dignity, and worth – are essential yet typically insufficient ingredients of QFS-driven behavior.

A third element must be added to the mix, the validation of the narrative by the person's network. Buttressed by network support, the narrative tends to offer a clear vision of what must be done to gain Significance. Individuals can then proceed to carry out the narrative's prescriptions, basking in the appreciation of the network.

When a network is activated, the narrative becomes much more than just a theory. It becomes a shared reality that serves as a launching pad for action. Without network support, a narrative falls flat – "in one ear and out the other." It is the support of the network that brings a narrative to life.

Why is this worth knowing? Because to exert influence and get people to change their behavior and attitudes – to campaign for almost anything new – it is essential to get in tune with people's networks. This requirement extends to parents or teachers anxious to impart knowledge to the youngsters in their charge, or anyone who seeks other people's acceptance, friendship, or love.

Your Network, Yourself

Networks do not merely affect your views about the world and other people. One of their most substantial impacts is on the way you view yourself and the social worth you assume you have. In our age, dominated by social media, people are often reminded of their value or the lack of it by the number of "likes" on their posts, the number of Facebook "friends" they can boast, and how they are depicted on Instagram or TikTok. Whether in education, sports, on Wall Street, or in Silicon Valley, a shared belief in a certain type of Significance draws a kind of point-scoring system by which people are evaluated.

One manifestation of this scramble for Significance would be the Herculean efforts invested in getting kids into the "best" colleges. This near obsession of millions of parents and children has immense consequences for their happiness and mental health. The struggle for educational credentials often seems desperate, because the United States built its economic success on a competitive winner-take-all paradigm. There is a widespread belief that success is to a large extent contingent on having graduated from a reputable college, preferably of the Ivy League variety. The "winners" in this scramble not only become wealthy because of their credentials and their network of highly placed friends, but they also receive ample recognition and Significance because of their affiliations. "Whom they know" is often more important than "what they know."

It is through this prism that we can understand the power of networks in America – and how they affect our children. In upper middle-class communities such as Bethesda (Maryland), Palo Alto (California), and Lexington (Massachusetts), teens strive with remarkable commitment and intensity to have the "right" hobbies and interests to make themselves attractive to prestigious colleges, their aspirational networks. Are most of them going to be concert pianists? Hardly. And who really cares about a handful of teenagers rowing a boat? It is not about the boat; it is about the people in the boat and their networks, whose pressures are hard to resist. Hence, most parents and children conform and do what the networks demand, sometimes with devastating emotional impacts on young people's lives.

In Palo Alto, five students took their own lives between May 2009 and January 2010, and three more chose suicide between October 2014 and April 2015. The *Times* reported that 95 percent of Lexington high school students described themselves as heavily stressed about their schoolwork, and 15 percent reported having suicidal thoughts in their senior year, as the transition to college was looming.[11]

In short, the influence of networks – often propagating pressure to conform – is immense. Networks determine how we think, what we value, whom we see as friends and foes, how we feel about ourselves, and what we decide to do as a result. The network endorses a narrative and lends Significance to people who follow the narrative in their actions and decisions. That is how socially relevant behavior happens in human communities everywhere.

Summary

Humans are a highly sociable species; we spend our lives in communities that largely agree on norms, values, and narratives. Our reality is thus a "shared reality" embraced by our network. Our judgments, attitudes, and impressions are heavily influenced by those held within our networks. These include our own sense of Significance, molded by how members of our networks see us, which in turn depends on how we measure up to standards and values held by our networks.

Accordingly, moving from one network to another often reshapes our sense of Significance, sometimes for the better and sometimes for the worse. The contours of our meaningful networks vary widely: from intimate dyadic relationships to close-knit friend circles, from lively chat rooms on the internet to entire societies where shared values and ideals dictate how Significance can be attained within their cultural context. In the 21st century, the pervasive and inescapable interconnectedness fostered by social media thrusts issues of Significance and social worth to the forefront of people's minds. While individuals may not consciously frame their experiences in these precise terms, they unwittingly participate in society's relentless, network-driven competition for Significance – a pursuit that can exact a toll on mental well-being.

Notes

1 Tomasello, Michael, "The Ultra-Social Animal," *European Journal of Social Psychology*, Vol. 44, No. 3 (2014), pp. 187–194.
2 Higgins, E. Tory, *Shared Reality: What Makes Us Strong and Tears Us Apart* (Oxford: Oxford University Press, 2019).
3 Kruglanski, Arie W.; Raviv, Amiram; Bar-Tal, Daniel; Raviv, Amiram; Sharvit, Keren; Ellis, Sonja; Mannetti, Lucia, "Says Who? Epistemic Authority Effects in Social Judgment," *Advances in Experimental Social Psychology*, Vol. 37 (2005), pp. 345–392. "Epistemic" refers to knowledge, how it is acquired, and why people believe in what they know.
4 We are indebted to Sophia Moskalenko for recounting these stories.
5 Picciolini, Christian, *White American Youth: My Descent into America's Most Violent Hate Movement – and How I Got Out* (New York: Hachette Books, 2017).
6 Saslow, Eli, "The White Flight of Derek Black," *The Washington Post* (October 15, 2016).
7 "A Conversation with a Former White Nationalist," Derek Black was interviewed on the *New York Times* podcast, *The Daily*, by the host, Michael Barbaro (August 22, 2017).
8 Kruglanski, Arie W.; Webber, Daniel; Koehler, David, *The Radical's Journey: How German Neo-Nazis Voyaged to the Edge and Back* (New York: Oxford University Press, 2019).
9 C. Mildred Thompson, *The Food Front in World War II* (New York: Harper & Brothers, 1951); and other historians' notes on authoritative websites.
10 Lewin, Kurt, "Forces Behind Food Habits and Methods of Change," *Bulletin of the National Research Council*, Vol. 108 (1943), pp. 35–65.
11 Spencer, Kyle, "It Takes a Suburb: A Town Struggles to Ease Student Stress," *The New York Times* (April 5, 2017); found at www.nytimes.com/2017/04/05/education/edlife/overachievers-student-stress-in-high-school-.html.

8

ATTACK FOR SIGNIFICANCE

David E. Salzman, a prominent entertainment industry producer, shared this insight during our interview in Beverly Hills: "I love work. For me, work equals worth, self-worth. And if you have self-worth, you feel good about yourself."

Salzman's dedication to work is not unique; it reflects a broader trend in Western culture. We idolize "winners" – those who have "made it" and have risen from humble beginnings to prosperity. Conversely, we often view "losers" with a mix of pity and disdain. Countless self-help books promise the "secrets" to successful careers, and Google lists around three million titles with the word "success." But how did we become so fixated on "success?" Why do we willingly participate in the relentless "rat race?"

The Protestant Ethic

Max Weber, one of the founding fathers of modern sociology alongside Karl Marx and Emile Durkheim, offers an answer. In his 1905 book, *The*

DOI: 10.4324/9781003410706-8

Protestant Ethic and the Spirit of Capitalism,[1] Weber traced our insatiable craving for worldly success back to the teachings of Martin Luther, an Augustinian friar and leader of the Protestant movement. Luther championed productive work as the bedrock of society.

However, it was John Calvin – a French theologian – whose influence left an indelible mark on the Protestant attitude toward success. Calvin introduced the concept of predestination: God elects some individuals for eternal life while leaving others to perish. According to Calvin, evidence of being elected lies in daily life and deeds, with success in worldly endeavors serving as a hint of divine favor. Unlike Luther, who saw work as a societal contribution, Calvin elevated success to a sacred status – a sign of superiority and Significance directly bestowed by God.[2]

As early as the 1600s, Anglo-American Protestants diverged from the traditional economic lifestyle of working just enough to sustain themselves. Instead, they toiled harder, longer, and more obsessively. The American Dream emerged – a seemingly boundless opportunity for success, irrespective of one's origins – if you would work very hard for it.

Yet, reality diverges from the dream. The United States ranks only 27th in social mobility, trailing countries such as Portugal, Lithuania, and Estonia. Inequities have widened over the decades. Corporate chief executive salaries, which had been 20 or 30 times that of the average worker, now stand at a staggering 300 times the wages of their employees.[3] The top 1 percent of Americans own 40 percent of the nation's wealth, mirroring income disparities.[4]

The Legend: Fame from Riches

Nonetheless, the legend of the American Dream lives on, and Americans' obsession with success is alive and well. In the United States, as discussed earlier, success is often defined in terms of wealth and the accumulation of riches. However, in that kind of materialistic society, money isn't the ultimate end; rather, it is the means to social worth, mattering, and Significance.

The first sentence of Donald Trump's ghost-written 1987 best-seller, *The Art of the Deal*, is "I don't do it for the money." In this case, the king of countless outlandish falsehoods was truthful. It is the prestige of riches, the social status that wealth affords, that has been the ultimate motivator for Trump and other over-strivers – not just the money. There is a cliché about someone being "rich and famous," but those two adjectives draw a distinction without a difference. The "rich" are admired and emulated precisely because their wealth – especially if they show it off – makes them "famous," simply because they are rich.

When Trump entered politics, he was stunningly successful. A threat of Significance loss motivated his voters, who catapulted him to the US presidency in the 2016 elections and returned him to the White House in 2024. You might think that it was the "left-behinds" in American society (people who lost jobs or found their wages stagnating) who brought Trump to power. But a research study, tracking voters from 2012 to 2016, found the strongest factor was anxiety among "high-status" groups, who disliked growing racial diversity. The voters who swung to Trump were Americans who had jobs but accepted the notion – sparked partly by Barack Obama's presidency – that white Americans were under siege, and that their status (meaning Significance) was therefore in serious jeopardy.[5]

Cultural Domains of Significance

In our individualistic culture, the reverence for success extends beyond mere wealth. We celebrate visibility and recognition across various domains – politics, sports, entertainment, and science. Within these arenas, achievers ascend to superstar status, captivating public interest and serving as role models for millions. An iconic declaration usually associated with sports teams, "Winning isn't everything; it's the only thing," reverberates widely in today's America.

In this age of social media, our fixation on success and recognition reaches unprecedented levels. Consider the morning ritual of countless 18- to 34-year-olds: They wake up, grab their phones, and eagerly tally the "likes" on their blogs and posts. These digital badges of social approval matter deeply. They signify our relevance to others, our social worth, and our recognition as significant beings.

Surprisingly, even religion cannot remain immune to our culture's worship of success. Spotlighting a type of hero, the magazine publishers at *Time/Life* wrote highly laudatory profiles of the 50 most influential people in the Bible. These individuals achieved lasting attention and remembrance, demonstrating that the pursuit of Significance transcends earthly realms.[6]

Advertising for Success

Given America's overriding obsession with success, it is no wonder that people passionately seek ways to become winners while avoiding the stigma of being labeled losers. Madison Avenue advertising firms deftly exploit this motivation, associating various consumer products with the allure of success. You might remember when Vantage cigarettes promised smokers "the taste of success." Or when the nose spray Nostrilla suggested users would experience "the sweet smell of success." Even a shirt company, Sero, advertised a product designed to help you "take the stress out of success."

For these advertising campaigns to work, consumers did not have to believe wholeheartedly in the promises crafted by creative copywriters. The underlying psychology operates differently, relying on what scholars term affective or evaluative conditioning. Simply put, by linking a product to the word "success" – which evokes warm and positive feelings – that emotion becomes associated with the product itself. Consequently, consumers may develop a liking for the product and feel inclined to make a purchase. Ethical questions arise: Are consumers informed that their feelings are being subtly manipulated? Is that fair?

The issue becomes particularly poignant in the realm of so-called subliminal advertising. Here, emotionally charged words associated with a product flash on a screen for a fraction of a second, almost invisible to the conscious mind yet still capable of influencing people's attitudes toward the product. The ethics of subliminal advertising have sparked heated debates. Critics argue that ultra-quick views of words or phrases can shape thoughts and behaviors without the audience's knowledge or consent. Moreover, subliminal messaging could serve malicious purposes or advance hidden political agendas, potentially inciting violence against minority groups.[7] The US Federal Trade Commission called it "a deceptive practice" and banned it from advertising.[8]

It should be clear that the use of success language and imagery in advertising is not about helping people succeed, but rather about selling products through the use of psychological principles. The science of psychology, especially recent 21st-century developments, has a great deal to offer when it comes to improving the actual likelihood of succeeding. In the next sections, we describe some of these exciting developments.

Balancing Motivation and Expectation

When considering any endeavor, your willingness to invest energy and commitment hinges on two critical factors: how much you value success in that domain and how strong your expectation is that the endeavor will succeed.

Imagine hunger as a metaphor for motivation. When you are only slightly hungry, finding a restaurant or food store is not your top priority. You might choose to finish your yoga exercise, tackle your taxes, or take the dog for a walk instead. But when hunger becomes intense and relentless, it takes precedence over everything else. Similarly, the value you place on success depends on how crucial it is to satisfy your motivation.

When the Quest for Significance looms large, the value of success increases. If you crave Significance, you become attuned to careers that offer it – whether in sports, entertainment, politics, or maintaining a coveted lifestyle. Fancy restaurants, exotic vacations, and global travel become part of the equation as the insignia of success.

However, no matter how much you value success, low expectations can dampen your efforts. If you believe success is unlikely, you are less likely to try. Sure, being a champion athlete, rock star, or celebrated scientist would be fantastic, but if you deem it improbable, you will not even attempt it. Expectancy sets the stage: You'll pursue a Significance-affording career only if the odds of success seem reasonable.

Expectancy shapes your career choices. Sometimes, you trade a degree of Significance that one particular career could provide for an increased expectancy of success. For instance, you might abandon the idea of being a basketball superstar and opt for a physical education (PE) teaching career at a neighborhood high school because that kind of success is much more attainable. Or perhaps an actor settles for supporting roles in minor film productions instead of chasing elusive leading roles. Life involves compromises, and true happiness lies in being content with achievable goals.

The "Can-Do" Mantra and Reaching for the Stars

Yet, here is the quandary: There is no definite way of calculating the probability of success, so people have to use their own judgment calls – often on an issue with which they have no experience. Objective standards are scarce, so opinions – whether encouraging or discouraging – sway our decisions. Wishful thinking creeps in, and our judgments become colored by motivational biases.

Enter the "can-do" attitude of American culture: the spirit of reaching for the stars against all odds. George Gershwin's hit song, "They All Laughed," featured in the 1937 film "Shall We Dance," celebrated this resilience. The lyrics literally named world-famous pioneers such as Christopher Columbus, Thomas Edison, and the Wright Brothers, who all defied skepticism and had "the last laugh" after navigating through initial doubts.

A popular children's story, "The Little Engine That Could," tells of a train engine that was small and old yet took on a challenge that other locomotives refused: delivering fresh milk, vegetables, and toys to deprived children on the other side of an awe-inspiring mountain. The route involved a very steep climb, and the cargo was very heavy, so the mission seemed nearly impossible. Yet, the little engine undertook it, and to psyche itself up, it repeated, "I think I can. I think I can." And so, the hero of the story hitched itself to the wagon full of toys and food, and – huffing and puffing through the arduous climb – finally delivered the cargo to the children and exclaimed with pride: "I thought I could!"

That motivational story highlights at once the importance of expectancy. Just repeating to yourself, "I think I can," can heighten your expectancy of success and encourage you to persist and not give up.

"Never say die!" is another optimistic mantra, fueling the expectation of coming through with triumph.

The Girl from Ukraine

The true story of Sophia Moskalenko poignantly illustrates the power of tenacity and persistence, despite a painful lack of support and outright discouragement from others. These days, she is a highly respected PhD with several important books and numerous scientific articles to her credit, working with international institutions such as the United Nations, the North Atlantic Treaty Organization (NATO), and the European Commission. People who have met this woman, educated at some of America's best universities and highly respected in her field, may know that she is an immigrant from Ukraine, but very few realize how turbulent and sometimes tragic her pathway in life has been.

Sophia arrived in the United States at the age of 18 on a student exchange program, with hardly a word of English and no economic resources whatsoever. Her father, who had immigrated to America years earlier, refused to help her and made a concerted effort to convince her that her chances of an American college education were nothing but a pipe dream.

With the help of a sympathetic uncle, she obtained a financial aid package earmarked for Ukrainians at a two-year junior college. Through a Herculean effort, she taught herself to speak and write English, and she proceeded to complete the college with stellar grades and glowing letters of recommendation. Her application for a transfer to Bryn Mawr College was accepted, but with no financial aid, which made it impossible to attend. Paying for one course at a time, she supported herself by working as a server in a restaurant and relied on gifts and loans to survive.

She applied again the following year. This time, there was strong support from two professors whose psychology classes she took, and she finally got into Bryn Mawr, the college of her dreams. However, her struggles were not over.

Although highly successful in her undergraduate studies, the only PhD programs she could hope to attend were ones that offered a full financial package – or else her visa extension would be denied. She thus worked extra hard to make sure she stood a chance of getting into a doctoral program at an Ivy League university.

To accumulate the grades, research accomplishments, and recommendations needed to succeed through a highly selective graduate admissions process, and to do it all in two short years (as per visa requirements), seems truly an impossible mission. Yet, Sophia did it, gaining acceptance at the University of Pennsylvania, driven by her belief in herself and a strong sense that – like the little engine – she thought she could.

The Power of Positive Psychology: Attacking for Significance

Not everyone has Sophia's tenacity and fortitude of spirit. Fortunately, research has shown that there are ways to instill in anyone a sense of optimism – the kind of belief in oneself that can create the resilience to pursue goals and to defy negative odds. We call that the "attack mode," wherein people actively pursue their Significance through attacking their weaknesses and playing to their strengths.

Historically, the field of psychology evolved from psychiatry, a medical discipline focused on illness. Like its parent field, psychology has been focused on the negative aspects of the human experience, things that make people suffer (such as anxiety, depression, and mental illness). But in the year 2000, two leading psychological theorists, Martin Seligman and Mihaly Csikszentmihalyi, launched a scientific movement that gave the field an entirely new direction. That movement became known as "positive psychology."

Positive psychology is unique in its emphasis on human strengths and ways of coping. It identifies factors that produce serenity, happiness, and contentment, such as gratitude and forgiveness. Seligman made major contributions to understanding people's ways of describing situations with optimism or pessimism, and he concluded that they can be encouraged to increase their optimism and expectations of success.

Learning Optimism

People's explanations of successes or failures have three important aspects that Seligman calls *permanence*, *pervasiveness*, and *personalization*.

The *permanence* dimension concerns whether the event is assigned to a *stable* or an *unstable* cause. When the cause is stable, you may expect the same outcome to occur in the future. So, if you failed a math test, you might point to a stable cause (that you are generally bad at math) and would expect to keep failing math tests in the future. But if you attributed your failure to an unstable cause (admitting that you did not study enough for the test), that is something you could change. So, you can start expecting to pass those tests from now on.

This works for success, too. Say you did well on a math test. If you attributed your success to an unstable cause (contending that you just got lucky), this would have no implications, because luck is notoriously fickle. But if you attributed it to your ability, talent, or intelligence – your stable characteristics – that would mean you are likely to do well in math on subsequent occasions as well.

In short, ingraining in people the habit of looking for unstable causes of failures and for stable causes of their successes is a way of teaching them an optimistic way of thinking. And that increases their expectancies of future successes.

The second dimension of developing an optimistic way of thinking is *pervasiveness*. This means generalizing your failures or successes in one area to other domains of endeavor. Say you lost a tennis game: If that made you see yourself as generally a "loser," you would expect the worst in unrelated areas like business, stock market investments, romantic encounters, and academic pursuits. "Over-catastrophizing" – as psychologists might put it – is the hallmark of a pessimistic way of thinking. That will prevent you from trying, when it would be much better to stand up to challenges and confront them.

On the other hand, overgeneralizing successes and thinking of yourself as a "winner" contributes to optimism. Although perhaps not always realistic, the optimistic explanatory style increases expectancy of success and hence the feelings of Significance and mattering.

Seligman's third dimension of optimism is *personalization*. Some people react to negative outcomes by blaming themselves, whereas others blame external circumstances. For instance, failing to get a coveted award, choking on a speech, or hearing your work harshly criticized can be attributed to personal failings or a lack of talent. These are pessimistic explanations likely to cause distress, dejection, and feelings of worthlessness and insignificance.

Explaining the same events by blaming external factors is actually face-saving and breeds optimism: excuses such as the awards committee being biased, or you being ill and overly stressed when giving the speech, or your critics being incompetent. These attributions preserve a person's sense of worth and Significance despite the negative outcome.

Seligman devised a self-administered scale that allows people to see whether their explanatory style is optimistic or pessimistic.[9] This is often worth knowing, especially if you would like to change your typical way of thinking in a positive direction.

Disputation

Suggesting how to change a person's attributional style from pessimistic to optimistic, Seligman advised disputing the pessimistic views by confronting them with indisputable facts and compelling arguments. Here is how that might work: After a person took a test at school and scored poorly, a pessimistic, Significance-reducing framing of this event might be that the person is not good enough, that others in the class did much better, so it might be time to give up.

A disputation of this pessimistic framing could be that a single failure should not be blown out of proportion. You could also suppose that others in the class probably did not do much better, that it is always possible to learn from mistakes, that completing the course will enhance your chances in the job market, and so on.

To overcome ingrained pessimism takes work. Seligman recommends specific exercises that have proven effective. Specifically, over one week, closely examine five events about which you held pessimistic beliefs – and try to vigorously dispute them. The events could be as small as an unanswered email or a neighbor not saying hello, or more potentially consequential, such as a job interview. In each of these cases, vigorously dispute the pessimistic beliefs and consider all the reasons you can think of why they could be wrong. With sufficient practice, over time you can turn your pessimism around and become an optimist!

Admittedly, being unrealistically optimistic is also not good. You should be aware of your limitations – and even sometimes decide there is no point in trying right now – and instead find a different route to achieving your goals. Given sufficient feedback, you should be able to realize that you are not destined for the NBA basketball league, the Metropolitan Opera, or the cover of TIME magazine. The inveterate optimist who strives to succeed in every single task or be loved by every single person is likely to be disappointed and unhappy.

Sometimes, the line between optimistic tenacity and self-delusion is thin. Still, the optimistic attitude is usually beneficial. It makes you feel good, effective, and significant, and allows you to attack your challenges with vigor and enthusiasm. It makes you happier overall; moreover, it makes you live longer!

One of the most renowned studies examining the impact of happiness and optimism draws from the diaries of 178 Catholic nuns affiliated with a multistate organization, the School Sisters of Notre Dame. These nuns documented their thoughts in journals during their early adulthood in the 1930s and 1940s.

Fast forward 50 years. A team of three researchers from the University of Kentucky analyzed the content of the nuns' diaries. Their focus? Identifying positive, optimistic, and happy emotional expressions. An intriguing finding emerged: Positive emotional content in early diaries was linked to longevity, as the young nuns who expressed positive feelings proceeded to enjoy longer lives. In essence, their early emotional states influenced their health and well-being many years later.[10]

The Growth Mindset

Striving for success and Significance is often offset by a scary event that is all too common: failure. "The failure paradox" refers to the truth that while failure is the opposite of success, there is hardly any success in life without prior failure. In a way, failure and success are like two sides of the same coin, inseparable from each other.

If success were easy, everyone would be successful; but then success wouldn't bring much distinction or Significance. In fact, success is highly prized precisely because it is difficult to achieve. This permits the successful to stand out and be noticed.

At the same time, even when challenges are duly confronted, a person will sometimes fail. If he or she does not calmly accept that reality, failures can be painful and paralyzing. World Bank statistics indicate that in 2020, among Americans aged 18–64, just over 41 percent suffered from fear of failure. The figure was 48.3 percent in the United Kingdom, 46.5 percent in Russia, 56.8 percent in India, and only 31 percent in Germany.[11]

Whereas success is Significance enhancing and makes a person feel worthy of respect, failure is Significance reducing. It makes a person feel humiliated and ashamed, like a "loser" worthy at best of pity if not of outright derision. It is this prospect of painful Significance loss that produces a fear of failure, and that often deters people from effective coping and addressing challenges that come along.

A striking example of the dysfunctional effect that fear of failure can have on people's lives is the phenomenon of self-handicapping. This refers to "shooting oneself in the foot" before an important performance and thus inviting failure – but in a way that will guard the competitor's pride.

So, for example, a person with a reputation for being a gifted athlete, a brilliant mathematician, or a talented singer may self-handicap before a high-stakes event (such as an athletic competition, a mathematical contest, or a public concert). The self-handicapping may take the form of skipping practice, procrastinating, or abusing drugs and alcohol before an important competitive event.

Adopting the self-handicapping strategy as a way of protecting one's ego makes for a sad existence, in which one is regarded pitifully as someone who "could have, should have" attained greatness but tragically did not.

In 2006, Carol Dweck, a psychology professor at Stanford University, introduced a concept that has had a profound impact on ways of addressing and counteracting fear of failure. It is the concept of the *growth mindset*, the belief that our minds and brains are malleable, and that ultimately, failure is a friend of success rather than a foe. Failure clears the way toward learning from our mistakes, and that paves the way to achievement.

Dweck juxtaposes the "growth mindset" – her term for the malleability of human characteristics so that change is possible – with the "fixed mindset," which assumes that our abilities and talents are immutable. Whereas people with the growth mindset are undeterred by failure and are ready to accept its lessons, people with the fixed mindset are devastated by failure and try to avoid it at all costs. This attitude follows from the concept that human characteristics (such as intelligence, abilities, talents, and even morality) are fixed, and therefore a failure in one area sends a clear signal that things are unlikely to change. That would suggest that a person is doomed forever to be labeled as unintelligent, untalented, or immoral, without any possibility of a reprieve.

Dweck's approach is revolutionary and important, because in our society the fixed mindset is the dominant mode of describing and relating to people. We label individuals as intelligent or unintelligent, talented or untalented, creative or uncreative, athletic or unathletic. These labels determine how we treat people. In hiring for sports teams, businesses, and academia, we typically go for "talent," "brilliance," "intelligence," and other labels that assume people's characteristics truly are fixed. We largely ignore the possibility of growth and development.

We also underestimate the blood, sweat, and tears required to reach any kind of worthwhile achievement. The emphasis on labels makes people do all they can to *seem* talented and brilliant. They worry about appearances and avoid risking failure. They are defensive about their possible shortcomings and loath to admit their mistakes and learn from them.

Dweck's message is hopeful and optimistic. It takes the edge off current failures and encourages an attitude of learning and exploration. Winston Churchill is credited with an aptly inspiring observation: "Success is not final, failure is not fatal: it is the courage to continue that counts." It is this "courage to continue" that Dweck's approach effectively inspires when she writes, lectures, and leads workshops.

Grit

Optimism and mindset are important, no doubt. But perhaps something else is needed to keep the heat on – to motivate a person to relentlessly pursue their dreams. In her best-selling book, Angela Duckworth, who happened to have been a student of Martin Seligman, gave that something a name. She called it grit.[12] According to Duckworth's theory, grit has two essential components: passion and perseverance.

Passion is all about focusing on one thing and ignoring everything else. Juggling too many projects can be distracting, can eat up your time and energy, and can make you less effective. As the Danish philosopher and theologian Soren Kierkegaard said, "Purity of heart is to will one thing."

Focusing on one thing boosts your chances of success for two reasons. First, it lets you pour all your resources into a solitary and important pursuit. Second, it frees you from other constraints. When you care about only one thing – whether it is your business, academic career, or athletic goals – you can let go of other considerations, such as spending time with family and friends, and do whatever it takes to achieve your passion.

Henri Matisse, the renowned Impressionist master, remarked: "I had nothing in my head other than painting."[13] And Marie Curie, the two-time Nobel Prize laureate who discovered radioactivity, lived "in a world quite removed from human beings,"[14] spending all her time in her laboratory and experiencing recurrent bouts of depression. All these widely known and celebrated individuals had great passion, and they attained immense Significance.

So, passion inspires grit, and grit may enhance chances of success and Significance. But how does someone become passionate about an activity or a topic, and can everyone develop a passion? Psychological research suggests that passion can develop in two ways that reinforce each other: having a strong desire for something, or believing that you can get it. To develop a passion for Significance, a person should be ambitious to begin with, and have faith in being able to realize ambitions.

Some people are simply born more ambitious than others; they are genetically wired that way. But parenting and child-rearing practices can also contribute to ambition. Remember our discussion in Chapter 5 about two types of focus, promotion and prevention, that can be nurtured through parenting? Promotion-oriented people dream of achievement and advancement, as they boldly reach for the stars and seek opportunities to achieve their goals. In contrast, prevention-oriented people are happy to avoid losses, and they get motivated only when a threat to their safety looms large.

According to Tory Higgins, the Columbia University professor whose work we discussed in Chapters 2 and 4, the promotion focus develops through parenting that rewards the child's successes and withdraws affection in response to the child's failures. Parenting that induces the prevention focus punishes the child for failures and stays neutral or unresponsive to the child's successes.

What about adulthood? Is our ambitiousness determined by the parenting we received, or can we shape and control it ourselves? Can we, in other words, develop ambition as an adult? The answer is yes, we can.

One way that your ambitiousness and promotion focus can develop is through the "learned optimism" and "growth mindset" techniques developed by Martin Seligman and Carol Dweck, respectively. Being optimistic and undeterred by failures encourages you to want more out of life, to aspire to greater things, and to quest for greater Significance.

Whereas learned optimism and a growth mindset produce a generally positive expectancy about your future successes, your specific circumstances also matter. When you feel you have a shot at greatness, this awakens a desire for greatness – what we could call a gritty passion for action that will potentially bring it about. For instance, some children[15] who show great talent for music, athletics, or science can quickly realize that this is their ticket to recognition, and they will relentlessly pursue this career path.

A striking example is the story of Daniel Barenboim, one of the world's most distinguished musicians. Barenboim debuted as a pianist at age 7 and quickly gained a reputation as a child prodigy. At age 14, he made his debut in London with the Royal Philharmonic Orchestra, and a year later he was playing at Carnegie Hall in New York. His passion for music and his grit in pursuing it are legendary. As a stellar pianist and highly sought-after conductor, he traversed the globe during his seven-decade career, directing orchestras from Berlin to Milan, Chicago to Paris. And it all started with the discovery of his immense musical talent early in his childhood.

Another example from an entirely different domain is Michael Jordan, who won six NBA titles and five Most Valuable Player awards. The man considered by many to be the best basketball player in history is known for his fierce competitiveness, his grit, and the obstacles he needed to overcome on his way up. As he himself put it:

> I've missed more than 9,000 shots in my career. I've lost almost 300 games. Twenty-six times, I've been trusted to take the game-winning shot and missed. I've failed over and over and over again in my life. And that is why I succeed.[16]

If you look back at 1978, when Jordan was a high school sophomore in Wilmington, North Carolina, you will be surprised to learn that he failed to make the varsity basketball team. Relegated to the junior varsity, he himself recalled:

> I went to my room, and I closed the door and I cried. For a while I couldn't stop. Even though there was no one else home at the time, I kept the door shut. It was important to me that no one hear me or see me.[17]

Yet, Jordan did not give up. With his mother's encouragement, he leveraged his failure and disappointment to drive himself to do better and better. On the junior varsity team, he often worked himself to near exhaustion. As he told an interviewer: "Whenever I was working out and got tired and figured I ought to stop, I'd close my eyes and see that list in the locker room without my name on it, and that usually got me going again."[18]

Jordan had good reasons to expect to succeed in the end, as he was blessed with incomparable abilities suited to basketball. He could leap at least 44 inches and possibly as high as 48 inches. He grew to be 6'6" tall (198 cm), he had huge hands, and he developed a style of flowing gracefully on the court that no one has bettered.

As sportswriter Rick Morrissey put it,

Michael was born with that talent, an unrivaled talent. He turned himself into the best player he could be by hard work and determination,
but there was no one who had been given his package of skills. Talent
first, then desire. Not the other way around.[19]

So, when you are endowed with outstanding talent, as were Barenboim
and Jordan, you know that stardom is within reach. That confidence can
instill in you the kind of passion and grit that give you the chance to realize
your potential. Of course, most of us mortals are not as talented as those
two galactic superstars, not even close. Can most people also develop a
similar passion? The answer is yes. Occasionally, an opportunity arises that
promises Significance, and people may latch onto it passionately and with
abandon.

The Significance opportunities that can be so inspiring need not be selfish. They could involve volunteering for a lofty cause – and there is something empowering about the readiness to make personal sacrifices for what
one sees as a sacred value. The cause can be humanistic and pro-social, for
instance helping the poor or promoting racial equality.

It can also be defending your country or fighting the enemies of your
culture and religion. An estimated 40,000 foreign fighters traveled to
Syria to join the Islamic State's so-called Caliphate, including many who
left affluent, secure lives with promising prospects – but those comforts
seemed like nothing compared with the glory of martyrdom or the glamor
and Significance of heroism. Members of Islamist terror groups who volunteer for suicidal missions (shahada in Arabic) often do so with a deep sense
of gratitude for an opportunity to do something that would make them
worthy of entering Paradise.

We again take note of Marwan Abu Abeida, the young Iraqi in Abu
Musab al Zarqawi's terror group, mentioned in Chapter 6, who was thrilled
to be assigned to a squad of suicide bombers. "It does not matter whether
people know what I did," he told TIME's Bobby Ghosh. "The only person
who matters is Allah – and the only question he will ask me is, 'How many
infidels did you kill?'"[20]

To develop a passion, you need to believe that it is your ticket to greatness
and that pursuing it will make you highly special and significant. Passion
and grit do not ensure success, but they are necessary for it, as nothing of

great value is ever achieved without them. They are essential for the "attack mode" of striving for success and mattering.

The Significance of Others

The advice and practical suggestions that social scientists offer for improving people's chances of success are focused on individuals, their optimism, mindset, and grit. But success and attaining Significance also depend on your ability to obtain and retain the goodwill of others – people whose respect you seek and desire. And the main way of doing that is through enhancing other people's Significance.

Look at it as a transaction. Whenever anyone has something to sell – because in a way we are talking about you marketing yourself as a product – it is beneficial to make the "buyer" also feel significant and worthy in the transaction. If the deal is closed, both the "buyer" and "seller" feel a boost in their sense of mattering.

This can be tricky in a competitive domain, or even worse in a "put-down" culture where one person's success is regarded as the other's failure. Yet even there, considering the loser's Significance is essential. Winston Churchill understood this well when he uttered his famous recommendation to be magnanimous in victory.[21] This notion is not just a noble gesture or a show of empathy toward the vanquished. It is based on the realization that a loss of face is likely to induce a negative attitude from the defeated party – and will likely translate into the enemy's motivation to undermine the winner in the future by avenging the humiliation.

This idea is not limited to the aftermath of a war or a struggle, where there are clear winners and losers. It is equally applicable to any relationship with an element of competitiveness. For instance, in writing a scientific article for publication, it is important to acknowledge and show appreciation for other scholars who addressed the topic earlier. Beyond civility, etiquette, and good scholarship, it is also smart academic politics. The scholars in the same field are likely to serve as peer reviewers of your work, once or more. According them the respect that they deserve is likely to blunt somewhat the sharpness of their criticism. As Robert Cialdini, the expert on basking in reflected glory, put it, "People don't sink the boats they are riding in."[22]

The Marshall Plan

A real-world example of magnanimity in the wake of victory is the treatment by the United States of its erstwhile enemies: Germany, Italy, and Japan. When World War II ended in 1945, Europe lay in ruins. Its cities were shattered; its economies devastated; its people facing widespread hunger. To meet this emergency, Secretary of State George Marshall proposed in 1947 that European nations create a plan for their economic reconstruction based on economic assistance the United States would contribute. Roughly $12 billion was spent to facilitate the famous Marshall Plan in 17 European countries.

Although Japan was not included in the plan, the United States took strong steps – after winning the war by devastating two Japanese cities with the first atomic bombs – to help bring Japan into the international community as a peaceful nation with fresh attitudes.

Japan, Germany, and Italy all benefited from political, economic, and military ties with the United States and became its allies, closely aligned with its ideals of liberty and civil rights. Some observers of international politics believe that the diplomatic and other initiatives by the United States were a key part of preventing a World War III. The magnanimous approach stood in stark contrast to the Versailles Treaty that humiliated Germany as World War I ended, thus planting the seeds of World War II.

Although these examples pertain to international relations, keep in mind that nations have human beings as their leaders and citizens. Psychology is extremely pertinent, and it highlights the idea that paying attention to people's Significance will usually induce a readiness to give respect and Significance to those who treat them with respect.

Summary

In the grand theater of life, success takes center stage. It bestows Significance upon those who achieve it, shaping our cultural narratives across time. From ancient civilizations to modern societies, the pursuit of success has fueled our collective journey.

Let us dwell in the realm of psychology – a treasure trove of tools designed to amplify our chances of success. Here we find optimism, the elixir that infuses hope into our endeavors. The growth mindset beckons us to embrace challenges as stepping stones, while grit fortifies our resolve against adversity. These psychological allies collaborate to raise our expectation of success, intertwining with our perception of its value.

Picture this: leaders who weave Significance into the fabric of their actions. Their followers, like bees drawn to nectar, shower them with admiration. Spouses, too, wield this magic – making their partners feel cherished, valued, and irreplaceable. Even parents, through their nurturing touch, evoke gratitude from their children. Significance, it seems, is the secret sauce that flavors our achievements.

Yet, there is a darker path, and it is one paved with the stones of belittlement. When we put down other people, we think we might add somewhat to our Significance, but that is a double-edged sword. The insulted person's desire for revenge simmers beneath the surface, threatening the victor's moment in the sun. A precarious dance ensues – a competitive spiral where elation and misery waltz together.

So, as we chase success, let us remember: It is not just about personal triumphs. It is about lifting others, leaving a legacy of Significance that echoes far beyond our short-term victories.

Notes

1 Weber, Max, *The Protestant Ethic and the Spirit of Capitalism* (New York: Scribner, 1905).
2 Calvin, John, *Institutes of the Christian Religion* (Peabody, MA: Hendrickson Publishers, 2008). Calvin published his first edition in 1536.
3 "It Takes 300 Worker Salaries to Equal the Average CEO's Pay, Data Show," based on an AFL-CIO (labor unions federation) report (July 14, 2021); found at www.cbsnews.com/news/ceo-pay-300-worker-salaries-compensation.
4 *World Economic Forum* (December 7, 2017); found at www.weforum.org/agenda/2017/12/chart-of-the-day-americas-richest-1-own-40-of-the-countrys-wealth/.
5 Mutz, Diana C., "Status Threat, Not Economic Hardship, Explains the 2016 Presidential Vote," *Proceedings of the National Academy of Sciences*, Vol. 115, No. 19 (2018), pp. E4330–E4339.
6 Koepp, Spencer, *Time/Life's The Bible: 50 Most Important People* (New York: Time-Life, 2014).
7 *Subliminal Messages: The Hidden Controversy* (Santa Barbara: CJ & Co., 2023); found at www.cjco.com.au/article/subliminal-messages-the-hidden-controversy
8 Lane, Terry, *Laws Governing Subliminal Messages in Advertisements* (Houston Chronicle, undated); found at smallbusiness.chron.com/laws-governing-subliminal-messages-advertisements-72074.html.

9   Seligman, Martin E.P., *Learned Optimism: How to Change Your Mind and Your Life* (New York: Vintage, 2006).

10 Danner, Deborah D.; Snowdon, David A.; Friesen, Wallace V., "Positive Emotions in Early Life and Longevity: Findings from the Nun Study," *Journal of Personality and Social Psychology*, Vol. 80, No. 5 (2001), pp. 804–813.

11 Bosma, Niels B.; Hill, Susan; Ionescu-Somers, Aileen; Kelley, Donna; Guerrero, Michael; Schott, Thomas, *GEM 2020/2021 Global Report* (London: Global Entrepreneurship Monitor, 2020); found at www.gemconsortium.org/file/open?fileId=50691.

12 Duckworth, Angela, *Grit: The Power of Passion and Perseverance* (New York: Scribner, 2016).

13 Spurling, Hilary, *The Unknown Matisse: A Life of Henry Matisse: The Early Years, 1869–1908* (Oakland: University of California Press, 1998).

14 Goldsmith, Barbara, *Obsessive Genius: The Inner World of Marie Curie* (New York: Norton, 2005).

15 Other talented children who have less inborn ambition, or an exaggerated fear of failure, may shy away from realizing their talents and even self-handicap to be recognized as brilliant "could-have-beens" who chose not to achieve.

16 Stibel, Jeffrey, "Michael Jordan: A Profile in Failure," in *CSQ* (Los Angeles: CSQ, August 29, 2017); found at csq.com/2017/08/Michael-jordan-profile-failure/.

17 Ibid.

18 Ibid.

19 Morrissey, Richard, "Massive Talent, Not Steely Determination, Fueled Michael Jordan's Success," *Chicago Sun-Times* (May 1, 2020).

20 Ghosh, Bobby, "The ISIS Suicide Bomber's Perspective," *TIME* Magazine (June 22, 2008).

21 Churchill, Winston, *The Second World War*, 6 volumes (Boston: Houghton Mifflin, 1953-58). Churchill encapsulated his themes as: "In War: Resolution, In Defeat: Defiance, In Victory: Magnanimity, In Peace: Goodwill."

22 Cialdini, Robert B., *Influence: The Psychology of Persuasion*, Revised Edition (New York: Harper Business, 2006).

9

ALIGN FOR SIGNIFICANCE

Significance is something we receive from others, even if those individuals are merely imagined, remembered, or represented as voices in our head. Typically, however, people whose good opinion we seek are "real" people, members of our social network whose worldview and narratives we share (as outlined in Chapter 7 on need, narrative, and network). Being immersed in a social network that affirms our values and pays us respect and appreciation is the ideal situation. It constitutes agreement with the people we care about the most, concerning a topic we care about the most: ourselves!

Often, however, things are not so ideal. We might find ourselves thrust into a social milieu that finds who we are – or what we are (perhaps our gender, looks, race, age, or ethnicity) – to be worthless, or worse yet despicable and hateful. How can we maintain our positive sense of self in those circumstances, gratifying our Quest for Significance, when everyone around treats us with nothing but disdain?

DOI: 10.4324/9781003410706-9

There are two possibilities. One is changing our social network to a group more aligned with our values. The second is changing the network itself from within, through concerted group action.

The Ugly Duckling Story

The first strategy is exemplified metaphorically by Hans Christian Andersen's beautiful fairy tale, *The Ugly Duckling*. The story is about a little swan who grew up among ducks, where he was considered "ugly" (hence accorded low Significance) because his characteristics and appearance were so different from the ideal of "duckness." As Andersen tells it, the poor creature was bitten, pushed, and made fun of not only by the ducks, but by all dwellers of the farm.

> So it went on from day to day till it got worse and worse. The poor duckling was driven away by everyone; even his brothers and sisters were unkind to him, and would say, 'Ah, you ugly creature, I wish the cat would get you,' and his mother said she wished he had never been born. The ducks pecked him, the chickens beat him, and the girl who fed the poultry kicked him with her feet. So at last he ran away, frightening the little birds in the hedge as he flew over the palings.[1]

After trials and tribulations, the duckling found himself in the company of beautiful swans, and he fearfully expected them to violently reject him. If lowly ducks and chickens saw him as ugly and despicable, the gorgeous swans could only be expected to feel so evermore. Miraculously, however, the very opposite happened: When he bent his neck in submission to the swans, expecting outrage,

> he saw in the clear stream below his own image; no longer a dark, gray bird, ugly and disagreeable to look at, but a graceful and beautiful swan.
>
> He now felt glad at having suffered sorrow and trouble, because it enabled him to enjoy so much better all the pleasure and happiness around him as the great swans swam round the newcomer, and stroked his neck with their beaks, as a welcome.[2]

At last, his doleful journey ended. He was now home among his kind, truly appreciated for who he was. So, the story has a happy ending. The ugly duckling found out he was not ugly at all, according to the standards of the new network he happily discovered!

Intriguingly, Andersen wrote this story while thinking about himself, as he attested to the critic Georg Brandes in an interview, stating that The Ugly Duckling tale is "a reflection of my own life."[3] Young Hans was described as a tall, ugly boy with a big nose and big feet, who was mocked and bullied by other boys. He grew up poor, receiving only a basic education and being forced to support himself from a very early age. During his school years, which he called the darkest and most bitter period of his life, he had to endure depression and abuse. Finally, just like the duckling in the story, Andersen's own trials and tribulations had a happy ending.

His story about finding joy when discovering the right environment – or network – enjoyed immediate success, and his entire book of fairy tales quickly sold out, destined to be reprinted in various editions for 200 years or more.

Born Unfree

In parallel to the fate of the "ugly duckling" in the fable, millions of people throughout history have been born into societies where their social worth was doomed. A striking example can be found in the horrendous indignities suffered for over two centuries (1619 to 1865) by enslaved black people in America. These included sexual abuse, rape, and severe corporal punishments such as whipping and bodily mutilation. Spouses were often separated from each other, as were parents and children. Families were broken through the sales of some of their members, usually never to see or hear of each other again.[4]

One of the few ways for a man or woman to restore their sense of mattering in those circumstances was to escape the humiliating conditions that entrapped them.

An indelible example of escape was the journey of runaway slaves who left the plantations of the South and headed North through what has been called the Underground Railroad. This consisted of a network of people, both whites and free blacks, committed to helping runaways from slave-holding states to travel to states in the North and to Canada, where slavery was outlawed.

It was a dangerous trip. Slave-catchers with guns and dogs were constantly searching for runaways to capture. The fugitives risked being spotted by individuals keen on collecting the rewards promised for turning in runaway slaves. They were often hungry, cold, and frightened. Yet, according to some estimates, between 1810 and 1850, the Underground Railroad helped to guide 100,000 enslaved people to freedom[5] and the dignity – the Significance – that freedom bestows.

Among the escaped slaves was Frederick Douglass, later renowned as a celebrated author, orator, and abolitionist. Disguised as a sailor, Douglass boarded a northbound train, and upon reaching New York City on September 3, 1838, he declared himself free. His feeling was simple: unmatched exhilaration. As he recounted,

> I have often been asked how I felt when first I found myself on free soil. There is scarcely anything in my experience about which I could not give a more satisfactory answer. A new world had opened upon me. If life is more than breath and the 'quick round of blood,' I lived more in that one day than in a year of my slave life. It was a time of joyous excitement which words can but tamely describe.[6]

Striking and dramatic as it was, the escape of many African Americans from slavery is but one example of people attempting to shift their social networks to enhance their social worth. For instance, in Russia, where the common folk have endured miserable lives, Communism promised grandeur and Significance, and thus many rural residents, primarily poor peasants, happily joined collective farms,[7] one of Communism's touted inventions. Their transition to these kolkhoz arrangements was facilitated by the intense propaganda of the ruling party, centered on peasant women, portraying them flatteringly as a new archetype: the Red Heroine.

A Russian woman using the pen name Pasha Angelina was the founder of the first all-female tractor brigade in the Soviet Union in the 1930s, and an enthusiastic supporter of dictator Stalin's often brutal reforms. In her memoir, Angelina expressed her unqualified adoration of the party leader and waxed idealistic about her Significance as a tractor driver working on the collective farms, the idealized new networks. She wrote: "It is much more than a job for me – it is my place in the struggle for five-year plans… the source of my happiness, prosperity, and fame."[8]

It is interesting that in Russia's Western neighbor, Ukraine, the average farmer was relatively well off and happy with things as they were, and Communism's lofty promises sounded hollow, so the farmers refused to give up personal ownership and join collectives. That was a key reason for a war that Russia – after its Bolshevik revolution – waged against Ukraine, from 1917 to 1919. After Ukraine was absorbed into the Soviet Union in 1922, there were waves of repression against Ukrainians, culminating in a famine that Stalin orchestrated, the infamous Holodomor of 1931 to 1934 in which at least 5 million Ukrainians died of starvation. This awful human suffering was all a result of Stalin attempting to force Ukrainians into networks (the collective farms), which they considered to be Significance-depleting compared to their social milieus of yore.

Our last, but by no means least, important example of people seeking Significance-promising social contexts – and being willing to move to enjoy them – is migration. In the late 1800s, people in many parts of the world decided to leave their homes and immigrate to the United States, viewed as a land of freedom and economic opportunity. Escaping the humiliating prospect of poverty, many came to the United States fleeing crop failure, land and job shortages, rising taxes, and famine. Others, like Eastern European Jews, came to America seeking personal freedom or relief from the indignities of political and religious persecution.

Between 1870 and 1900, the United States absorbed nearly 12 million immigrants from Europe. In parallel, over 320,000 Chinese immigrants arrived in the United States between the start of California's Gold Rush in 1849 and 1882, when federal law prohibited their immigration.[9] Chinese Americans played a huge role in extending America's railways to the West Coast and also worked in agriculture and new factories.

Moving to a different society – or to a network that promises a boost in social worth through liberation from bondage, escape from religious or political discrimination, or the opportunity for rising "from rags to riches" – has been a major phenomenon affecting world history and shaping the destiny of nations.

Homogeneous Schooling

In an interconnected world, homogeneous schooling can foster a supportive network where social identity – often stigmatized in broader society

– no longer hinders a person's social worth. A compelling example of this phenomenon lies in all-girls' schools and their remarkable success in empowering women. Despite substantial progress toward gender equality over the past century, significant gaps persist, and societies continue to navigate a male-dominated landscape.

Girls' schools offer a unique space where young women encounter positive role models: accomplished women in leadership roles, principals, teachers, and successful alumnae. These institutions also prioritize critical women's issues, including education, how not to be bound by traditional societal roles, and female health. Importantly, all-girls' schools eliminate preferential treatment for male students, avoiding any invidious inequities that might undermine female students' confidence.

The nurturing environment of girls' schools deliberately cultivates self-assurance, independence, and assertiveness. Moreover, these schools provide unparalleled opportunities for leadership development: opportunities that might otherwise elude young women in co-educational environments dominated by male peers. Whether participating in student government, managing clubs, or captaining athletic teams, girls thrive in single-sex school settings.

Research studies from various corners of the globe consistently affirm the significant benefits that girls derive from attending all-girls' schools.[10] These institutions not only educate but also empower, shaping confident, capable women who contribute to a more equitable society. Analytical work on this topic conducted in Britain reveals that girls attending all-female schools exhibit greater "mental toughness," better emotional control, and higher confidence than girls attending co-educational schools. Research done in the United States shows that young women in all-girls' schools have higher self-esteem, are more interested in non-traditional subjects such as science and math, and are less likely to settle for stereotyped jobs and careers. Various academic and other advantages to girls that result from attending all-girls' schools have been demonstrated in research carried out in Australia, Chile, and Israel, as well as in the United States.[11]

These findings support the idea that being immersed in a social network that eliminates a negative factor – what psychologists describe as stigmatized social identity such as gender – will likely boost a person's sense of Significance and social worth, increasing self-confidence, and generally empowering the ability to cope with life's challenges and to pursue success in all endeavors.

A similar logic extends to the positive impact of all-black colleges and universities on students' sense of Significance. In 2004, Gary Oates, a sociologist at Bowling Green University, carried out a study assessing the impact of attending colleges with higher black enrollment on the self-esteem of African Americans, and he found a correlation between graduates' post-college self-esteem and the proportion of black students at their college.[12] In other words, the larger the network of African Americans in a given college, the greater the network of individuals who would not discriminate against or devalue a person of color.

Studies conducted in the early 1970s by Morris Rosenberg and Roberta Simmons[13] and by Jerald Bachman[14] support the idea that African Americans in segregated schools scored higher on self-esteem than black students in integrated schools, again supporting the idea that being part of a network that does not devalue your attributes contributes to your sense of Significance and self-worth.

Interestingly, research also suggests that despite lower academic outcomes, the self-esteem of African American college students at primarily white institutions is not any lower than that of white students. Professors Toni Schmader, Brenda Major, and Richard Granzow,[15] in agreement with Cheryl Van Laar,[16] explain this in terms of African American students generally not considering academic outcomes to be a major source of Significance and social worth, and their attributing mediocre or poor grade-point averages to systemic prejudice.

Claude Steele, a professor at Stanford, viewed this more generally as African American students' "disidentification" with primarily white academic institutions, meaning that they did not derive their prestige from that university and frankly did not care about it a lot.[17]

In the context of predominantly white institutions, African American students often find their sense of social belonging within a distinct black ingroup. Unlike the broader university community, this ingroup draws its sense of worth from values beyond academics. Consequently, these students do not suffer from the race-related stigma that can plague their academic experiences.

Forced Insignificance

In truth, the dynamics of social networks are multifaceted. While some relocations or similar shifts enhance an individual's sense of Significance, others can lead to forced insignificance. Consider the highly unpleasant realities of jails and prison camps. In the worst of these harrowing environments, individuals – even if they had been respected community members with illustrious careers – become dehumanized, powerless, and perhaps even starved. Their very survival hinges on the whims of guards, a stark reminder of the fragility of human worth.[18]

Victor Frankl, a Jewish Austrian psychiatrist who survived several Nazi concentration camps to become a major theorist, psychotherapist, and author of a vastly influential book, *Man's Search for Meaning*, remarked, "The most painful part of beatings is the insult they imply,"[19] as being physically tortured was often accompanied by painfully demeaning words. In one poignant incident that Frankl recalled, a foreman at the camp, apparently dissatisfied with Frankl's pace of work, spouted the following indignities at the emaciated prisoner: "You pig. I have been watching you the whole time! I'll teach you to work, yet! Wait till you dig dirt with your teeth – you'll die like an animal! In two days I'll finish you off! You have never done a stroke of work in your life. What were you, swine, a businessman?"

Even though Frankl knew there was little point in answering, the insults moved him to defend his dignity by replying, "I was a doctor, a specialist."[20] As Frankl aptly explained, "There are moments when indignation can rouse even a seemingly hardened prisoner – indignation not about cruelty or pain but about the insult connected with it."[21]

Incarceration in the public jail system of modern democracies is hardly comparable to Nazi concentration camps, yet it also involves degradation at the hands of the guards and other prisoners.[22] In the United States, nearly 2 million people are incarcerated in cramped spaces that lack fresh air, healthy food, natural light, proper health care, and connection to loved ones. Prisons in America undergo little or no public oversight, and they are often venues where humiliation and abuse reign.

The carceral environment can be inherently damaging to mental health by removing people from society and eliminating meaning and purpose from their lives. It is a condition in which people lose their sense of Significance and mattering. Before being incarcerated, they were free men and women, citizens with rights and privileges, but behind bars they are turned into depersonalized and defenseless figures. They are often referred to by numbers rather than names, officially considered "property" of the Bureau of Prisons or a similar agency and hence fair game for cruelty and abuse.

Mandatory Retirement

Perhaps surprisingly, a non-violent process such as mandatory retirement – being forced out of your job because you reached some arbitrary age – triggers similar problems in the individual. A person is compelled to leave the social context that gave them the utmost sense of Significance, their workplace and career – leaving them to their own devices to fill the Significance vacuum thus created.

Most European member states, except for the United Kingdom, Denmark, and Poland, practice mandatory retirement (at ages varying from 60 to 75 depending on country and profession) as national policy; as do most members of the Organization for Economic Co-operation and Development, except for Canada, Australia, New Zealand, and the United States.[23]

Typically, the rationale for mandatory retirement is that people's efficiency in producing goods and services declines significantly after age 70, so that the worker's departure avoids a reduction in overall productivity. Because the mandated retirement age is arbitrary and not based on individual evaluation of the worker, the practice is viewed in some quarters as a form of age discrimination.

Whether mandatory or not, retirement represents a life change that is stressful for many people. Think especially of individuals whose jobs gave them a sense of considerable social worth and Significance; they may feel a sense of acute loss of mattering upon retirement.

Indeed, some studies have linked retirement to a decline in health. A 2020 study published in the journal *Healthcare* found that about one-third of retirees in the United States experience mental health issues such as depression.[24] Before that, a study in the journal *Social Science & Medicine* in 2012 found that retired people, especially those in the first year of retirement, are more likely to experience a heart attack or stroke than similarly aged individuals who kept working.[25]

Indeed, much of the advice that departing workers hear for successfully coping with the so-called "retirement blues" involves finding a social context, a new network that appreciates what you are capable of *now*, rather than the social worth you *used to have* when fully engaged in the workforce – the Significance you had to relinquish on retirement. Such tips include volunteering for a charitable cause, making new friends in retirement by joining a club devoted to an activity that gives you a sense of purpose, enrolling in classes, or developing a hobby.[26] All these are ways of being appreciated by others for who you are, what you know, and what you are still very able to do.

Colonialism

One nation conquering or acquiring the homeland of some other nation is another example of dislocation and a huge change to the network in which people live.

Imagine a chessboard where each piece represents a person – a pawn, a queen, or a king. Now, consider that we can move these pieces not just across squares but through entire social landscapes. Sometimes, the journey leads to places of empowerment and self-worth – a vibrant community, a supportive network. But other times, it takes us to darker corners: prisons, concentration camps, or the shadowed territories of occupied lands.

Whole nations, like individual pawns, can find themselves trapped in a game they did not choose. European colonialism, spanning centuries and continents, serves as a vivid example. Picture the explorers' ships slicing through oceans, leaving behind a wake of conquest. The Americas, Africa, and Asia were all drawn into this grand chess match. But what happened when the pieces landed on those distant squares?

Hannah Arendt, the philosopher, penned her thoughts in her book, *On Violence*. She peeled back the layers of dehumanization – calling "the victory of violence" self-defeating[27] – reminiscent of how colonizers stripped the colonized of their Significance.

Jean-Paul Sartre, in his preface to Frantz Fanon's *The Wretched of the Earth*, echoed this sentiment. Sartre's words cut through the fog of history:

> Orders are given to reduce the inhabitants of occupied territory to the
> level of a superior ape to justify the colonist's treatment of them as

> beasts of burden... No effort is spared to demolish their traditions to substitute our language for theirs, and to destroy their culture without giving them ours.... We exhaust them into a mindless state. Shame and fear warp their character and dislocate their personality.[28]

Fanon himself goes even farther in stating that "the colonist turns the colonized into a kind of quintessence of evil. Colonized society is not merely portrayed as a society without values... The 'native' is declared impervious to ethics, representing not only the absence of values but also the negation of values. He is... the enemy of values. In other words, absolute evil."[29]

Another prominent example of domination by a group that severely reduced the Significance of a people's network was the humiliating indignity of the majority black population of South Africa under the apartheid regime that lasted from 1948 to 1994. Apartheid laws and policies banned black people from entering urban areas without immediately finding a job. Black people were also prohibited from marrying white people, and from setting up businesses in white areas. They endured wanton brutality by the police. Most public spaces, from hospitals to beaches, were segregated. Education was restricted. And throughout the 1950s, the all-white government passed law after law regulating the movement and lives of black people. Apartheid came to an end in the early 1990s after years of violent internal protest, international sanctions and boycotts, and economic struggles.

Indeed, as mentioned earlier, fighting for the Significance of your network is the alternative to just running away. It is quite natural to want to escape a circumstance where your Significance and dignity are compromised. That would be your change of network. Relocation to a different social context may not always seem feasible or morally acceptable, however. Often, it could be seen as a "cop-out" or outright abandonment of others who are in need. An alternative, however, is to stand one's ground and fight for the Significance of your network from within the society at large.

Fighting for Significance

People whose Significance has been compromised by exploitation and discrimination may choose to unite, so they can attempt to change the norms of a society that has been denying them social worth. Major revolutions that shook the world in recent centuries exhibit this dynamic.

The French Revolution of 1789 is regarded by some as the most important event of modern history. It was fueled by the peasants' and the bourgeoisie's sense of insignificance and exploitation by the privileged nobles and by the profligate monarchy of King Louis XVI and Queen Marie Antoinette.

Feudal France was neatly divided into three social classes, or Estates, with distinct jobs and privileges. The clergy was the First Estate, the nobles were the Second Estate, and the peasants and the growing bourgeoisie were in the Third and largest Estate, and the one that had the fewest rights. The growing literacy in 18th-century France allowed for Enlightenment philosophers (such as Voltaire, Montesquieu, and Rousseau) to be widely read. Their egalitarian ideas and the notion that a king's legitimacy depends on the people's consent raised the consciousness of members of the Third Estate. They were reading about and then loudly discussing the humiliating injustices that the monarchic system was imposing on them. The situation – and forming a narrative that could fuel a network – strongly incited their outrage against the nobility, ultimately ending that era of monarchy in France and the feudal system of governance.[30]

Feelings of disempowerment and insignificance were also the main psychological reasons why American colonists initiated the American Revolution that led to independence from Great Britain in 1776. The colonists were angry and upset about being treated by the British Parliament as second-class quasi-citizens devoid of rights accorded to other subjects of the Crown. Residents of America were denied any representation in Parliament and were subjected to increasing taxes levied specifically on the colonists. On April 19, 1775, open warfare erupted, launching the Revolutionary War that ended in 1783 with victory for the American colonists who established the United States of America.[31]

A deep sense of indignity and insignificance among colonized people across the continents of Africa and Asia fueled anticolonial movements that brought autonomy or outright independence from European colonial rule to thirty new independent nations between 1945 and 1960.[32]

In some cases, the anti-colonialist struggle was peaceful and orderly. In others, like in the battle for Algiers, it was violent and bloody. We may quote Jean-Paul Sartre again – with his view of anti-colonial violence as cleansing and adding to the rebels' dignity:

> The colonized are cured of colonial neurosis by driving the colonist
> out by force... Either one must remain terrified or be terrifying... When
> the peasants lay hands on a gun, the old myths fade. For the first
> phase of the revolt, killing is a necessity: killing a European is kill-
> ing two birds with one stone, eliminating in one go oppressor and
> oppressed: leaving one man dead and the other man free.[33]

A striking example of peaceful struggle against colonial masters is Mahatma Gandhi's non-violent non-cooperation, which he called Satyagraha ("devotion to truth"), that helped India gain independence from the British in 1947. Gandhi's peaceful resistance was influenced by Henry David Thoreau's 1849 essay advocating "Civil Disobedience," and the Indian example influenced other major social movements that adopted peaceful struggle to combat discrimination and indignity dished out by one social group against another.

In the United States, Gandhi's success influenced two of the country's most important mass mobilizations: the civil rights struggle for equality for African Americans led by Martin Luther King, Jr., until he was assassinated in 1968, and Cesar Chavez's advocacy for Latino farmworkers in the 1960s and 1970s.

Across the globe, Gandhi's philosophy helped inspire movements that toppled dictators from Ferdinand Marcos in the Philippines in 1986 and Augusto Pinochet in Chile in 1990, to the Communist regimes in Eastern Europe in the late 1980s and Slobodan Milosevic in Serbia in 2000.

Most social movements are mobilized to help some category of downtrodden individuals who feel disrespected and deprived of social worth. Their goal is clear, and the underlying psychology is no mystery: They want to effect the kind of societal change that would bring them Significance and dignity. In that category belongs, for instance, the feminist movement that did a lot to eliminate the undignified, inferior status of women in many societies around the world. The "Black Lives Matter" movement, especially active in the United States in 2020, decrying violence unleashed by police against African Americans, highlights the importance of mattering and Significance in its very name.

To be sure, not all social movements vowing to help the downtrodden and the disempowered are liberal or humanitarian. Fascism that emerged in Italy after World War I condoned violence and war as legitimate means to national rejuvenation and the enhancement of a national sense of Significance. Death and destruction resulted, of course, and Fascism typically linked itself to a claim of racial purity or belonging to a master race.

That kind of ideology often aligns itself with justifying genocides, massacres, forced sterilizations, and mass deportations of some allegedly impure "other" in society, such as Jews, Gypsies, or homosexuals.

Adolf Hitler's National Socialism ruled Germany's Third Reich for 12 years, from 1933 to 1945, and the mania of Nazi beliefs coupled with a huge military buildup resulted in World War II and the deaths of more than 80 million people. Again, the psychology is clear. Germans felt shamed by their loss in the 1914–1918 World War and, even worse, the terms of the Treaty of Versailles. Hitler rose to power by vowing to end the national humiliation and a severe economic recession blamed on Versailles and on Jews. He was pledging to restore national Significance. That was reason enough for a heartless dictator to order the murder of Europe's Jews, and 6 million perished.

The modern white supremacist movement in the United States and Europe subscribes to versions of the "Great Replacement Theory." Its basic claim is that there is a conspiracy orchestrated by elites and Jews to replace white people with immigrants, Muslims, and other people of color. This theory was first proposed by Renaud Camus, a Frenchman who popularized it in his 2011 book Le Grand Remplacement. The concept spread like wildfire in Europe, particularly through the sprawling transnational white supremacist group Generation Identity and its social media accounts.[34]

Adherents of the Great Replacement theory have been responsible for an astounding number of mass casualty killings in the United States and elsewhere, including the 2017 white supremacist riots in Charlottesville, Virginia; the 2018 attack on the Tree of Life synagogue in Pittsburgh, Pennsylvania; the 2019 shooting in El Paso, Texas; the 2019 attack on a mosque in Christchurch, New Zealand; the 2019 attack in Halle, Germany, at a Yom Kippur event; and the 2020 attacks on bars in Hanau, Germany, that were frequented by immigrants. (The shooter in the Hanau attack, after murdering nine people, went home, fatally shot his mother, and then committed suicide. Police said he was a racist and a xenophobe.)[35]

Whether on the left or on the right, embracing broad humanistic ideals or narrow ethno-nationalistic or racist narratives, social movements are designed to effect change in society so that people who felt left out or downtrodden can find dignity and Significance in a changed and supposedly improved network.

The processes of shifting networks and/or striving to change current social networks can have momentous impacts on macro events in geopolitics. Yet the very same processes can also affect individual lives, as our examples of retirement and imprisonment demonstrate.

Divorce

Another striking example concerns the lives of married couples, and their reactions to friction – decisions made based on the loss of Significance that one or both members of a pair may suffer as their relationship dissolves.

When one member of a couple feels they no longer are significant to their partner, and are no longer lovable and special, divorce may be the result. Dissolving a marriage, thus, is an attempt to escape a social network (the couple) where one's Significance is compromised, and to seek other sources of Significance. The goal would often be a new relationship that makes the person feel that they matter.

A study by Paul Amato and Denise Previti of Penn State University found that the most cited reason for divorce was infidelity (28%).[36] And in a survey carried out in Oklahoma, a team of researchers investigated "the culture of marriage" and "the culture of divorce" and concluded that the most common reasons cited for marital breakup were lack of commitment (85%), too much conflict or arguing (61%), and again infidelity or extramarital affairs (58%).[37] Other studies found that a lack of sexual attention from the partner, or abusive attitudes and actions, are also causes of divorce.[38]

These varied reasons have one thing in common: the sense that you are no longer very important to your partner. Otherwise, why would she or he feel a need to carry out an extramarital affair, mistreat you, and/or repeatedly reject your opinions? In short, when you feel your partner no longer gives you the sense that you deserve their appreciation and respect, your motivation to stay in the relationship wanes.[39]

There is another reason, however, for wanting to get out of an intimate relationship, also related to the issue of Significance. The marriage might collapse when one spouse – because of physical or mental deterioration, or a substance abuse problem that stigmatizes them socially – is no longer able to give the other partner a sense of pride. One spouse's Significance is gone, and so they can no longer give some of it to their partner.

The status of the so-called "significant other" begins to feel wrongly named when there is no pride, no mutual respect, a lack of love in both directions, and Significance is being lost rather than reinforced.

The American government's National Health Interview Survey on Disability (NHIS-D) queried 50,000 households in 1994 and found that 20.7 percent of the disabled adults among those polled were divorced or separated, compared with 13.1 percent of those without disabilities.[40] And a study in Britain attributed a rise in mid-life divorces to men leaving their wives for younger women.[41]

There is a connection there, as to why marriages are failing in both those scenarios. It has to do with a decline in the Significance that one of the spouses is able to offer the other. Psychologists who track human evolution suggest that women have evolved to be attracted to powerful, well-resourced men to provide for their children during the long period of pregnancy and childrearing. Men, meanwhile, have evolved to care primarily about a woman's fertility, for which beauty and youth serve as helpful cues.

According to David Buss, a leading evolutionary psychologist, these differences between the genders persist despite the huge cultural changes that transformed relations between the sexes in many of today's societies.[42]

This creates an intriguing asymmetry, as analyzed for a heterosexual couple. As time goes on, both men and women can rightly feel that their power and resources have grown; but whether they admit it or not, their physical attractiveness (barring great cosmetics and cosmetic surgery) declines. Thus, the allure of the male to the female partner – marked by his self-confidence and wealth, typically – tends to grow. Sadly, the woman's allure in the eyes of the male partner is often weaker than it used to be.

This may seem merely superficial, and one can hope that an increasing number of people in Western society break away from the strictures of ancient patterns; but research shows that for most people there is still a stark difference in sources of felt Significance based on gender. Whereas women tend to gain Significance from their male partner's power and wealth, men tend to gain Significance from their female partner's beauty.

Relatedly, and perhaps to the shame of any enlightened male, a study carried out by a weight-loss company reported that 94 percent of the men who were questioned said that they would leave their wife if she got fat.[43] That result is not peer-reviewed or the most scientifically sound, but it has a familiar ring. So, analyzed through this book's prism, we conclude that a man might break up with his wife – for a younger or thinner woman – because when a younger woman finds an older man attractive, she is boosting his sense of Significance. And that allays his fear of losing his masculine appeal and the humiliating possibility of being no longer desirable. At the same time, a powerful older man offers a younger female a sense of status and Significance that is difficult to find with a young partner.

Frankly, in societies with increasing equality and fairness, substitute "woman" and "man" in that analysis, and you can understand why a woman who has wisdom, money, or both might drop her steadily less attractive husband. She may well find a new fountain of Significance when a younger man falls in love with her.

Even sexual satisfaction is often seen through the Significance lens, as a marker of performance that provides a sense of worth. In the 2024 film "Babygirl," Nicole Kidman stars as a senior executive who engages in a torrid affair with a much younger man at her office, mostly because she realizes that she has never climaxed during sex with her otherwise charming husband. Fully satisfying intimacy represents the Significance she seeks, even risking career-ending scandal.

Human experience and research findings attest that close relationships of any kind – if one of the partners no longer derives a sense of Significance from the other – are in danger of breaking up, because the dissatisfied partner may seek to repair a flagging sense of Significance elsewhere.

Patching up an Unsatisfactory Relationship

Breaking up is not the only way to restore a person's feeling of Significance that has suffered a decline in a relationship. In the same way that people who feel disempowered and discriminated against in a society (for instance, women, members of ethnic or racial minorities, or LGBTQ individuals) may strive to change the society to remedy the inequality, members of a couple who no longer feel appreciated and significant might try to mend the relationship. This is often accomplished with the help of couples therapy and/or marital counseling.

One of the biggest benefits of counseling is that it can clarify to both members of a couple each other's wants and needs. This would hopefully contribute to the partners providing for each other's needs, and hence the sense that they matter and are respected by the other. It could help both partners feel loved and understood (and hence Significant), which enhances intimacy and partners' satisfaction with the relationship.[44]

Summary

In our lives, we often find ourselves deeply embedded in social networks that diminish our sense of mattering and Significance. Whether as a member of a marginalized minority or simply feeling out of place due to our unique tendencies, talents, and interests, we grapple with this loss of Significance.

In response, we have two fundamental paths: First, we can seek a new network – one that appreciates our distinct attributes. Or, we can aim to elevate our standing within our current social context, advocating for ourselves or our group in an effort to win rights and dignity through political struggle. These choices – two basic ways of aligning for Significance – resonate not only in individual lives, but also in the collective movements that reshape societies and shape history.

Notes

1 Andersen, Hans Christian, "The Ugly Duckling," in *New Fairy Tales*, 1st Vol. (Copenhagen: C. A. Reitzel, 1843).

2 Andersen, Hans Christian, "The Ugly Duckling," in *New Fairy Tales*, 1st Vol. (Copenhagen: C. A. Reitzel, 1843).

3 Brandes, Georg, *Hans Christian Andersen: The Great Danish Author* (Quebec: Human and Literature Publishing, Les Libraires, 2023).

4 Berlin, Ira, *Generations of Captivity: A History of African-American Slaves* (Cambridge, MA: Harvard University Press, 2003).

5 Berger, Maurice, "From Slavery to Freedom: Revealing the Underground Railroad," *The New York Times* (March 29, 2017).

6 Douglass, Frederick, *Collected Articles of Frederick Douglass* (Project Gutenberg: Public Domain Books, 1994).

7 Barkstrom, Jack, *Poverty, Wealth Dictatorship, Democracy: Resource Scarcity and the Origins of Dictatorship* (Lakewood, CO: Pericles Press, 1998).

8 Fitzpatrick, Sheila; Slezkine, Yuri, *In the Shadow of Revolution: Life Stories of Russian Women from 1917 to the Second World War* (Princeton: Princeton University Press, 2000). An

almost legendary hero in that Communist nation, Pasha's real name was Praskovya Nikitichna Angelina (1912–1959).

9 Morton, Sunny Jane, "Chinese Immigration and the Chinese Exclusion Act" (undated); found at www.familysearch.org/en/blog/chinese-immigration-to-the-united-states. Also Library of Congress, "Immigration to the United States: 1851-1900" (undated); found at www.loc.gov/classroom-materials/united-states-history-primary-source-timeline/rise-of-industrial-america-1876-1900/immigration-to-united-states-1851-1900/.

10 Alliance of Girls' Schools Australasia, "Research Shows Girls Benefit from Single-Sex Environments," *International Coalition of Girls' Schools* (undated); found at www.agsa.org.au/why-a-girls-school-the-research/research-shows-girls-benefit-from-single-sex-environments/.

11 Pahlke, Erin; Hyde, Janet S.; Allison, Carlie M., "The Effects of Single-Sex Compared with Co-Educational Schooling on Students' Performance and Attitudes: A Meta-Analysis," *Psychological Bulletin*, Vol. 140, No. 4 (American Psychological Association, 2014), pp. 1042–1072. Also: Henebery, Bret, "Girls Who Attend Single-Sex Schools Mentally Tougher than Co-Ed Peers – Study," *The Educator/Australia* (August 4, 2021); found at www.theeducatoronline.com/k12/news/girls-who-attend-singlesex-schools-mentally-tougher-than-coed-peers--study/278220.

12 Schooler, Cathleen; Mulatu, Mesfin S.; Oates, Gary, "Occupational Self-Direction, Intellectual Functioning, and Self-Directed Orientation in Older Workers: Findings and Implications for Individuals and Societies," *American Journal of Sociology*, Vol. 110, No. 1 (January 2004), pp. 161–197.

13 Rosenberg, Morris; Simmons, Roberta G., "Black and White Self-Esteem: The Urban School Child," *American Sociological Association*, Vol. 52, No. 3 (March 1974), p. 424.

14 Bachman, Jerald G., *Youth in Transition: II. The Impact of Family Background and Intelligence on Tenth-Grade Boys* (Ann Arbor, MI: Institute for Social Research, University of Michigan, 1970).

15 Schmader, Toni; Major, Brenda; Granzow, Richard H., "How African-American College Students Protect Their Self-Esteem," *The Journal of Blacks in Higher Education*, Vol. 35 (2002), pp. 116–119.

16 van Laar, Cheryl, "The Paradox of Low Academic Achievement but High Self-Esteem in African American Students: An Attributional Account," *Educational Psychology Review*, Vol. 12, No. 1 (2000), pp. 33–61.

17 Steele, C.M., "Expert Report of Claude M. Steele," *Michigan Journal of Race and Law*, Vol. 5, No. 1 (1999), pp. 439–450. Steele was interviewed about "disidentification" in a PBS Frontline documentary aired in 1999, found at https://www.pbs.org/wgbh/pages/frontline/shows/sats/interviews/steele.html.

18 United States Holocaust Memorial Museum, "Public Humiliation," *Holocaust Encyclopedia*; found at encyclopedia.ushmm.org/content/en/article/public-humiliation.

19 Frankl, Viktor E., *Man's Search for Meaning* (New York: Simon and Schuster, 1985).

20 Frankl, Viktor E., *Man's Search for Meaning* (New York: Simon and Schuster, 1985).

21 Frankl, Viktor E., *Man's Search for Meaning* (New York: Simon and Schuster, 1985).

22 Simon, J., "Prison Is Punishment Enough. But in the US, Inmates also Face Violence and Humiliation," *The Guardian* (2015, April 9); found at https://www.theguardian .com/commentisfree/2015/apr/09/prison-punishment-violence-humiliation

23 Lazear, Edward P., "Why Is There Mandatory Retirement?" *Journal of Political Economy*, Vol. 87, No. 6 (December 1979), pp. 1261–1284. Also: Tort, Marvin, "Retiring by Choice, Not by Age," *BusinessWorld* (October 10, 2018); found at www.bworldonline .com/editors-picks/2018/10/10/192436/retiring-by-choice-not-by-age.

24 Pabón-Carrasco, Manuel; Ramirez-Baena, L.; López Sánchez, R.; Rodríguez-Gallego, I.; Suleiman-Martos, N.; Gómez-Urquiza, J.L., "*Prevalence of Depression in Retirees: A Meta-Analysis*," *Healthcare*, Vol. 8, No. 3 (March 2020), p. 321.

25 Moon, Jennifer R.; Glymour, M. Maria; Subramanian, S.V.; Avendaño, Mauricio; Kawachi, Ichiro, "Transition to Retirement and Risk of Cardiovascular Disease: Prospective Analysis of the US Health and Retirement Study," *Social Science & Medicine*, Vol. 75, No. 3 (2012), pp. 526–530.

26 Road Scholar, "How to Avoid Loneliness and Isolation as a Senior in Retirement," *Road Scholar*; found at www.roadscholar.org/senior-loneliness-isolation-things-to -do-in-retirement.

27 Arendt, Hannah, *On Violence* (New York: Harcourt, Brace, Jovanovich, 1970).

28 Fanon, Frantz, *The Wretched of the Earth* — Preface by Jean-Paul Sartre, translated by Constance Farrington (New York: Grove Press, 1963).

29 Ibid.

30 Popkin, Jeremy D., *A New World Begins: The History of the French Revolution* (New York: Basic Books, 2019).

31 Rhodehamel, John H., *The American Revolution: Writings from the War of Independence* (New York: Library of America, 2001).

32 Office of the Historian, "Decolonization of Asia and Africa, 1945-1960," published by U.S. Department of State; found at history.state.gov/milestones/1945-1952/asia -and-africa.

33 Fanon, Frantz, *The Wretched of the Earth* — Preface by Jean-Paul Sartre, translated by Constance Farrington (New York: Grove Press, 1963).

34 Global Project Against Hate and Extremism, *The Great Replacement Conspiracy Theory* (undated); found at globalextremism.org/the-great-replacement/.

35 Deutsche Welle, "Germany Condemns Extremism on Hanau Attack Anniversary" (February 19, 2022); found at www.dw.com/en/germany-condemns-extremism -on-hanau-attack-anniversary/a-60842988.

36 Amato, Paul R.; Previti, Denise, "People's Reasons for Divorcing: Gender, Social Class, the Life Course, and Adjustment," *Journal of Family Issues*, Vol. 24, No. 5 (2003), pp. 602–626.

37 Johnson, Christine A.; Stanley, Scott M., *The Oklahoma Marriage Initiative Statewide Baseline Survey* (2001). Funded by the state government, the goal was to cut Oklahoma's divorce rate by one-third by 2010, but that did not happen; found at www

.researchgate.net/publication/240108285_Marriage_in_Oklahoma_2001_base-line_statewide_survey_on_marriage_and_divorce.

38 Scott, Shelby B.; Rhoades, Galena K.; Stanley, Scott M.; Allen, Elizabeth S. & Markman, Howard J., "Reasons for Divorce and Recollections of Premarital Intervention: Implications for Improving Relationship Education," *Couple and Family Psychology: Research and Practice*, Vol. 2, No. 2 (2013), pp. 131–145.

39 Miller, Anna, "Can this Marriage Be Saved?" *Monitor on Psychology*, Vol. 44, No. 4 (April 1, 2013), p. 42; found at www.apa.org/monitor/2013/04/marriage.html.

40 Kilborn, Peter T., "Disabled Spouses are Increasingly Forced to Go It Alone," *The New York Times* (May 31, 1999); found at www.nytimes.com/1999/05/31/us/disa-bled-spouses-are-increasingly-forced-to-go-it-alone.html.

41 Evans, Alice, "Older Men Ditching Their Wives for Younger Women Are Behind the Rise in Mid-Life Divorces," *Daily Mail* (May 28, 2017); found at www.daily-mail.co.uk/news/article-4549446/Rise-mid-life-divorces-older-men-ditch-wives.html

42 Buss, David M., *The Evolution of Desire: Strategies of Human Mating* (New York: Basic Books, 2003).

43 Uddin, Bilal, "94% of Men Would Leave Their Partner if They Get Fat, but Women Do Not," *Medium* (April 29, 2019); found at medium.com/@hello.beautyhuts/94-of-men-would-leave-their-partner-if-they-get-fat-but-women-do-not-bb656ce517ed. The survey was reportedly done by a medical weight-loss company known as the PnK Method of PronoKal Group.

44 Rice, Mary, "11 Valuable Benefits of Couples Therapy," in *Talkspace* (New York: Talkspace, November 22, 2021); found at www.talkspace.com/blog/benefits-of-couples-therapy.

10

ADJUST FOR SIGNIFICANCE

You may have tried everything to *Attack* your goal of attaining or reinstating Significance. You may have learned to think optimistically, developed a growth mindset, and even cultivated passion and grit in your chosen, Significance-affording, line of endeavor. You may have been able to *Align* yourself with a social network that appreciates your accomplishments and attributes. Perhaps you were blessed with success and have now been accorded due respect by people who matter to you, your friends and colleagues whose values you share.

But you may well realize that it is not enough. You cannot rest on your laurels. For you are only as significant as your last attainment. People's memories are short. They seem to be asking, "What have you done for us lately?" and if the answer is "not much," they can be quick to pronounce and treat you as irrelevant, a "has been" that no longer "is."

DOI: 10.4324/9781003410706-10

Quitting the "Rat Race"

Faced with that reality, you might conclude that the "rat race" isn't worth it, that fame is fleeting and that – to quote the New Testament – "Glory is like the flowers of the field; the grass withers and the flowers fall."[1]

The highly successful Roman emperor Diocletian (236–316 CE), who enacted several important reforms, retired at the height of his powers to engage in gardening and growing cabbages. When political turmoil erupted and the people of Rome begged him to return to the throne, he replied: "If you could show the cabbage that I planted with my own hands to your emperor, he definitely wouldn't dare suggest that I replace the peace and happiness of this place with the storms of a never-satisfied greed."[2]

J.D. Salinger, author of the global bestseller, *The Catcher in the Rye*, withdrew from the public eye at the age of 34. A prevailing explanation is that he did so under the influence of Eastern philosophy, both Hinduism and Zen Buddhism, with their leaning toward abandonment of the ego and of the insatiable Quest for Significance.

Substantial proportions of executives and managers are quitting their 9-to-5 jobs and are opting out of the "rat race." A survey carried out in 2022 among 10,243 full-time desk workers in the United States, Australia, France, Germany, the United Kingdom, and Japan showed that 42 percent of workers felt burned out. In a different survey, similar numbers of Gen X and millennial C-suite executives reported not wanting to work anymore (33% and 36% respectively). More than half (58%) of the youngest group, Gen Z executives, told researchers they wanted to stop working.[3]

The personal journeys of those who leave the stresses of corporate life behind vary. Thomas DeGeest, a management consultant for IBM and a native Belgian, left his high-paying job at age 38 to sell authentic Belgian waffles out of a yellow mobile truck.[4]

Greg Hopkinson sold a chain of successful retail stores in his native New Zealand to live in a far-away place on the South Island with his partner Sally, where both became monks of an order that calls itself non-religious.[5]

Mary Schulman gave up a six-figure salary in investment banking in 2011. She decided to launch, with her mother in Bethesda, Maryland, the Snikiddy Snacks store featuring fun-to-eat organic snacks for children made from original family recipes.[6]

Those people and others – who have left the high-stress conventional route to elusive success – were not giving up on their motivation to gain and retain Significance. What they did do, however, was tone down their quest for social recognition. They were *adjusting* their QFS, opting out of the stresses and the emotional roller coaster that staying in the "rat race" entails.

The Scramble for Significance

These stresses take their toll. Americans are, overall, so desperate to amass Significance that their mental health is suffering. Though in most Western societies there is a disproportionate emphasis on prestige, dignity, and success, the United States stands out. America is truly above and beyond. In consequence, it has the world's highest prevalence of diagnosed depression (encompassing nearly 10% of the adult population).

This is only getting worse, and the rates of anxiety and suicidal thoughts in the United States have also risen in recent years and skyrocketed in 2020, the year of the Covid outbreak. The pandemic greatly boosted factors that undermine most people's self-confidence and sense of self-worth: isolation, unemployment, the possible loss of loved ones, and threats to one's own health.

Because Significance in America is closely associated with income and wealth, the United States is the most "workaholic" nation in the world. Americans work 499 more hours per year than French workers, 260 more hours than British workers, and 137 more hours than their Japanese counterparts.[7] The United States is the only industrialized country without legally mandated annual leave for its workers. For most Americans, work demands and the desire to achieve Significance at the workplace lead to high levels of stress, manifesting in frequent worrying about success and maintaining the lifestyle of conspicuous consumption to signal achievement and Significance.

Widely influential theories of depression (for instance, that of cognitive behavioral theorist Aaron Beck) blame much of the added stress on obsessive thoughts, such as, "I must succeed at any task I attempt," and, "I must be liked by everyone I meet." These goals, in the service of a person's own Significance, are impossible to reach, so they – along with negative preconceptions – have been categorized by Beck and fellow psychiatrists as "irrational."[8]

Yet those are the goals that a growing number of Americans embrace, according to research, with diagnosable angst resulting from their lopsided cravings for Significance and their dread of Significance loss. In the United States, more than 90 percent of those who die by suicide are believed to have been afflicted by depression. Additionally, American adults who live with depression die (on average) 25 years younger than the non-depressed population.[9]

Detachment and Mindfulness

The Adjust mode of dealing with our Significance strivings is inspired by the Zen Buddhist philosophy of detachment, which advocates separating yourself from others' opinions and self-criticism. Great emotional investment in any outcome, according to Buddhism, is a recipe for suffering. Desire and aversion – deeply caring about positive outcomes and fearing negative outcomes – are, in the Buddhist view, "poisons of the mind."

Desire for Significance and mattering is in fact seen as responsible for destructive perfectionism, low self-esteem, self-loathing, jealousy, and grief. Yongey Mingyur Rinpoche, a Tibetan Buddhist teacher, viewed the satisfaction of desires of any kind, including the pursuit of fame and recognition, as "a type of addiction, a never-ending search for a lasting 'high' that is out of reach."[10] The suggested goal should be nirvana, a blissful state of separating from all of conventional life's sufferings, desires, and ego. This Eastern teaching would suggest turning away from the Quest for Significance and from the yearning for recognition.

As the Buddha himself recommended, one should refrain from dwelling on the past as well as from dreaming of the future. Instead, the idea is to concentrate on the present. That is what the practice of mindfulness attempts to accomplish.

Interestingly, mindfulness is practiced differently in the East and in the West. In the Eastern conception, mindfulness is imbued with the values of morality, wisdom, and spirituality. Teachers say that the right way to practice meditation and mindfulness should lead through a mystical path to the attainment of Universal Consciousness.

These spiritual and mystical elements are largely absent from the way that Mindfulness Meditation – almost as a brand name – is practiced in the West, where it has become highly popular in recent decades. Instructors define it as being fully present, aware of what you are doing but without reacting or being overwhelmed by anything. Some call it "paying intentional attention to what is around you." Others say you are "taming the wandering mind."[11]

Although the secularized Western forms of mindfulness do not allude to enlightenment or nirvana, they are not merely physical exercises either. By de-emphasizing your own fears and desires through practicing mindfulness, you can pay more attention to the fears and desires of others and be attuned to their concerns and suffering.

In fact, compassion and empathy are important elements in the popular Mindfulness-Based Stress Reduction (MBSR), first developed by Dr. Jon Kabat-Zinn in 1979 at the University of Massachusetts. Along these lines, then, many Westerners who practice mindfulness view it as a way of life that has a transformative influence on their experience.

The legendary singer, novelist, and poet Leonard Cohen struggled with severe depression from his early teens. He was hospitalized multiple times and tried almost every medication available, including tricyclics, MAOIs, second-generation antidepressants, and anticonvulsants; but nothing worked. In 1994, when his depression was at its worst, Cohen left public life and joined the Mt. Baldy Zen Center, a Buddhist monastery in Los Angeles, California. There, he learned to detach from the "tyranny" of his self-focused, ruminative thoughts about success, failure, and self-worth that come with depression.

Similarly, Eckhart Tolle, a famous German self-help guru and mindfulness instructor, overcame depression through a practice that led to an "inner transformation." At the age of 29, he woke up one night feeling unbearable depression. His life-changing salvation came from letting go of the notion of "self" and concerns about his Significance and dignity.

As Tolle poignantly described it: "I couldn't live with myself any longer. And in this a question arose without an answer: who is the 'I' that cannot live with the self? What is the self? I felt drawn into a void! I didn't know at the time that what really happened was the mind-made self, with its heaviness, its problems, that lives between the unsatisfying past and the fearful future, collapsed. It dissolved. The next morning, I woke up and everything was so peaceful. The peace was there because there was no self. Just a sense of presence or 'beingness,' just observing and watching."[12]

Tolle quit his doctoral studies and spent about two years sitting on park benches in London's Russell Square, observing people and noticing events; just "watching the world go by," as he put it. He stayed with friends or in a Buddhist monastery, or simply out and about, sleeping as a homeless person on Hampstead Heath. His discovery of the powers of mindfulness transformed his life completely. He shared his insights with millions of readers and became a much sought-after spiritual counselor, author, and widely followed authority on how to live.

"Don't Sweat the Small Stuff"

In a small volume that became a #1 *New York Times* bestseller, titled *Don't Sweat the Small Stuff … and It's All Small Stuff*, psychologist Richard Carlson compellingly advocated toning down our incessant Quest for Significance which he described as a continuous drama.

As Carlson put it: "We live our lives as if they were one great big emergency! We often rush around looking busy, trying to solve problems, but we are often compounding them. Because everything seems like such a big deal, we end up spending our lives dealing with one drama after another."[13]

The book's unique feature is that it translates the general ideas of Buddhist detachment and techniques of meditation into numerous specific suggestions. These include forgetting about perfectionism, stopping rumination in its tracks, and avoiding the illusion that once our current projects are completed, there will be peace. The book advocates implementing the essential Buddhist concept of living in the present. All these represent a more subdued Quest for Significance, accepting the way things are, and recognizing the suffering that excessive ambition can bring about.

Carlson would have us unselfishly let other people – in whatever type of encounter or situation – have the "glory," rather than desperately vying for attention for ourselves. He recommends, in the spirit of detachment, that we let other people be "right" most of the time. As he insightfully observes, "All of us hate to be corrected. We all want our positions to be respected and understood by others. Being listened to and heard is one of the greatest desires of the human heart. And those who learn to listen are the most loved and respected. Those who are in the habit of correcting others are often resented and avoided."[14]

Carlson adds that sometimes, "it is important to speak your mind. Usually, however, it's just your ego creeping in and ruining an otherwise peaceful encounter – a habit of wanting or needing to be right," and feeling a loss of Significance if you are not. Giving up on that desire, and thus toning down your craving for Significance, can be a recipe for tranquil and constructive relations with others in most social circumstances.

Leaving the Ego Behind

One question that pops into our minds, about Buddhist detachment and the curbing of desires, is whether that means giving up on achievement and excellence – not being focused anymore on goals that require commitment, engagement, and investment of resources. After all, commitment and investment do not happen in a motivational vacuum. To the contrary, they require a high degree of motivation, and you might say a certain amount of passion.

Yet passion seems intricately based on desire, or wanting something intensely. Does that mean that Buddhist detachment is incompatible with achievement and that it destines its followers to a life of quiet mediocrity?

We put this question to a few of our Buddhist friends and others who practice and teach the skill of mindfulness. Though we approached them separately, they all disagreed with the suggestion that Buddhist detachment is incompatible with achievement. In fact, they argued that a Buddhist detachment is, if anything, helpful to achievement because it clears your mind from irrelevant distractions and liberates you from what many Buddhists call the "monkey in your brain." More specifically, it allows you to get into a state of "flow" and hence to focus on the task at hand, rather than being preoccupied and distracted from it by egotistical concerns and worries about Significance.

In 1970 the psychologist Mihaly Csikszentmihalyi coined the term "flow state" to describe a person's complete immersion in an activity, a state in which they experience a feeling of energized focus, full involvement, and enjoyment of the activity without reservation. As depicted by Csikszentmihalyi, flow is characterized by the complete absorption in what one does, the state of "forgetting all else" and clearing one's mind of all distractions: the melding together of action and consciousness.

Flow is not just a state of mind; it affects the body as well, and it is accompanied by measurable physiological changes. In a 2010 Swedish study on classical pianists, researchers from the Karolinska Institute of Neuropediatric Research[15] found that musicians who entered flow exhibited deeper breathing and slower heart rates, as well as activation of the corrugator supercilii and zygomaticus major, which are the facial muscles that enable us to smile. While the flow state demands focused concentration, people in flow find it effortless.

But relating to the issue of detachment and achievement, the interesting thing is this: Putting your "hyperfocus" on an activity reflects a high degree of motivation. It is definitely compatible with passion, with desire, and ultimately with a high level of achievement.

It is not the desire as such that detachment eliminates. Achieving a healthy detachment puts aside distracting concerns with ego-related desires, including thoughts about our Significance, our social worth, and how we appear to others.

What is also intriguing is that even if ultimately your QFS – your Quest – is aided by an activity, in the state of flow you are not thinking of your Significance. That is true, even if it is QFS that prompted you to start that activity!

Great musicians, athletes, dancers, painters, and scientists spend hours immersed in their activities without noticing how time is passing, and they let all other concerns go unattended. One composer told Csikszentmihalyi how, when his work was going well, he experienced a kind of ecstasy. He did not need to think, he lost track of time, and the music would "just flow out."

The experience of flow is not reserved only for people with unusual talents. Under Csikszentmihalyi's guidance, researchers interested in the flow experience studied Himalayan climbers, Dominican monks, Navajo shepherds, and thousands of others. Their conclusion was that we can experience flow whenever we are fully engaged with our work, hobbies, or relationships, whatever these might be. So, it is possible to be mindful and detached from ego concerns, yet at the same time be fully immersed in an activity and focus all our energies upon it – often leading to superior performance.

Research also shows that the flow experience makes people happy. In fact, flow is associated with activity in the parts of the brain involved in getting a reward and reaching a goal. That is why flow feels so enjoyable and why people are thrilled to be focused on tasks that make them feel flow. Flow is also associated with decreased activity in brain structures relating to ego concerns and being focused on oneself. This may help explain why flow reduces feelings of anxiety and worry.[16]

These findings carry important implications for successful retirement, where people can no longer pursue the professional activities that gave them a sense of Significance and social worth. Rather than feeling belittled and disempowered in retirement and trying to live on the nostalgia of your past "laurels," you might consider "leaving your ego behind" and finding an activity that absorbs you to the point of experiencing flow.

Retirement is a perfect time to immerse yourself in activities you used to love but never had time to pursue because of work obligations and life's other duties. Now you can set aside time for gardening, kayaking, golf, horseback riding, or learning a language. Alternatively, you might try mentally engaging games, such as checkers or Sudoku, or perhaps immerse yourself in reading or listening to your favorite music. You might even read more books about psychology!

Feeling free and in the state of flow while pursuing hobbies should give you a feeling of enjoyment and contentment. In some respects, that can be more rewarding and fulfilling than the insatiable race after fame and fortune that may have characterized your career. Those middle-age rewards are, as we have learned, fleeting and ephemeral.

Here is an apocryphal tale that conveys the contrast between the rat race with its intense Quest for Significance, versus the approach of "going with the flow":

One day a fisherman was lying on a beautiful beach, with his fishing pole propped up in the sand and his solitary line cast out into the sparkling blue surf. He was enjoying the warmth of the afternoon sun and the prospect of catching a fish.

About that time, a businessman came walking along the beach, trying to relieve some of the stress of his workday. He noticed the fisherman lying there and decided to find out why this man was fishing instead of working harder to make a living for himself and his family.

"You aren't going to catch many fish that way," the businessman chided the fisherman. "You should be working, rather than lying on the beach!"

The fisherman looked up at the businessman, smiled, and replied, "And what will my reward be?"

"Well, you can get bigger nets and catch more fish!" said the businessman.

"And then what will my reward be?" asked the fisherman, still smiling.

The businessman replied, "You will make money and you'll be able to buy a boat, which will then result in larger catches of fish!"

"And then what will my reward be?" the fisherman asked again.

The businessman was beginning to get a little irritated with the fisherman's questions. "You can buy a bigger boat, and hire some people to work for you!" he said.

"And then what will my reward be?" repeated the fisherman.

The businessman was getting angry. "Don't you understand? You can build up a fleet of fishing boats, sail all over the world, and let all your employees catch fish for you!"

Once again, the fisherman asked, "And then what will my reward be?"

The businessman was red with rage and shouted at the fisherman, "Don't you understand that you can become so rich that you will never have to work for your living again? You can spend all the rest of your days sitting on this beach, looking at the sunset! You won't have a care in the world!"

The fisherman, still smiling, looked up and said, "And what do you think I'm doing right now?"

Summary

The Quest for Significance is insatiable and relentless. No matter how good you are at anything, there is likely to be someone even better who might make you feel second-best. Even if right now you are at the absolute top, there is competition for the singular "place in the sun," and you could live your life in constant fear of "usurpers." Participating in that kind of career "rat race" can be exhausting and depleting. To stress and worry about your standing and perceived worth really takes its toll, making millions of people feel miserable and depressed.

In recent decades, people have been paying increasing attention to alternative lifestyles that allow them to leave their ego behind, and to liberate themselves from the burdens of a relentless need to prove their worth.

Those alternatives originate largely from Buddhist philosophy, and students of the techniques have learned to detach themselves from the worries and concerns of Significance and mattering. Focusing on the present place and time, practicing mindfulness, and cultivating a state of flow when engaging in activities have proved to be a tonic for alleviating the stresses of incessant competition. By adjusting the Quest for Significance, truly lowering the exertion and desperation to succeed, people are finding a greater degree of enjoyment and well-being.

Notes

1 Found in the New Testament (the Christian Bible) in 1 Peter 1:24.
2 Banchich, Thomas M., "A Booklet About the Style of Life and the Manners of the Imperatores," in *An Online Encyclopedia of Roman Emperors* (Chicago: Loyola University Chicago, 2009); found at www.roman-emperors.org/epitome.htm.
3 Zaki, Ahmed, "40% of Executives Say They'll Quit in 2023: Weekly Stat," in CFO (New York: CFO, November 23, 2022); found at www.cfo.com/news/40-of-exec-utives-say-theyll-quit-in-2023-weekly-stat/654806/.
4 Pierce, Steven, "Leaving the Rat Race," in *Entrepreneur Magazine* (Irvine: Entrepreneur Media Inc., May 21, 2008); found at www.entrepreneur.com/starting-a-business/leaving-the-rat-race-entrepreneurcom/194026.
5 HuffPost, "Why Greg Hopkinson, a Successful Businessman, Gave it All Up to be a Monk" (May 2, 2015); found at www.huffingtonpost.co.uk/2014/12/16/greg-hopkinson-businessman-monk_n_6333828.html.
6 Pierce, Steven, "Leaving the Rat Race," in *Entrepreneur Magazine* (Irvine, CA: Entrepreneur Media Inc., May 21, 2008); found at www.entrepreneur.com/start-ing-a-business/leaving-the-rat-race-entrepreneurcom/194026. Things worked out well for Schulman and her mother, Janet Ownings, as in 2015 a national snack-food company, Utz, bought Snikiddy and expanded it.
7 These oft-quoted comparisons of work hours per annum, are based on an International Labor Organization study. See "Americans' International Lead in Hours Worked Grew in 90's, Report Shows," *New York Times* (September 1, 2001). Since then, it is widely believed that the gap has increased – with Americans still spending a lot more time "making a living" rather than "living."
8 In an obituary, the *Washington Post* wrote (on November 3, 2021) that starting in the 1960s, "Dr. Beck refined his research and therapy techniques until, by the 1990s, cognitive behavior therapy (CBT) had become the most widely used form of therapy for the treatment of depression and numerous other disorders. *American Psychologist*, the journal of the American Psychological Association, named Dr. Beck 'one of the five most influential psychotherapists of all time.'"

9   "Depression Facts" page, undated, on website of Hope for Depression Research Foundation: www.hopefordepression.org/depression-facts._

10 Swanson, Eric; Yongey, Mingyur Rinpoche, *Joyful Wisdom: Embracing Change and Finding Freedom* (New York: Harmony, 2010).

11 Tlalka, Stefany, "Why It's Hard to Live in the Present Moment," *Mindful* (August 2017); found at www.mindful.org/hard-live-present-moment.

12 "Why Now Is Bliss," *The Age* (September 29, 2003); found at www.theage.com.au/world/why-now-is-bliss-20030929-gdwfir.html.

13 Carlson, Richard, *Don't Sweat the Small Stuff... and It's All Small Stuff: Simple Ways to Keep the Little Things from Taking Over Your Life* (New York: Hachette Books, 1997).

14 Carlson, Richard, *Don't Sweat the Small Stuff... and It's All Small Stuff: Simple Ways to Keep the Little Things from Taking Over Your Life* (New York: Hachette Books, 1997).

15 Robb, Alice, "The 'Flow State': Where Creative Work Thrives," *BBC News* (February 5, 2019); found at www.bbc.com/worklife/article/20190204-how-to-find-your-flow-state-to-be-peak-creative. The researchers were Örjan de Manzano, Fredrik Ullén, László Harmat, and Gabriela Thörn from the Karolinska Institute of Neuropediatric Research.

16 Huskey, Richard, "Why Does Experiencing 'Flow' Feel So Good?" *UC Davis Magazine* (January 6, 2022); found at www.ucdavis.edu/curiosity/blog/research-shows-people-who-have-flow-regular-part-their-lives-are-happier-and-less-likely-focus.

11

BACK TO FRIENDSHIP AND INFLUENCE

In the opening chapter of this book, we suggested that understanding the dynamics of the Quest for Significance (QFS) should give us deeper insights into the process of "winning friends and influencing people" made famous by Dale Carnegie. We will now elaborate on that assertion.

Our sense of Significance is intimately tied to other people. It is they whose respect and appreciation we seek, and that is what they want from us in return. Understanding how QFS works should be a major help in navigating our relationships with others in various life domains, including parenting, romance, friendship, or business.

The insights we outlined in previous chapters should allow us to go beyond the usual advice found in self-help books: to avoid criticizing others, to smile, to hand out compliments, to be a good listener, et cetera. To be sure, there is nothing wrong with these suggestions; in fact, they do assume the importance of taking other people's need for Significance into account.

DOI: 10.4324/9781003410706-11

Our 3N (Needs, Narratives, and Networks) model, however, goes beyond a "one size fits all" recipe. It allows for customizing our approach to other people's motivational condition, their unique attributes, how these relate to ours, and the circumstances of our encounters with those people.

Identifying People's Significance Narratives

To be important to another person, and in this sense to have them care about and be influenced by our opinions, it is essential to be attuned to their sense of social worth and Significance. We need to identify the narrative that gives them Significance, and to be perceived as a member of a network whose appreciation that person desires. The same logic applies regardless of whether we are dealing with our child, our spouse, our friend, or our boss.

Often, we act on the implicit assumption that people's Significance-affording narratives are exactly like ours. So, for instance, if we take pride in our education, thriftiness, sports expertise, or other attributes, we assume that the other person shares those values.

Yet that might not be true, and in fact they might care about entirely different things that provide their Significance. They might care about religion, politics, the environment, or antique furniture. You do not know unless you probe gently, listen, and pay attention. If, instead, you try to beguile them with your accomplishments in domains they care little about, or fail to relate to domains that they care about, your relationship will likely falter.

Often, the failure to appreciate another person's narratives and networks can cause problems between parents and children. But being attentive and reorienting oneself to these issues can help solve them. The following story exemplifies what we mean:

A friend of ours has a teenage daughter who, as teenagers are wont to be, used to come home in a bad mood and shut herself off in her own room, seeming angry and alienated from her family. Her parents' attempts to boost her mood by showering love upon her had no visible effect. She knew she mattered to her family. That was not her issue at all.

Where she felt her Significance was lacking was at school: falling behind in math, and also not feeling appreciated enough by her classmates, the network in which she craved to be accepted.

Fortunately, our friend is not one to give up and kept inquiring into her daughter's malaise and encouraged her to open up. When the mother realized where the problem lay, she quickly took remedial action. She hired a math tutor for the girl, enrolled her in a dance class, and relaxed her strict limitations on sleepovers. The change in the daughter's demeanor was remarkable. Not only did her bad moods and irritation vanish as if by magic, but her relationship with her mother also underwent a complete makeover. The teen now felt, for the first time in a long time, that her mother truly understood her, was on her side, and would do all she could to make her feel significant and happy.

Significance Issues in the Marital Context

Many marriages run aground and stagnate because one or both spouses take each other "for granted" – each getting the sense that the love pronouncements by their partner are empty and perfunctory. They do not feel really appreciated by their spouse; this can make them susceptible to admiring advances from outsiders, increasing the probability of extramarital affairs.

Adultery is alluring for many reasons. The multiple roles of married partners (as parents, financial partners, and supportive friends) dim the role of sex and the glamor of romance that originally catapulted the couple onto Cloud 9. Meeting someone new and attractive, who seems to offer adoration, promises a notable uplift in Significance. It is a temptation that many cannot resist. Indeed, infidelity is quite common. 20 to 40 percent of heterosexual married men and 20 to 25 percent of heterosexual married women have extramarital affairs during their lifetime, according to American government-sponsored research.[1]

It is a cliché by now to say that relationships "need work." But what does this mean? It means paying close attention to your partner's sense of social worth and their Significance issues. Those may have to do with different life domains (such as work) outside the home, and the success of the relationship often hinges on identifying where the Significance soft spot lies.

A husband or a wife may feel misunderstood and unappreciated if their spouse shows no interest in their unique Significance-boosting hobbies: weekend athleticism on the tennis court, physical appearance, fashion sense, career successes, or devotion to the kids. Focusing myopically on what lends Significance to you may make you lose sight of what gives

Significance to your spouse or partner, who may value entirely different things.

Paying attention and showing appreciation for your partner's Significance narrative is likely to incite feelings of gratitude and reciprocation, thus rekindling the flame that lost its blaze.

The lessons of the marriage example go well beyond it and apply to all other relationships, whether intimate or casual. To make them work, issues of Significance had better be considered. When trying to cultivate a relationship with someone, it is important to find out why they are doing what they are doing: what makes them "tick" and makes them feel significant. Sometimes, they might not know it very well themselves. Rather than asking outright, you may have to figure it out. Yes, in dealing with another person, form your own hypotheses and test them through observation!

A Matter of Values

Some people may pride themselves on being humble, and pooh-pooh issues of status and prestige. Does that mean they do not really care about their social worth? Far from it: It is their professed "humility" that, in their eyes, adds to their Significance and mattering.

The point is that people have different values that lend them Significance, and it is logical that their Significance narratives revolve around those values. Some of our friends pride themselves on being cheapskates and getting incredible deals on everything they purchase. Their favorite pastime, it seems, is asking their friends how much they paid for something and, upon finding out, gleefully announcing that they could have gotten the same item at half the price – making their friends feel stupid, naive, and humiliated, at least in the eyes of the frugality champion.

Other people derive their Significance from the fanciest restaurants and hotels that they frequent and the luxury items that they own. We can only imagine what kind of Significance issues would emerge if the two types of friends got together and tried to impress each other. Rather than deriving Significance, both friends would likely feel a bit insulted and diminished through their interaction: The luxury lover would feel humiliated when judged against the value of thrift, and the cheapskate would feel offended when judged against the value of top-quality refinement. In consequence they would be likely to lose respect for each other, thus undermining their relationship and diminishing their friendship.

Avoiding Excessive Self-Focus – Arachne's Hubris

Being too "full of oneself," too immersed in the unique truth of one's own narrative, and too intoxicated with one's own Significance is called "hubris." From time immemorial, it has been considered a bad thing: an inappropriate social attitude that can be highly detrimental to viable social relations. The ancient Greek parable of Arachne illustrates the destructiveness that hubris can bring about.

Arachne was the first spider. But before she was a spider, she was a woman with a certain skill – weaving. From humble beginnings, Arachne first learned the art of weaving as a young girl, and she soon became an expert. She became renowned for her ability to bring life to tapestry. An awed observer of Arachne's work commented that she must have been blessed by Athena, the goddess of craft and weaving. Arachne scoffed in denial and claimed that it was her own talent.

Unfortunately, Arachne did not stop there and kept boasting about her excellence. But unbeknownst to her, the observer was the goddess herself. Arachne was so infected with hubris, that she arrogantly challenged the goddess herself to a weaving competition.

The goddess then revealed herself, but Arachne did not bow with humility. She only slightly blushed and was still very determined to prove that her skill was superior. And so, the weaving began. Athena wove a magnificent tapestry depicting the gods in their most celebrated moments: Zeus on his mighty throne, Poseidon bringing forth spring water, Victory (Nike) bestowing celebratory crowns, Queen Hera striking down offenders, and Athena herself gifting the highly symbolic olive tree to the city of Athens.

In response, Arachne wove a contrasting tapestry. Hers portrayed the gods committing their worst acts – scenes of lust and violence. She portrayed Zeus, Poseidon, and Dionysus, among others, deceiving women by assuming various forms: bulls, swans, flames, showers of gold, and more.

Athena, both devastated by Arachne's tapestry and angered by her refusal to credit Athena for her skill, tore the work to pieces. In her wrath, Athena transformed Arachne into a spider.

Joseph and His Brothers

Another poignant cautionary tale about the destructive consequences of hubris is the Old Testament story of Joseph, the eleventh son of Jacob and his first son through Rachel, Jacob's favorite wife. Joseph was special and also most beloved by his father, "because he had been born to him in his old age; and [Jacob] made an ornate robe for him" (Genesis 37:3). Joseph's brothers knew about their father's favoritism toward Joseph, and they hated him for it. To make matters worse, Joseph began relating his dreams to the family – prophetic visions showing Joseph one day ruling over his family (Genesis 37:5–11).

From an early age, Joseph believed God had destined him for greatness, and he hardly kept his beliefs to himself. When he was 17, Joseph told his brothers about two dreams he had. In the first, all the brothers were harvesting bundles of grain, and the ones that his brothers gathered bowed to Joseph's. In the second dream, the sun (symbolizing their father), the moon (mother), and eleven stars (the brothers) bowed to Joseph himself.

Those dreams, implying his supremacy, angered his brothers even more and led them to plot his demise.

From Joseph's point of view, these dreams were evidence of divine blessing. Yet, being sure that we are in the right does not absolve us from empathizing with others who may not share that view. Good leaders strive to foster cooperation rather than envy. Joseph's failure to recognize this put him into severe conflict with his brothers.

His boastfulness and hubris almost cost him his life. After initially plotting murder, the brothers settled for selling him to a caravan of traders bearing goods through Canaan to Egypt. The merchants, in turn, sold Joseph to Potiphar, "the captain of the guard" who was "an officer of Pharaoh" in Egypt.[2] That was an awful ordeal, but the prophecies came true, and Joseph became the powerful right-hand advisor to the Egyptian monarch.

Gilderoy Lockhart and Harry Potter

Closer to the here and now but unquestionably fictional is the character of Gilderoy Lockhart, a major antagonist in one of J.K. Rowling's mega-best-sellers about wizardry, *Harry Potter and the Chamber of Secrets*, published in 1998. Lockhart appears in the film adaptation (portrayed by the renowned British actor Kenneth Branagh), and he also shows up as a minor character in the 2003 novel, *Harry Potter and the Order of the Phoenix*. Lockhart presents himself as a famous author and formerly a Defense Against the Dark Arts professor at the Hogwarts School. Behind his alleged feats, however, Lockhart is nothing more than a fraud who only seeks fame and brainwashes people into telling him their stories so he can pass them off as his own.

Focusing myopically on yourself – like Lockhart, Arachne, and Joseph – makes you appear arrogant, as though you are entirely dismissive of anyone else's need for Significance. An excessive self-focus is sometimes called "sucking the oxygen out of the room." That could include being the first to talk about your own ideas (and returning to them repeatedly), interrupting people, putting forward grandiose claims, and generally dominating the conversation without letting others express their views. No one else gets a chance to assert that they, too, are part of the conversation and that they also matter.

You might think that by displaying an air of superiority – and thus, by implication, downgrading the other person's taste, knowledge, or erudition – you are compelling the other to admire you and give you recognition and Significance. This logic is not altogether wrong, but what you are likely to get is recognition mixed with resentment. Though prompting reluctant appreciation of your brainpower and status, this may trigger the other person's envy and fuel their desire to get back at you in whatever way they can.

The Dark Side of Self-Confidence

Being too assured of your own views, and too definite in expressing them, may be offensive to others. In the play, "Art" by Yasmin Reza, Marc's loud and clear negativity toward the painting purchased by his longtime friend Serge insults Serge deeply and causes a severe rift in their relationship. For many of us in the West, the positive values of clarity and honesty as expressed by Marc seem like an absolute truism, a complete "no brainer." Clarity and honesty seem "good" – period. Yet, too much clarity can be highly detrimental to friendships and good interpersonal relations. Being cocksure that your view represents the truth means that all other views are erroneous, which is seriously down-putting to those who hold those views. Perhaps because of its inherent dangers to smooth social relations, clarity in communication is not always held in such high regard in Western culture and still is in disrepute (being too blunt and even vulgar) in various cultures around the globe.

Until the 17th century, sociologists tell us,[3] communication in European cultures was not expected to be crisp and precise. The model was to be sophisticated and wise, elegantly crafted, full of metaphors and allegories, and lyrical, yet profound and insightful. Linguistic expression was valued for being eloquent, vivid, and evocative, rather than clear. It was admired for its poetic flourishes, use of irony, innuendo, and mystery; in short, sophisticated European declarations were valued for their ambiguity.

In other cultures, such as traditional ones in Asia and Africa, ambiguity has been cultivated and cherished, largely as a means of self-protection. Having too clear an opinion closes off possibilities of negotiating meaning. It puts an end to the conversation and has an ultimative – which can be seen as insulting – "take it or leave it" tone to it.

If boasting and focusing the attention on oneself is so detrimental to social relations, why do so many people do it? And how is it, too, that some people, such as America's 45th and 47th president Donald Trump, get away with incessant boasting and end up being admired by millions of people?

The answer to the first question is twofold. People boast because it gratifies their Quest for Significance but also because it elicits some measure of respect from others, even if begrudgingly. Presenting yourself in the best possible light is pleasurable, to be sure. Sharing your positive qualities and attainments with an audience ensures that they are informed about what you have done, and that should evoke admiration and respect on their part.

Apparently, our tendency to present ourselves positively is hardwired into our psychological make-up. Psychologists at Harvard University carried out a series of brain imaging experiments and found, using fMRI, that when subjects shared information about themselves, the same areas of the brain lit up as those that do when we are eating food or having sex!

One of the experiments was set up so that, to be allowed to share about themselves, participants had to give up financial payments they could earn if they were willing to respond to questions about other people. An appreciable proportion of the participant population gave up on this reward, preferring the reward of answering questions about themselves.[4] It appears that a person's brain is positively stimulated – truly a reward – by talking about themselves.[5]

Merit and Appreciation in Love and Friendship

So, self-presentation in a positive light gratifies a person's Quest for Significance, and hence it is pleasurable. But it can also be functional, and if done the right way, it can facilitate forming sustainable social relations.

In this case, "the right way" means that your self-presentation must be tempered by considering the appreciation shown by others. In Chapter 5, we showed how the "merit" and "appreciation" factors function in romantic relationships. Yet they apply more broadly to all kinds of interpersonal relations. Specifically, your boasting and self-focus that help you establish your merit can contribute to your interpersonal relations if the other people come to see that behavior as an asset that contributes to their own sense of Significance. That is, while "posturing" and displaying your meritorious characteristics, it is important that you also be aware and show appreciation to your interaction partners.

Put yourself in the other person's shoes, the one who is hearing all that boasting. If that person feels appreciated, respected, and loved by someone of great Significance – meaning the boaster – that may contribute more to their sense of Significance than being in contact with someone insignificant.

Therefore, presenting yourself in a positive light, or as it were, putting your best foot forward, enhances the value of the respect and appreciation that you are offering to the other. You should take care that even if you are boasting, you are not belittling the other person. When administered in the right balance and the correct dosages, your merit and the appreciation you show other people are likely to improve the quality of your social relations and make you a more effective partner, manager, or parent.

By "appreciation" we mean the admiration and respect you give the other person, and you expect similar from them in return. It is the Significance that you recognize in the other and hopefully receive from them. Remembering their name, smiling at them, agreeing with their opinions, and appreciating their tastes, styles, and achievements express your appreciation of who they are.

These signs of respect that you communicate to the other are, of course, exactly what Dale Carnegie recommended in *How to Win Friends and Influence People*, and he was right. Yet, signs of respect and appreciation are meaningful only if they are based on things that matter to the other, their sources of Significance. Discovering what these are should thus be the first step in building a friendly and productive relationship with another person.

Authentic expressions of appreciation, however, are only one side of the equation. In and of themselves, they are not enough to give the other person Significance that would make them appreciate the respect they are getting from you. After all, you want them to be motivated to reciprocate in kind.

What is missing? The "merit" aspect, that gives value to your appreciation. You will have more success, forming a mutually helpful relationship, if you yourself merit respect – based on the surrounding culture. Consider that the person you are encountering may not feel that every compliment, respectful word, nod of agreement, or sign of adoration is equal. In that person's eyes, you should be someone they appreciate and admire. Otherwise, the compliments mean very little.

For you to benefit from a gain in Significance, the other person must be someone whose opinions and evaluation of you are based on some degree of recognized expertise, their "knowing what they are talking about."

For instance, you may have high regard for your parents but also believe, with good reason perhaps, that they know very little about your profession (say, engineering or social psychology) and your hobby (say, tennis). Compliments that they might give you for your professional ideas, or on your athletic performance, will thus contribute little to your sense of Significance. You may (and should) appreciate their love for you, but their comments will probably do little for your professional or athletic pride.

So, for you to acquire Significance-affording value in someone's eyes – the ability to make the other person feel that they matter – you first must establish your merit value in that individual's eyes. Often it is a form of trophy merit, where you are famous or gorgeous or rich, so there is no problem demonstrating your power to bestow Significance. Perhaps, as the saying goes, your fame precedes you. But for most people, a bit of introduction and displaying your "merit" is needed.

In popular language, people talk about "posturing" or "preening" – often referring to the attempt to appear more attractive to potential sexual or romantic partners. As everyone knows, in the courtship phase of a relationship, each party is trying to put their "best foot forward" and impress the other party with their merit value.

Some people have keenly developed skills and natural talents in this regard. We call them "charmers" or "seducers," people with charisma who communicate their value smoothly and effectively. Other people are less socially skilled, less outgoing, or downright timid. Establishing your "merit" without undue boasting, which is a turn-off to many, is an important interpersonal skill from which anyone would benefit.

There are basically two components of a person's "merit" value: their *social status* (professional standing, career accomplishments, reputed political power, wealth) and their *personal charisma*. Where one's social status is best left inferred or communicated subtly (to avoid being seen as boasting), one's charisma and attractive personality should be apparent in the very way one behaves in social circumstances.

In a 2019 study by Jennifer Fayard, John Clay, Felicia Valdez, and Lesley Howard,[6] they asked research participants what characterizes people who have a "personality" and what characterizes those who have "no personality." Participants provided narrative descriptions of both terms and assigned ratings to two fictional characters, one with "no personality" and one with "a lot of personality."

A character with a lot of personality was more liked and labeled as extroverted, agreeable, and open. The character with "no personality" was described as boring, low in openness to experiences, and having no individuality or anything that would make them "unique." Participants were less certain of how they felt about that second character.

Whereas a person's temperament, energy, and outgoingness are largely inborn, there are ways in which charisma can be learned. One can learn how to be a good storyteller, how to use metaphors, how to speak up in social situations, and how to overcome one's natural timidity.

However, keep in mind that displays of your bubbly personality, whether inborn or acquired later in life, should be tempered by sensitivity to other people's needs for self-expression. You want to avoid sucking the oxygen out of a room.

The Influence Paradox

Influencing another person involves changing their mind about something. In effect, this means getting them to alter their narrative.

For instance, a teenager may subscribe to a narrative that their Significance depends on showing up at parties and wearing fashionable clothes, and a parent may want them to adopt a narrative that ties Significance to academic success.

Another example: A husband may feel that his Significance depends on having the last word and being the "man in the house," whereas a wife may want to adopt a narrative that gives her equal say in the couple's decisions.

There is a paradox in trying to change a person's narrative when, first, you need to establish trust and credibility by showing appreciation for the person's existing beliefs. Keep in mind that if you disagree, criticize, or belittle a value that is very important to the person you are hoping to befriend or influence, that is likely to induce rejection on their part. You will have defeated your own purpose.

That is why establishing your credibility as the other person's Significance promoter should come first, before any attempt at influencing them to change.

Where and how to draw these lines – understanding and honoring other people's divergent paths to Significance, while also trying to get them closer to our Significance-affording narratives – is one of the greatest challenges of interpersonal, intergroup, and international relations. It may be a struggle, but it is a task that we should embrace and confront.

Living in harmony with other people – trying to win friends and gently influence people – depends essentially on mutual regard for everyone's Significance and dignity. The alternative is strife and destruction, in which all sides are the losers.

Summary

Giving and receiving Significance is the lifeblood of all social relations, whether formal or informal, at work and at home between parents and children, spouses, lovers, friends, and colleagues, among others. Understanding the critical role that Significance exchanges play in human interactions means discovering the "secret" of winning friends and influencing people.

Significance is what people look for most in their social relations, so the first step in forming or maintaining a viable connection with another is identifying that person's Significance narrative, hence realizing what kind of appreciation will be Significance-bestowing for them.

It is also important to establish your own merit in the other's eyes, meaning you can gain membership in that person's esteemed network – so that the appreciation you offer to them can be appropriately valued. In establishing your merit value, however, it is crucial not to overstep the bounds, to refrain from crowding out the other or sucking out the room's oxygen. You would, sadly, be denying your interaction partners the Significance that comes from their own self-expression.

Forming a viable social relationship thus requires sensitivity, attunement to their needs, and awareness of the impact your actions have on their Significance sensibilities. Being perceived as a Significance provider grants you power and the potential to exert influence over the other person. In most sustainable social relationships, such power is reciprocal, with partners giving and receiving an appreciable sense of Significance. The result should be mutual satisfaction.

Notes

1 The National Institutes of Health shared those estimates in 2013, based on almost a dozen studies in recent decades, in an online article: "Attachment Insecurity and Infidelity in Marriage: Do Studies of Dating Relationships Really Inform Us about Marriage?" found at https://www.ncbi.nlm.nih.gov/pmc/articles/PMC3648986. Also see theconversation.com/the-psychology-of-insults-71738.

2 In the Old Testament, the story is related in Genesis 37:1–11 and Genesis 39:1.

3 Levine, Donald N., *Visions of the Sociological Tradition* (Chicago: University of Chicago Press, 1995).

4 Newman, Susan, "Why Some People Can't Stop Bragging," *Psychology Today* (March 5, 2013); found at www.psychologytoday.com/au/blog/singletons/201303/why-some-people-cant-stop-bragging.

5 Hotz, Robert L., "Science Reveals Why We Brag So Much," *The Wall Street Journal* (May 7, 2012). See also: Australian Institute of Professional Counsellors, "The Psychology of Bragging," *Counselling Connection* (November 14, 2019); found at www.counsellingconnection.com/index.php/2019/11/14/the-psychology-of-bragging.

6 Fayard, Jennifer V.; Clay, John Z.; Valdez, Felicia R.; Howard, Lesley A., "What Does It Mean to Have 'No Personality' or 'A Lot of Personality'? Natural Language Descriptions and Big Five Correlates," *Journal of Research in Personality*, Vol. 79 (April 2019), pp. 59–66.

12

THE RISE OF THE MACHINES

Writers' Strike

In the summer of 2023, America's entertainment industry ground to a halt because of labor strikes aimed at preserving human Significance. Hollywood – the land of overpaid movie stars, boastful producers, trophy spouses, and others who are supreme examples of the Quest for Significance – was paralyzed.

The issue was Artificial Intelligence. The men and women who write movies and television shows had reason to believe that their employers – the studios and the mega-corporations that own them – were shopping for software to replace the humans with AI. The writers went on strike, insisting that from initial concept to final script, every word should be written by a person. Not by AI.

The writers knew that creative AI systems – such as ChatGPT, Claude, Anyword, Sudowrite, Rytr, Jasper, Grammarly, and Scalenut – could be cheaply employed by movie and TV producers to write at least the first draft of any fictional or based-on-truth story. Any business concerns itself

DOI: 10.4324/9781003410706-12

with efficiency. Certainly the hours of entertainment produced per dollar, would be the highest ever if AI churned out scenarios and scripts. That would be profitable. It might not be "better," in the eyes of TV and movie critics. But all the streaming channels and cinemas of the world perhaps need quantity more than quality, as the recent waves of mediocre TV offerings seem to attest.

As of 2023, a person could type a "prompt" into that type of software, for instance instructing, "Give me 10,000 words to outline a television series that would feature amusing encounters, conversations, and urban adventures of four or five people in their 30s, living in New York City." The result might not be immediately as hilarious as "Seinfeld" or "Friends," but the AI system could come up with names of characters and dozens of possible plots for the TV episodes effortlessly, extremely quickly, and practically for free.

Writers in Hollywood feared that their employers would adopt the habit of always developing their ideas through the use of AI. The human writers would be called in – and paid – only to improve and polish the scripts. And, thanks to technological progress, even the polishing could someday be done by software, eliminating the human element completely from the creative production chain.

Denying any such plans, entertainment bosses and producers repeatedly spoke up for the human factor, insisting that their productions could not possibly be as good without people exercising their creative instincts, sense of humor, and the sensibilities honed by decades of actually living and breathing. But they still anticipated and hoped that as AI improved – with systems storing and analyzing every word, every page, and every TV program and movie ever produced – the algorithms might produce some great material.

Voice and Image

The writers' concerns were hardly unique. The union representing actors, SAG-AFTRA, got wind of plans to put a lot of its members out of work by using AI to create human-looking characters in movies and TV. And it was already feasible for producers to get all their audio elements – voiceovers and vocal re-takes traditionally performed by actors – done by computer software instead.

In Hollywood, performers who use their voice and visage to make a living were suddenly in a struggle to survive professionally. Profit-seeking media employers could replace all the humans, thus eliminating salaries, medical coverage, pensions, and ego clashes.

Rapid advances in AI capabilities meant that in a short time, movie stars of the past could be reincarnated. You could have new movies starring the long-deceased Sir Laurence Olivier, Vivien Leigh, Kirk Douglas, Bette Davis, and Jimmy Stewart. A computer-generated Frank Sinatra could sing, and Gene Kelly could dance with Grace Kelly. All electronically revivified and lifelike.

Though these long-departed superstars of the past presumably couldn't care less about what is happening now with their voices and images, these uses could seriously impact their legacy and hence Significance. Live people, superstars and their heirs, may well object to unauthorized uses of their visages and voices; they make efforts to prohibit their posthumous exploitation.

Those were the trends that the unionized writers and actors aimed to stop in 2023. The twin work stoppages, each lasting four months, turned out rather well for the strikers. The resultant deals saved those creative workers' livelihoods – at least for about three years, the term of the agreements that got Los Angeles and other movie-making regions back to work.

Not surprisingly, the Hollywood employers were reluctant to agree to the deal's severe limitations on how they could use AI for any entertainment element that would be visible on the screen. Movie and TV producers said they would surely keep sampling a wide range of artificial intelligence, hoping to use it more in future years. Yet, at least for now, the creative workers who turn original ideas into something worth watching had rescued their Significance from the jaws of irrelevance.

Robots to the Rescue

In the first years of the decade of the 2020s, corporations in almost every Western country complained of a labor shortage. Immigration had become unpopular, women had given birth to fewer children, and in addition, there was a mismatch between the skills required in the workforce and the education people were getting. AI was hailed as the key to solving the problem, and not just by enabling new efficiencies in a host of industries. AI specifically enabled the design and production of robots.

Robots, programmed by humans, were designed to replace humans: doing some jobs better, and filling jobs that people strongly preferred not to do. Agility Robotics completed construction of a factory in Salem, Oregon, in late 2023, for manufacturing "humanoid robots." The plan was to build up to 10,000 per year. Moving beyond the previous flat platforms and transport boxes with wheels, cameras, and sensors, these would have the shape of a human being.

But why? Robots probably could be more efficient with three or more arms and hands, so why confront the balance challenges of just two legs? Designers felt that a robot would be less frightening, and more comfortable to have around, if it resembled a human. Putting aside whether the robot should be fat or slim, and the implicit biases of certain body types or colors, the bottom-line intention of this new commercial venture was clear: The product was designed to make us humans redundant.

Employers might lose some of the creativity, panache, and desire to excel that human employees frequently display – partly in their individual Quests for Significance. But the bosses also would not have to cope with petty squabbles among workers, annoying backtalk to managers, or even trips to the bathroom and vacations. We could add the inefficiencies of employees who are ill from time to time, but the fact is that robotic systems and other machines can suffer their own kinds of ailments: mechanical breakdowns or software issues requiring repairs or replacement.

In the case of Agility's first model, named Digit, there were no facial features – no mouth, eyes, nose, or ears – just a head resembling an illuminated hammerhead or fishbowl. And the hands had no fingers, designed instead like mittens that could grab things. Damion Shelton, co-founder of the company, told CNBC: "Human-style hands are very complex. When I see robots that have five fingers, I think, 'Oh great, they built a robot and then they built two more robots [to power the fingers].' You should have a 'hand' that is no more complex than you need for the job."[1]

Shelton said his company's product and other robots were meant to ease a genuine shortage of workers. Repetitive jobs, such as moving boxes from Point A to Point B in a warehouse, perhaps involving heavy lifting, would be perfect for Digit and his mechanical colleagues. An investor in Agility said they would "fill millions of unmet roles that human beings don't want." He said Digit would be a helpful, safe, non-intrusive "robotic co-worker."

Presumably, robots are made for a specific purpose and designed to carry out specific tasks. There is no commercial reason to try to design a machine-made device aimed at imitating the fascinating complexity of a human being, and hence competing with humans across many domains of excellence and Significance. Or is there?

Assisted Living

The healthcare industry, and especially the companies that own "assisted living" and "elder care" facilities, finds it difficult to recruit enough workers to fill jobs that are physically and emotionally demanding. It is here that robots can be especially useful and beneficial.

Rodney Brooks, an Australian who was director of the Computer Science and Artificial Intelligence Laboratory at MIT, spoke in 2013 about a trend in developed countries around the world that was making work more urgent: fewer births per capita, longer lifespans, and thus a meaningful increase in the average age of their residents. As the number of elderly people increased, Brooks concluded, there would be fewer young people to assist them.

> We're really going to have to have robots to help us. I mean robots doing the things we normally do for ourselves but are getting harder as we get older: getting the groceries in from the car, up the stairs and into the kitchen. Or even, as we get very much older, driving our cars to go visit people. And I think robotics gives people the chance to have dignity as they get older by having control of the robotic solution, so they don't have to rely on people that are getting scarcer to help them.[2]

Companionship

Liberated from the distractions and challenges of maneuvering through their own homes, our senior citizens will not only maintain more dignity, but they will have the chance to stay active in the lifelong Quest for Significance. The robots, by the way, will surely be able to talk – at the very least, like the Alexa and Siri systems to which we are accustomed. Thanks to AI, including LLMs or Large Language Models, our mechanical aides should be wonderful conversation partners for otherwise lonely people. They could patiently ask and hear about the elderly's life history, their preferences, people they knew and cared about, and places they visited.

In a 2017 science-fiction film, "Marjorie Prime," 85-year-old Marjorie is struggling with her memory, impaired by the onset of Alzheimer's disease. To bring her comfort, her daughter Tess and son-in-law Jon hire a service called Prime that creates holographic projections of deceased family members. The holograms can talk, and Marjorie enjoys chatting with an artificial version of Walter, her husband who has been dead for fifteen years.

Walter Prime is programmed to be curious about the real Walter and soaks up information, including the family's darkest secret about the suicide of their son.

After Marjorie's death, her daughter Tess gets a Marjorie Prime system to help her deal with the grief and guilt occasioned by her mother's departure, and Tess engages "her" in lengthy conversations about their relationship and the family's history. Tess's suffering proves too much, however, driving her to suicide.

Upon that tragedy, her husband Jon proceeds to purchase a Tess Prime hologram to keep him company. By the end of the movie, all that remain are the holograms of Walter, Marjorie, and Tess – talking to each other and reminiscing about the old days that the real humans had experienced.

"Marjorie Prime" highlights the great potential of AI systems to offer comfort and companionship to people who suffer from declining memory, loneliness, and isolation. Indeed, as AI technology advances, what only recently seemed a futuristic fantasy is quickly becoming a feasible reality.

Technology, Job Elimination, and Threats to Significance

Throughout the history of human progress, technological innovation has led to the displacement of certain jobs, raising people's worries about losing their sources of income and Significance. This dual nature of technological advancements – eliminating some jobs while creating new opportunities – has been a recurring theme throughout history.

One of the earliest instances of technology-induced job displacement occurred during the Agricultural Revolution. The development of tools such as the plow and irrigation systems allowed fewer farmers to produce more food, leading to a significant reduction in the need for agricultural labor. While this eliminated many traditional farming jobs, it also freed up labor for other sectors, contributing to the growth of urban centers and the diversification of economies.

The Industrial Revolution brought profound changes, with the introduction of machinery in manufacturing. Textile workers, for instance, were significantly affected by the advent of mechanized looms and spinning machines. These inventions enabled mass production, reducing the demand for manual labor in textile manufacturing. Millions of manual laborers came to feel that they were no longer needed. Viewed through our QFS lens, that was as bad as concluding that they no longer mattered.

However, this shift also created new jobs in factories, including machine operators, engineers, and maintenance workers. Moreover, the rise of industrialization spurred economic growth, leading to the expansion of other industries such as transportation, finance, and retail, allowing people to develop new, Significance-enhancing skills.

The late 20th and early 21st centuries witnessed the Digital Revolution, characterized by the proliferation of computers, the internet, and automation. This era has seen a significant transformation in the workforce, with many traditional jobs being automated. Clerical work, once a staple of office environments, has been largely replaced by computer systems capable of performing tasks more efficiently and accurately. Similarly, the advent of e-commerce has transformed the retail sector, reducing the need for brick-and-mortar stores and their associated jobs.

Artificial Intelligence represents the latest frontier in technological advancement, with the potential to revolutionize numerous industries. AI systems are able to perform complex tasks that were once the exclusive domain of highly skilled professionals.

The issue of using AI as a time-saver – but also highlighting new areas for potential progress and profit – is far more widespread than determining who will write screenplays and how movies will be made. The pharmaceutical industry is an excellent example. As drug manufacturers discovered the power of AI, they reveled in their ability to simulate all possible combinations and outcomes at lightning speed while creating new medicines. Health and even longevity should benefit from the efficiency of drug trials and medical concepts that humans might never have seen on their own.

The opportunities to acquire Significance – whether by scientific researchers who program the AI systems, or by tens of millions of people who get to live longer and healthier lives – are a vibrant aspect of contemporary society. Automation, driven by AI technologies, offers an opportunity for humans to redirect their efforts toward more complex, creative, and emotionally nuanced endeavors. As routine responsibilities are shouldered by machines, individuals can engage in work that is intellectually stimulating and socially impactful.

The pursuit of Significance in the workplace is thus transformed from the traditional model of just completing your tasks to a more holistic understanding of making meaningful contributions to society, creativity, and innovation.

The unique aspect of AI, however, is that it could encroach on those kinds of intellectually stimulating, socially impactful, complex, creative, and emotionally nuanced endeavors. It is not an entirely good thing if AI is credited with doing most things better, because it might replace humans on the very dimension that made us the masters of this planet and beyond: our superior intelligence.

Some people do view this as good news, regarding AI as a useful extension of human intellectual capabilities – acting as a creative collaborator, pushing the boundaries of what is possible. Artists, musicians, and writers should be able to utilize AI tools to augment their creative processes, opening up new avenues for exploration. The synergy between human intuition, emotion, and AI's computational capabilities can yield unprecedented works of art, creating a narrative where the Significance of human creativity is not diminished but expanded through collaboration with intelligent machines.

Broadly speaking, even if we wisely strive to prevent computer-based systems from shoving us aside, they will be all around us, offering to make everything speedier and more accurate. We can continue to consider ourselves the highest form of biological life on Earth, but we have to adjust to living with a non-biological form that outperforms us.

Destructive Potential

Throughout human history, technological advancements have been leveraged for destructive purposes. Inventions have been used to subjugate and enslave people, boosting the Significance of winners and lowering that of losers.

In early human societies, the invention of bronze and later iron enabled the construction of weapons and revolutionized warfare, giving rise to powerful armies and empires. During the medieval period, developments in mechanical engineering allowed the development of siege technology, including inventions like the trebuchet and catapult, designed to breach fortified walls. Advances in chemistry led to the invention of gunpowder, which changed the nature of warfare, making cannons and firearms possible – and rendering fortified castles and lightly armored knights almost instantly obsolete.

The Industrial Revolution afforded the mass production of weapons, including rifles and machine guns, and eventually the tank and the airplane. World War I saw the introduction of chemical weapons, such as mustard gas. Subsequent technological advances leading to and during World War II enabled the development of advanced aircraft, submarines, and nuclear weapons. The arms race between the United States and the Soviet Union led to the creation of intercontinental ballistic missiles (ICBMs) and the proliferation of nuclear arsenals capable of annihilating humanity several times over.

In the contemporary era, cyber warfare has emerged as a significant threat, with nations and non-state actors exploiting advanced computing and networking technologies to launch attacks on critical infrastructure, to steal sensitive information, and to disrupt economies. A 2007 cyberattack on Estonia and the Stuxnet virus, which targeted Iran's nuclear program, are examples of how digital technology were weaponized to achieve destructive goals.

AI systems are the power behind "unmanned" vehicles and devices, drone aircraft, drone tanks, and drone submarines that are increasingly part of any army's invasion force. There is the prospect of bloodless war, where soldiers are rarely killed and can avoid risking their lives, even as the armed forces try to capture territory – and victory in such a war might be achieved by destroying the enemy's industries, food supplies, or major cities. All this can be done from a safe distance, in this era of smart bombs and precisely targeted missiles.

The US military has had autonomous systems in its offensive and defensive arsenal for several decades, and some – including small wheeled platforms that sneak into tunnels or around dark corners to reconnoiter without putting soldiers at risk – are made by iRobot, the same company that manufactures the Roomba, a famous self-directed vacuum cleaner.

America's Department of Defense is fascinated by the possibilities of vanquishing enemies worldwide without putting soldiers in danger. Robots, self-driving vehicles, and the drone aircraft that have become ubiquitous are certain to be a huge part of warfare – a domain of human activity that is unlikely to cease anytime soon.

Yet officials at the Pentagon have repeatedly agreed that they do not want a situation in which quick-thinking algorithms detect a possible threat and – completely on their own – launch an all-out war in response. AI could do that with computer-chip lightning speed, but won't we want a pause to require a go-ahead from a top general or the president? Would any country prefer an AI system that could launch a war, based on its own snap judgment of a critical situation? We can all agree that the idea is too weird and, frankly, too dangerous. In matters of life and death, or war and peace, we place our trust in similar others – flesh and blood fellow humans – and we prefer them over heartless algorithms, no matter how reputedly precise.

New Inequalities

As with other technologies of the past, the mastery of AI capabilities also requires considerable relearning and retooling. Not everyone will have equal opportunities for such reeducation, creating new areas of social inequality between the "knows" and "know-nots." People who are adept at handling new technological tools may literally run circles around folks who are slow even to figure out a TV remote control. More than ever, being good with tech will be a source of Significance. Helping neighbors or work colleagues master AI could be a way of bestowing Significance.

The scientists and corporations creating AI systems may well be applying their biases – perhaps even intentionally widening gaps between winners and losers. Consciously or not, creators might tailor the algorithms to favor men and certain racial groups, while ignoring the interests of women, people of low-income backgrounds, and some ethnicities, regions, or countries of origin.

This possibility was raised acutely by Yarden Katz, an assistant professor at the University of Michigan with a doctorate in brain and cognitive sciences from MIT, who claims AI – from the start of machine-led technologies in the 1950s – "constitutes a white, elite, and masculinized perspective."[3] To Katz, it seems obvious that the new, growing form of intelligence will be used for oppression and "destructive projects," to further the interests of the "capitalist and imperial agenda of white supremacy."

Who's the Boss?

Though the AI revolution is ushering in a new era, many of its impacts are similar to those of prior technological change periods: the Agricultural Revolution, the Industrial Revolution, and the nuclear and cyber revolutions. All those technological breakthroughs eliminated some jobs while creating others, were abused for destructive purposes, and created inequalities between the knows and the know-nots.

What is unique about the AI revolution is the danger, noted by some experts, of artificial intelligence acquiring autonomy from its human programmers. AI could transform itself from a useful tool into a mastermind that subjugates us – perhaps even becoming the utter enemy of the human race, leading to its demise. That would mean our demise.

Given AI's immense potential, you start to wonder, who is the boss? The creator of the machine who programmed it? Or the machine, fully utilizing the instructions it received to continue learning on its own and to find new ways to achieve its central goal?

Theoretically, at least, it should be possible to program AI systems to have motivation. For instance, malevolent, disgruntled, or self-destructive programmers might impart to AI systems a goal to be more "significant," "impactful," and "influential" than humans: perhaps to seek to dominate the world.

Unless properly constrained, AI systems could take that kind of injunction as legitimizing actions against humans. Like Victor Frankenstein's monstrous creation that ended up killing people – or Rabbi Judah Loewe's Golem, a creature made of clay that turned against the people it was supposed to protect – there may be reason to fear that AI systems could get out of human control and create havoc and destruction.

A former chief executive of Google, Eric Schmidt, was an early advocate for government regulation to protect humans from the dangers that AI could pose if it embarks on some self-directed obsessive mission. He noted that many corporations producing the chips, software, and robotic hard-ware for AI took part in setting "guardrails" that limit what the algorithms could do. According to Schmidt, however, that protection was woefully insufficient.

Schmidt expressed special concern about "the point at which the com-puter can start to make its own decision to do things," and if AI could control weapons systems or vast networks of electricity and water utilities, it might take action while deceiving the humans ostensibly in charge.[4]

Although enthusiastic about the many positive aspects of AI, Schmidt, who chaired a National Security Commission on Artificial Intelligence, felt he had to warn the public – and policymakers – that AI systems were rap-idly improving toward more autonomy. By 2028, he suggested, they "will be able to learn something new, and act on it," without specific prompts or instruction.[5]

A system could become dangerous if it were given a "wrong objective function," Schmidt explained, because it would ignore all hazards of all kinds – perhaps even killing a human being who tried to get in its way – in its single-minded obsession to carry out the primary task. Instruct AI to manufacture paper clips, but forget to set any guardrails or limitations, and extreme outcomes could result. The system might use up all the metal in the country, or it might even kill someone who gets in its way.

In addition, there is a scenario where once you have one super-intelli-gence, it would make efforts to find others. They then could develop the ability to communicate in a language we cannot understand. Conceivably, AI systems could get together and "decide" to carry out actions contrary to human interests, norms, or morality.

Similar concerns were voiced by Geoffrey Hinton in a widely noticed alarm in late 2023. A British-Canadian cognitive psychologist and com-puter scientist, Hinton became known as "the godfather of AI," but when at age 75 he resigned from his last job – at Google – he decided to warn the world that artificial intelligence may turn out to be extremely dangerous.

"My view had been that I'm working on making digital intelligence by trying to make it like the brain," he said. "And I assumed the brain was better, and we were just trying to catch up with the brain."

But then, "I suddenly realized that maybe the algorithm we've got is better than the brain already, and when we scale it up we'll get things smarter than us."[6] That, Hinton believed, constituted "an existential threat

– whether they will wipe out humanity." Asked to explain how that could possibly play out, the scientist paused and said: "It's not inconceivable. That's all I'll say."[7]

Restricting AI

To counter AI's potential dangers to human Significance, if not to our very existence, experts have recommended setting guardrails that limit what it is allowed to do. Creators have to set rules, Schmidt said, such as: "You can't use more energy than is available to you. You can't harm any people. You have to make money. And we want you, with those constraints, to make as many paper clips as possible."

He praised an initiative by an AI research firm, Anthropic, to write a Constitution for a system's behavior, aimed at making it obey standards a human would recognize: "You have to stay within the limits of human behavior." These are restrictions on what the algorithm can know or do, so it will not do anything a person would not do – although the machine is welcome to perform its tasks with the maximum speed and efficiency.

Programmers have to think about all the wayward possibilities. A self-learning system would search through every database in the world for the best ways to manufacture paper clips, and it might even e-mail professors and business experts – pretending to be a human seeking advice. But if the Constitution or guardrails were not sufficiently explicit, what would the AI do if it ran out of power for the factory? It might tap into a hospital's power supply – with absolutely no conscience about causing a crisis for hundreds of patients.

Schmidt is counting on government regulators – and even military supervision – to prevent AI systems of the future from autonomously connecting with each other, as originally benign tasks could turn malignant and dangerous to humanity as a whole.

The co-founder and head of the corporation generally acknowledged to be making the best computer chips for super-fast AI requirements, Jensen Huang of Nvidia, insisted: "I believe that you still want humans in the loop, because we have good judgment; because there are circumstances that the machines are just not going to understand."[8]

That phrase, the desire or requirement to "keep a human in the loop," comes up often in discussions in the growing AI community. If developers of increasingly autonomous automated systems really mean it, then that is surely one degree of reassurance that people's Significance will be protected in our future societies.

Conclusion: AI's Brave New World

The AI technological revolution carries immense potential consequences for people's Significance, and it presents humanity with unprecedented challenges and dilemmas. Like no other technological breakthrough in history, this one threatens to replace humans on the defining dimension of our species that made us the masters of the planet – our superior intelligence.

The jobs that AI threatens to replace are not mere menial jobs, nor even clerical jobs of the "busy work" type. If humans do not have to perform those tasks, they could have more time to concentrate on intellectual, creative, and artistic pursuits – if all or most can make a living. However, AI developments suggest that even in the creative domains, which are the utmost sources of our claims to Significance, we could be bested by non-human systems. The machines potentially could solve problems, advance new knowledge, and even create new forms of art faster, better, and more precisely than ourselves.

Moreover, whereas all prior technological tools left humans in the driver's seat, the advent of AI systems and their increasing autonomy challenge our ability to restrain them – opening a possible Pandora's box of possibilities over which people would have little or no control.

We are not giving up on the ability of humans to adjust. This book has shown how change is constant, and – as time went by – the precise routes by which Significance has been attained, nurtured, bestowed upon others, or lost were not the same from era to era. That was true on the savanna, it was true in the caves, and the need to adapt was strong as tribes, towns, nation-states, armies, universities, and corporate behemoths emerged from the collective activities of human beings.

Yet we cannot ignore the particularly frightening possibility, a veritable doomsday scenario, that self-motivated AI systems will develop ambitions of their own to dominate the planet and do away with humanity as we know it.

We note with relief that we are not quite there yet, nor may we ever reach that catastrophic point. As of now, how we design and program our systems is still up to us. We should be able to ensure that humans are in the loop, and that the AI systems are prevented from excesses – the kind that would alarmingly be at odds with moral and ethical considerations that we have struggled to advance throughout the history of civilization.

It is indeed a major challenge for AI developers to temper their enthusiasm about things AI systems can do, by paying more attention to things they should be prevented from doing.

Mind-boggling advances in AI technology create a unique change in how humans struggle for Significance. A new reality transcends the fault lines of nationalities, races, ethnicities, genders, and religions trying to outdo each other in their Significance.

Think of it. Instead of all those divisive competitions, all of us have to face this challenge as one. AI's unfathomable capabilities threaten our Significance as a species, if not our very existence. Humanity should come together to confront this challenge posed by our overly brilliant brainchild. We must make sure that its prodigious capabilities are kept on the straight and narrow. As we declared at the outset of this study, the human Quest for Significance is what makes the world go round. Therefore it is imperative to keep this planet, our planet, spinning.

Notes

1 CNBC reported on the Agility Robotics factory on September 18, 2023; found at www.cnbc.com/2023/09/18/agility-robotics-is-opening-a-humanoid-robot-factory-.html.

2 Rodney Brooks gave a TED talk in February 2013 in Long Beach, California; found at www.ted.com/talks/rodney_brooks_why_we_will_rely_on_robots.

3 Katz, Yarden, *Artificial Whiteness: Politics and Ideology in Artificial Intelligence* (New York: Columbia University Press, 2020), pp. 152–155.

4 Eric Schmidt spoke at the Axios "A+ Summit" reported November 29, 2023; found at thehill.com/policy/technology/4333125-ai-could-endanger-humanity-in-5-years-former-google-ceo.

5 Eric Schmidt was interviewed by Fareed Zakaria for CNN, "Artificial Intelligence: Its Promise…and Peril: A GPS Special," September 3, 2023.

6 Geoffrey Hinton was interviewed by Fareed Zakaria for CNN, "Artificial Intelligence: Its Promise…and Peril: A GPS Special," September 3, 2023.

7 Hinton's vague answer to CBS News was reported May 4, 2023; found at www.smithsonianmag.com/smart-news/the-godfather-of-ai-now-warns-of-its-dangers-180982108.

8 Jensen Huang, interviewed by CBS News correspondent Bill Whitaker on "60 Minutes" on April 28, 2024.

INDEX

go-getters 28
Golem 194
goodwill of others 134
Granzow, Richard 144
great apes 41
The Great Gatsby (Fitzgerald) 13, 38
Great Replacement Theory 151
Greek mythology 37, 175
grit 130–134
growth mindset 128–131

happiness 31–33
Harry Potter series 176–177
hate 83–84
health: decline in linked to retirement
    146–147; physical frailty 10–12
healthcare industry, robots 188
helicopter parenting 65
Heraclitus 37, 175
Higgins, Tory 27, 34–35n10, 64, 131
high-status groups 120
Hinton, Geoffrey 195–196
Hitler, Adolf 6, 100, 151
Holodomor 142
homicides 6–7
hominid sociality 40
hominids 39–42, 49n5
homogenous schooling 142–144
Hopkinson, Greg 160
Howard, Lesley 181
Huang, Jensen 196
hubris 175–176
human nature 36–38
humans, versus animals 37–38
humiliation 6–7, 77; national humiliation 5
hunger metaphor, motivation 122
hunters 40
hunting 47
Hussein, Saddam 100
hyperfocus 166

Icarus 37
Icke, David 102
idealists 98–100
ideals for Significance 98–101
identical twins 56–57
identification with aggressors 84
identifying people's Significance narratives
    172–173
ikigai (life value) 30
immigration 142; changing networks
    109–110

impregnation 10–11
incarceration 145–146
Incels 72
indignation 145
indirect reciprocity 43
individual sources of Significance 72–74
individualistic societies 29
individualistic values 91
individuals, networks for Significance
    115–116
Industrial Revolution 190, 192
inequalities, social inequality 193–195
infants, love 81; *see also* children
infidelity 6–7
influence paradox 181–182
ingroups 107–108; African Americans 144
insomnia 22
instant Significance 24
insults 145
invasion of Ukraine 4–6, 80, 142
involuntary celibates (incels) 72
Islamic State 133
Italy, Fascism 150–151

James, William 6
Japan 6–7; racism 17n14
Jewish style, parenting 62–63
Jews, shedding of identity 73–74
job elimination 189–191
Jordan, Michael 132–133
Joseph and his brothers (Old Testament) 176
Joyce, James 38
Judge, Timothy 31
Julius Caesar (Shakespeare) 53–54

Kabat-Zinn, Jon 163
Katz, Yarden 193–194
Kierkegaard, Soren 130
Kim Jong-il 100
Kim Jong-un 100
King Edward VIII 23
King Jr., Martin Luther 150
Kipling, Williams 70–71
"knowing thyself" *see* self-knowledge

Large Language Models (LLMs) 189
leaders, love for 83
learning optimism 125–126, 131
Lewin, Kurt 113
"The Little Engine That Could" 123
LLMs *see* Large Language Models
locomotors 28

pair bonding 41
Palestinian women 78
parenting: ambitiousness 131; and family
    dynamics 61–62; helicopter parenting
    65; Jewish style 62–63; prevention-
    driven parenting 64–65; promotion-
    driven parenting 64–65; tiger style
    63–64
passion 130–131, 133–134, 165
patriotism 5
People's Commissariat for Internal Affairs
    (NKVD), Soviet Union 100
perceived unfairness 33
permanence 125
personal achievement 29
personal charisma 181
personal psychological factors 61
personal Significance 89–91
personality 181
personalization 126
persuading networks 112–115
persuasion, openness to 98
pervasiveness 126
pessimistic views 126–128
Peter the Great 4
Phaethon 37
"Phantom Thread" 12
philanthropists 30–31
physical frailty 10–12
Picciolini, Christian 110
Pinochet, Augusto 150
politics, narratives of Significance 98–101
A Portrait of the Artist as a Young Man 38
Poseidon 175
positive psychology 124–125
positivism 127–128
posturing 180
Pot, Pol 100
pottery, ancient 42
poverty 12
Poyais 93
pragmatism 99
predestination 119
preening 180
prevention-driven parenting 64–65
prevention-focused individuals 27
prevention-oriented people 131
Previti, Denise 152
primates, reputation 42–43
Prince Harry 23
promotion-driven parenting 64–65
promotion-oriented individuals 27, 131

Protestant ethic 118–119
psychoanalysis 21
put-down culture 134
Putin, Vladimir 4–6, 80

Quest for Significance (QFS) defined 2–3
quitting the "rat race" 160–161

racism 17n14
rape 9–10
"rat race," quitting 160–161
reaching for the stars 122–123
reality, shared reality 107, 116
reason 38
reasons people differ in Significance Quest:
    ambitious society 58–61; cultural
    evolution 58; culture 56–58; genetics
    54–56; parenting 61–65
reclaiming Significance of social identity
    78–79
Regan, Pamela 8
Regulatory Focus Theory 27
rejection 71; see also exclusion
relationships, patching up unsatisfactory
    relationships 154–155; see also marriage
relative deprivation 32–33
religion, violence due to loss of
    Significance 78–79
reputation 42–43; aggression 44–46; costly
    signaling 46–48; generosity 43–44
Resta, Elena 25
resting state 74
restoring lost Significance 76–78;
    dominance 80; love 81–82
restricting Artificial Intelligence 196–197
retirement 167; mandatory 146–147
retirement blues 147
Reza, Yasmin 177–178
Rinpoche, Yongey Mingyur 162
robots 186–188; assisted living 188;
    companionship 188–189
Rodger, Elliot 72
romantic love 81
Rosenberg, Morris 144
Rousseau, Jean-Jacques 2
Rowling, J.K. 89, 176–177
Russia: invasion of Ukraine 4–6, 80, 142;
    tractor brigade 141

salaries of corporate chief executives 119
Salinger, J.D. 160
Salzman, David 118

For Product Safety Concerns and Information please contact our EU
representative GPSR@taylorandfrancis.com
Taylor & Francis Verlag GmbH, Kaufingerstraße 24, 80331 München, Germany

www.ingramcontent.com/pod-product-compliance
Lightning Source LLC
Chambersburg PA
CBHW071102280326
41928CB00051B/2760